BRINGING MONTESSORI TO AMERICA

BRINGING MONTESSORI TO AMERICA

S. S. McClure, Maria Montessori, and the Campaign to Publicize Montessori Education

GERALD L. GUTEK AND PATRICIA A. GUTEK

The University of Alabama Press
Tuscaloosa

The University of Alabama Press
Tuscaloosa, Alabama 35487-0380
uapress.ua.edu

Hardcover edition published 2016.
Paperback edition published 2017.
eBook edition published 2016.

Typeface: Garamond

Cover image: Maria Montessori and S. S. McClure; courtesy of Bain Collection, Library of Congress
Cover design: Michele Myatt Quinn

Paperback ISBN: 978-0-8173-5908-9

A previous edition of this book has been catalogued by the Library of Congress as follows:

Library of Congress Cataloging-in-Publication Data
Names: Gutek, Gerald Lee, author. | Gutek, Patricia, 1941– author.
Title: Bringing Montessori to America : S.S. Mcclure, Maria Montessori, and the campaign to publicize Montessori education / Gerald L. Gutek and Patricia A. Gutek.
Description: Tuscaloosa : The University of Alabama Press, [2016] | Includes bibliographical references and index.
Identifiers: LCCN 2015031838| ISBN 9780817318970 (cloth : alk. paper) | ISBN 9780817389314 (e book)
Subjects: LCSH: Montessori method of education—United States. | McClure, S. S. (Samuel Sidney), 1857–1949 | Montessori, Maria, 1870–1952.
Classification: LCC LB1029.M75 G88 2016 | DDC 371.39/2—dc23
LC record available at http://lccn.loc.gov/2015031838

Contents

Illustrations

FIGURES

TABLES

Preface

This book tells the story of the meeting of two remarkable individuals, Maria Montessori and Samuel Sidney (S. S.) McClure, in the second decade of the twentieth century. Maria Montessori (1870–1952) is acclaimed internationally as one of history's great pioneering educators. Montessori schools operate worldwide in countries as culturally diverse as the United States, the United Kingdom, India, the Netherlands, Spain, and her native Italy, all nations in which she taught and lectured. Montessori's biographers agree that she was a unique individual, a remarkable woman, a physician, and an educator who used her medical and scientific training, her life experience, and her insights to construct a highly innovative philosophy and method of education. Her method challenged the conventional educational wisdom of the late nineteenth and early twentieth centuries. Not only did she have to challenge the rote and routines in schools, she had to overcome the late Victorian era's gender-based restrictions that defined women as wives, mothers, caregivers, and in some cases primary school teachers and nurses. Her biographers, especially Rita Kramer and Phyllis Povell, tell the life story of a determined woman who successfully surmounted the barriers that limited the freedom of women to chart new careers.

While the life story that Montessori's biographers tell is true, might there be something more to the woman whose students refered to her as *La Dottoressa* (the doctor)—the physician turned educator? The five years from 1910 to 1915 when she was connected with S. S. McClure, her American publicist, reveal a multidimensional woman who, while truly a great educator, was a complex personality, determined at all costs to control what she had created.

Montessori's relationship with S. S. McClure (1857–1949) provides a fascinating account of an initially promising, then tortured, relationship between two very strong but totally different personalities. While Montessori's biographers have stood in awe of their subject, history has not been as generous to McClure.

Today, books on American history, particularly on the Progressive Era, devote a few lines, perhaps a single short paragraph, to McClure and the journal he founded, *McClure's Magazine*. The energetic publisher and editor, once acclaimed as the pioneer of modern American publishing and journalism, certainly would resent his contemporary place at history's margins. However, when McClure met Montessori in 1910, his fame in the United States, perhaps even in Western Europe, overshadowed that of the Italian educator.

McClure commanded center stage in American journalism during the height of the Progressive Era, the years from 1890 to 1920. During these three decades, reform-minded political leaders, journalists, settlement house workers, conservationists, and educators formed a loose but broad coalition to root out political and corporate corruption and reform American life and institutions. The articles of leading Progressives such as Theodore Roosevelt and Jane Addams were featured in the pages of *McClure's Magazine*. When McClure brought Montessori to lecture in America's major cities in 1913, the Progressive former Princeton University president, Woodrow Wilson, was in the White House. Montessori's educational philosophy even reached the nation's first family as Wilson's daughter Margaret became an enthusiastic Montessori supporter and a founding member of the Montessori Educational Association established by McClure and Mabel and Alexander Graham Bell.

McClure, who came to the United States as an immigrant lad from Northern Ireland, epitomized the American model of the successful self-made man who climbed, in Horatio Alger style, from rags to riches. But in McClure's case the riches were transitory. As an enterprising and innovative publisher of a leading national magazine, McClure sought to dissolve the distinction between elite and popular literature. He introduced American readers to Rudyard Kipling, Arthur Conan Doyle, and Robert Louis Stevenson through the serialization of their novels. He hired the great investigative Progressive journalists Ida Tarbell and Lincoln Steffens as writers for his magazine. He possessed an uncanny acumen in searching out and popularizing talented authors and reporters. McClure believed that Maria Montessori was indeed a talented figure, a genius, in the usually staid field of education. With boundless enthusiasm, McClure developed an ambitious plan to bring Montessori to the American public with him on a joint lecture tour and, later, create a Montessori teacher training institute.

The story of McClure and Montessori is about the meeting, intersection, and interfacing of two highly interesting but very different persons. This intersection occurred in the twentieth century's second decade when prospects for progress seemed bright. But, halfway through that decade the lights would go out all over Europe, as World War I, the Great War, dimmed these prospects.

The relationship between McClure and Montessori went through stages that are examined in the chapters in this book. First, biographies of McClure and

Montessori tell readers about the lives and careers of these two main characters at the time of their relationship. However, other leading personalities come into and out of the McClure-Montessori saga: Alexander Graham Bell, inventor of the telephone, and his wife, Mabel; Gilbert Grosvenor, the editor of the *National Geographic* and the treasurer of the Montessori Educational Association; Carl Byoir, pioneer in American public relations; Dorothy Canfield Fisher, noted writer; Margaret Wilson, a daughter of President Woodrow Wilson; Anne E. George, the first American trained by Montessori; Lee Keedick, the lecture impresario; Helen Parkhurst, founder of the Dalton Plan of Education; and William Heard Kilpatrick, the Progressive Columbia University professor. These noteworthy persons of their times were drawn, like moths to a bright light, by Montessori. Much of the illumination of Montessori's ideas came from the series of articles about her in *McClure's Magazine* from 1910 to 1912. McClure's campaign to publicize Montessori in the United States led to her triumphal lecture tour in 1913.

Our book narrates the story of the dynamic but difficult relationship between McClure and Maria Montessori from 1910 to 1915; it describes and interprets the agreements, misunderstandings, and tensions between these two dramatically charged personalities. McClure, a publisher, had decided that he would capitalize on Montessori's method and become its leading proponent in the United States. Montessori, in turn, was determined that only she would control the method that she had developed.

The questions explored in the following chapters are:

1. How did such different personalities decide to cooperate in bringing the Montessori Method to America?
2. Did Montessori seek to use *McClure's Magazine* and connections to promote her method?
3. How did McClure seek to profit from his association with Montessori?
4. Did McClure's irrepressible enthusiasm and lack of attention to details doom the relationship with Montessori?
5. Did financial issues over the profits from the sale of Montessori's didactic apparatus and other items contribute to the disintegration of the Montessori-McClure relationship?
5. Why was the successful establishment of Montessori education in America delayed for three decades after the break-up of the McClure-Montessori relationship in 1915 until its renaissance in the mid-1950s?

Our research on the McClure-Montessori story has been enjoyable, entertaining, and challenging. We were helped along our way by the capable and highly professional archivists at Knox College in Galesburg, Illinois, and the Indiana University's Lilly Library in Bloomington, Indiana. Yolande Wersching, the Head

Librarian of Lewis Library at Loyola University, Chicago, was especially helpful in finding and assessing articles, books, and dissertations on our subject. We are very grateful for the superb translators who translated the French and Italian handwritten and hard-to-read correspondence of Maria Montessori and her associates. Dorina Spiering translated from Italian and Anie Sergis translated from French. Sabine Haenen of Legal Confidential Certified Translations in the Netherlands translated from French while using her knowledge of Italian to accurately interpret Montessori's meaning.

We are also grateful for the expert genealogical assistance on Anne E. George by our friend Joanne Periolat Siadak.

We hope that you will enjoy reading our book as much as we enjoyed researching and writing it.

1

S. S. McClure

Cyclone in a Frock Coat

Figure 1. S. S. McClure (*The Booklovers Magazine*, January 1903).

The personalities of S. S. McClure, editor and publisher, and Maria Montessori, physician and educator, made them the most unlikely of associates. Their short transatlantic alliance was both energized and flawed by their distinctive traits of character. The McClure-Montessori relationship, from 1910 to 1915 is a fascinating historical episode that reverberated with alternating currents of enthusiasm and depression, trust and mistrust, promise and failure.

Born in 1857 and thirteen years older than Montessori, McClure's life circumstances were dramatically different from the Italian educator. Unlike the gentility and security of Montessori's middle-class family, Samuel McClure, the son of Scots-Irish working-class parents, endured an insecure childhood. Born on February 17, 1857, at his maternal grandparents' home in County Antrim, in the northeast section of Northern Ireland, he was named Samuel after his paternal grandfather. Unlike Maria Montessori, an only child, Samuel was the oldest of Thomas and Elizabeth (Gaston) McClure's four surviving sons.

In 1858, Thomas bought a small nine-acre farm at Drumalgea from his father, Samuel McClure Sr. Because he could not support his family solely by farming, Thomas McClure left for Scotland to work as a laborer in the shipyards in Glasgow. An accident at work took his life at age 32, in November 1864. Thomas McClure's twenty-seven-year-old widow, Elizabeth, who was pregnant, returned to her mother's home with her sons. In addition to sons Samuel, John, and Thomas, a son named Robert died when he was one and one-half years old. Subsequently, the youngest McClure son, born in 1865 after Thomas's death, was also named Robert.

Facing a bleak future in Antrim, Elizabeth decided her only hope was in America. By selling her farm back to her father-in-law for one hundred pounds she was able to pay for the passage. On June 14, 1866, Elizabeth McClure and her four young sons sailed from Londonderry on the *Mongolia*, landing at Quebec June 26. She planned to go to Indiana where her two married sisters and two single brothers were living, in Lake and Porter Counties. After traveling by train for seven days, Elizabeth and her children arrived in Valparaiso, in northwest Indiana on July 3, 1866. Nine-year-old Samuel McClure now began his new life as an American.

With some reluctance Elizabeth's sister, married to a Mr. Coleman, took in the five McClures. The Colemans, who lived on a farm near Valparaiso with a large family of their own, were financially strained with the addition of the McClures to their household. To bring in desperately needed funds, Elizabeth hired out as a laundress; but as she was required to live in her employer's home, leaving the four McClure boys added an unwelcome burden on her sister.

Samuel McClure, in his *Autobiography*, published in 1914, largely shaped the narrative of his early life. He told the story of the Irish immigrant lad in Indiana, who in Horatio Alger style, went from "rags to riches." He relished telling of his upward climb from poverty and obscurity to wealth and fame. Like the Scottish Andrew Carnegie, McClure came as an immigrant child to the United States. As with Carnegie, McClure's account, though sometimes embellished, was largely true.

McClure, who would become an editor, said he had loved books and reading as long as he could remember. He had learned to read at age four as a pupil in a national school in Antrim. McClure remembered how as a child he searched for something to read: "During these years the lack of reading matter was one of the deprivations which I felt, most keenly. We had no books at home. . . . When I was about thirteen years old I first read, in the weekly edition of the *Chicago Tribune*, 'The Luck of Roaring Camp.'"[1] He made his fondness for literature the core of his editorial quest for talented writers of engaging stories.

McClure's childhood search for books and magazines made an imprint on his mind. For a time, he lived in the house of Dr. Orpheus Everts, a prominent physician, in Valparaiso, where his mother worked as a housemaid.[2] There, the doctor gave him access to his library. Sam remembered, "For the first time in my life I found myself in a house where there were plenty of books. I sometimes read two or three books a day."[3] He also recalled finding some books left at a deserted hunter's camp: "I . . . found . . . several old paper-backed novels and a few tattered magazines. These were a great find for me. Years afterward, the idea of forming a newspaper syndicate first came to me through my remembering my hunger, as a boy, for something to read."[4]

Like his appetite for reading, Sam McClure hungered for an education. Unlike Montessori, who had a complete education from primary school through medical school, McClure struggled to attend school. While the Montessori family could pay for Maria's education, McClure's widowed mother could not. In Antrim, Sam attended a national primary school when he was four. Never humble about his achievements, McClure claimed he excelled as a student, always first in his class. Passing two forms (classes) a year, at age eight he was in the sixth form with fourteen- and fifteen-year-old boys.

After immigrating to Indiana as a nine year old, McClure's formal education grew increasingly sporadic. Like many farm boys in rural America at the time, chores took priority over school. He had to work on his uncle's farm for over a year before attending the local Hickory Point School. Despite all the obstacles that blocked his path to an education, Sam managed to attend whenever possible. He recalled, "The second winter I attended school for the first time since we came to America. I went to the Hickory Point School. . . . I was so fond of school that, if I had to work at home for part of the day, I would go all the way to school to get the last hour, from three to four, there."[5]

Two years after her arrival in Indiana, Elizabeth McClure married a neighboring farmer, Thomas Simpson, an immigrant from Tyrone, Ireland. She and her sons moved to his one-hundred-acre farm. Elizabeth had four children from her second marriage, but only one daughter survived infancy. Samuel remembered his mother during these years as a hard worker who milked cows, made and sold butter, and was usually carrying a new baby or caring for a sick toddler.[6]

Though undereducated, Elizabeth McClure, valuing learning, encouraged her sons to go to school. In the 1870s, high schools were slowly being established around the country and Valparaiso opened one in 1871. The school, however, was over fourteen miles from the Simpson farm. McClure's ever-practical mother encouraged her fourteen-year-old son, Sam, to move to Valparaiso, enroll in the high school, and support himself by working in private homes for his room and board. A character trait that McClure developed as a child was to move head first into challenging situations and then figure out how to surmount them. Samuel, eager to attend high school, went to Valparaiso without money and only the clothes he was wearing. He knocked on doors offering to do chores in exchange for room and board and was hired first by the Cass family; then he worked for the Kelloggs during the winter term, and later for the Shreeves.

When he learned his classmates all had middle names, Sam decided he needed one too. Because he admired Civil War General William Tecumseh Sherman, he told his teacher his middle name was Sherman. Recalling how he came to be S. S. McClure, he said, "Later I changed the Sherman to Sidney. I am usually known now as S. S. McClure, but there never was any S. S. McClure until that morning."[7]

While Montessori's teaching experiences led her to create her own method of education, McClure's teaching experiences were less promising. During the summer vacation following his first year as a high school student, McClure, who needed to earn some money for his next year, tried teaching. At a time when credentialing teachers was a local matter, McClure passed the Porter County examinations and was hired as a teacher at a country school near his stepfather's farm. He decided to change the school's daily routine, "The custom was then in country schools to keep the little children in their seats all day, although they had only three or four recitations during the school period. This seemed to me inflicting a needless hardship, so I decided to give the youngest children eight short recitations periods a day and to let them play out of doors the rest of the time. . . . This was not the usual way of managing a country school, however, and a hired man who worked in the fields near the schoolhouse complained to the directors. . . . The school directors met and asked me what I had to say to this charge. I was then fifteen, had had no experience in teaching before. . . . The charge was dismissed. I could not, however, teach out my term of three months. The humdrum of teaching was more than I could endure. . . . One thing I could never do was teach a country school. I tried it twice afterward, but both times I had to run away from the job before the term was over."[8]

As an adolescent, McClure began to experience an unsettling feeling he called "attacks of restlessness." Most likely due to the onset of a psychological condition, perhaps manic-depression, McClure experienced this for the rest of his life. Not understanding what was happening, he wrote,

> I simply had to run away for a day, for half a day, for two days. It was not that I wanted to go anywhere in particular, but that I had to go somewhere,

> that I could not stay another minute. . . . These fits were apt to come on at any time; but in the spring . . . they were sure to come. . . . There was no standing up against them. . . . Usually I didn't try; I simply ran down to the station and took the first freight-car out of town. . . . I ran away like this, not once or twice, but dozens and dozens of time. It was a regular irregularity in my life. It was, indeed, more than most other things, a necessity of my life. . . . This restlessness was something that I seemed to have no control over. I have had to reckon with it all my life, and whatever I have been able to do has been in spite of it. As a lad I followed this impulse blindly, but later I realized that this restlessness was a kind of misfortune, and that it could be at times a hard master.[9]

As an adult, McClure periodically had to be on the move, either by train or steamer. He became so famous for his frequent Atlantic crossings that ship captains would signal to each other asking if McClure was aboard their ship.

After his stepfather, Thomas Simpson, died in early 1874, his twice-widowed mother asked seventeen-year-old Sam to leave high school in Valparaiso and come back to work the farm she had inherited. Though farming did not appeal to him, McClure returned reluctantly but hoped to find an escape so he could continue his education.

McClure's opportunity came when his uncle, Joe Gaston, Elizabeth's brother, a student for the ministry at Knox College in Galesburg, Illinois, urged him to go to Knox. Eager to leave the farm and needing little encouragement, McClure was ready to go to college. He recalled that his "vague project instantly became a definite plan. I was going to Knox College. . . . When September came I set off for Galesburg."[10]

Beginning the first of his seven years as a student at Knox College in September 1874, McClure would not graduate until June 1882. His extended time as a college student was due to his dire financial situation, which required absences to earn money for tuition and board, his deficiency in the academic prerequisites required for admission as a college student, and his bouts of restlessness.

Before being admitted as a freshman in the College, McClure had to pass a three-year classical college preparatory program. Knox, like many colleges at the time, had a preparatory department, the Knox Academy, in which students could fulfill their college-entry requirements. McClure recalled beginning his study at Knox: "I was seventeen, and it was a seven years' job that I was starting upon."[11] McClure credited Professor George Churchill, the Academy's principal, as being a positive influence on him.

McClure's move from northwest Indiana to Galesburg in northwest central Illinois kept him in the familiar small-town midwestern environment. As in his high school years in Valparaiso, Sam struggled financially and often lacked money for food and clothing. During his first year at Knox, he worked for room and board and stayed at the home of Galesburg's mayor, J. C. Stewart. He recalled, "I earned extra money for books and pocket-money by sawing wood about town. . . . I had no outside help at all; and at the end of the school year I had made my own way, and had six dollars left."[12]

A small coeducational college with religious origins and a faculty of fifteen professors and instructors, Knox College made a deep and lasting imprint on McClure. In 1895, *McClure's Magazine* published an article on Knox College and Galesburg by Madame Blanc (Therese Bentzon), a French writer who was studying coeducational institutions in the United States. Blanc's visit to Knox College in 1893, when it had an enrollment of 600 students, portrayed the college much as it was when McClure was a student. She found the "prairie college" inseparable from the little town of "pretty" painted wood houses, on maple-lined streets with board sidewalks. The town was named for its founder, Rev. George Gale, who, in 1836, led thirty families from upstate New York to settle on the western Illinois prairie. The college, supported by Congregationalists and Presbyterians, received a charter from the state of Illinois in 1837 and opened in 1838 with forty students.[13] Its goals were to prepare well-educated evangelical ministers and women as "worthy educators of future generations." In her article, Blanc referred to McClure as "the honest little peddler" who worked to pay his college expenses and one of "those late in beginning" who "are likely to show superior talents."[14]

Blanc noted a religious spirit pervaded the campus in which students and faculty attended a service each morning in the auditorium of Alumni Hall, a large brick and red sandstone building in modified Roman style, where there was prayer, Bible reading, and commentary. Attending the same classes, the young women and men voluntarily separated themselves on different sides of the classroom.

McClure recalled that "Four-fifths of the students at Knox . . . took the old-fashioned classical course, in which Greek was obligatory. . . . I enjoyed Greek and mathematics more than any other subjects." The "Classical Course" to which he referred was a four-year program consisting of Latin and Greek languages and literature; mathematics; geography and history; natural sciences; philosophy; and English language, literature, and rhetoric. With a strong concentration on academic disciplines, McClure found "there were no fraternities, no organized athletics, no student dances, no concerts, no students' orchestra or glee club. . . . A boy's standing among the other boys depended entirely upon his scholarship. . . . One felt that Knox College was a place set apart for boys to . . . develop in mind and body . . . a kind of monastic calm."[15]

Although he described Knox College as a place of "monastic calm," McClure, definitely not a monk, was rarely calm. He had a restlessness about him that required him to be on the move. He had to struggle for the basic necessities— food, clothing, and even enough coal to heat his room. Resourcefully joining his need for money with his need for movement, he became a door-to-door peddler, traveling through the Midwest. In his sophomore year, he started his journeys as a traveling salesman, "Whenever I ran short of funds, I shouldered my pack and went away into the country for a few days, and returned with money enough to go on for a while. I had at last found a vocation exactly suited to my nature and to my needs, that could be taken up and dropped again at will: a means of making money that was easy, pleasant, nomadic, and especially adapted to broken time," such as school breaks and summer vacations.[16]

McClure, whose vivacious personality attracted his classmates, enlisted his friend and roommate, Albert Brady, to join him the summer after their junior year, traveling around the Great Lakes selling microscopes. McClure recalled they "had traveled upward of three thousand miles, had made a little money, and were better friends than ever. Then [began] . . . senior work at Knox."[17] Brady, a lasting friend, would join McClure as the Advertising Manager of *McClure's Magazine*.

Years later, McClure, reflecting on his peddling experiences, felt that they had given him insights into publishing his popular magazine. The people of the small midwestern towns and farms subscribed to *McClure's Magazine* because they "were interested in exactly the same things . . . that interested me. . . . I could never believe in that distinction made by some editors that 'this or that was very good, but it wouldn't interest the people of the Middle West, or the people in the little towns.' My experience had taught me that the people in the little towns were interested in whatever was interesting—that they were just like the people in New York or Boston. I felt myself to be a fairly representative Middle-Westerner. I bought and printed what interested me, and it usually seemed to interest the other Middle-Westerners."[18]

Although both Montessori and McClure were ready to seize an opportunity when it came their way, their different personalities caused them to exploit it differently, sometimes successfully and others not. Both were bright intellectually but uneven in their dispositions. Montessori, as many said, was a near genius; McClure was an extraordinary innovative, but not systematic, thinker. Scientist and physician, Montessori was cautious and deliberate but also guarded and suspicious. McClure, excitable, typically acted quickly on his myriad ideas.

At Knox College, McClure met and fell in love with Harriet Hurd, the daughter of Albert Hurd, a highly respected Knox faculty member. Hurd, a graduate of Middlebury College in Vermont and a student of Louis Agassiz, the pioneer American natural scientist, had a long distinguished career at Knox. A professor of chemistry and Latin for forty-one years, Hurd also had served as Knox's acting president for three years.[19] The match between Harriet and Samuel, a most unlikely one, appeared doomed to failure. Like everyone else at the College, Professor Hurd was well aware of McClure. He did not find the penniless Irish immigrant, a restless part-time peddler who took seven years to earn his bachelor's degree, to be at all suited to his intellectual and capable daughter. The professor, determined to thwart his daughter's relationship with McClure, however, like others, underestimated his relentless determination. When McClure wanted something, even if it appeared unattainable, he persisted until he got it. McClure's two aims were to earn a college degree and to marry Harriet (Hattie) Hurd.

Like Professor Hurd, McClure's mother, Elizabeth, opposed her son's relationship with a college professor's delicate daughter. She developed a scheme to thwart the romance. In the summer of 1876, she had Sam accompany her on a visit back home to Northern Ireland. Elizabeth, who paid for the trip with funds from the sale of her husband's farm, had a plan. She would return to the United States, leaving Sam in Ireland without money for his voyage back home. Stranded, he would have no choice but to stay and work in Ireland. Sam, however, was more than a match for his mother when it came to devising strategies. Nineteen-year-old Sam McClure would not be left behind. He had his own plan; he would return to Knox College and to Harriet Hurd, with whom he was "very much in love."[20]

When an idea came to him, McClure acted on it. He attempted to stow away on a ship sailing to New York but was discovered and ordered off. Sam pleaded with the ship's first officer that he be allowed to stay on board. He earnestly told the officer that he was a medical student who needed to complete his degree in the United States so he could achieve his life-long dream of returning to Ireland to care for the poor. Impressed by the young man's altruism, the officer agreed to take him on as the assistant to the ship's doctor. McClure's lack of medical training was discovered after the ship had left port. He was put to work as a deck hand and mess server to pay for his passage.[21] Now that he had thwarted his mother, McClure would next deal with Professor Hurd.

Back at Knox for the beginning of the fall semester in September 1876, Sam McClure asked Harriet, "whether, if I turned out to be a good man, she would marry me in seven years. She said that she would."[22] When Sam was eligible to begin his freshman year in 1877, Harriet, the valedictorian of her class, graduated from Knox in July 1877. Professor Hurd, still determined to end his daughter's involvement with McClure, arranged for her to study French in Canada. Harriet reluctantly agreed to her father's plan. Parting with McClure, Harriet told him "that her father was going to send her away to school, and that she had promised him not to see . . . or . . . write to him." McClure "did not see her or hear from her again for four years and two months."[23] Despite his problems with the professor, the *Knox Student*, which McClure edited, praised Hurd for his "unfailing interest and labor" in assembling Knox's "mineralogical, geological, conchological, and botanical collections."[24]

McClure pursued his long and often interrupted courtship with the same determination he displayed in the seven years he spent earning his bachelor's degree. In 1882, Harriet, back in Galesburg, again began seeing Sam. McClure wrote, "On September 15 of my senior year I saw Harriet Hurd for the first time in nearly five years. . . . She . . . said that she felt that things had never changed between us. . . . We met again as if we had not been separated for nearly five years, with complete sympathy and understanding. . . . After that I saw Miss Hurd nearly every day until she left Galesburg in March" to take a teaching position at the Abbot Academy, in Andover, Massachusetts.[25] Professor Hurd had persuaded his daughter to take the job as a way of ending her involvement with McClure. Although Professor Hurd won this battle, he would lose the war—as Harriet would eventually marry Samuel S. McClure.

Despite his troubled relationship with Professor Hurd and his daughter, McClure's seven years at Knox College had a pronounced influence on his life, especially his career as the editor and publisher of *McClure's Magazine*, the journal that won his place in the history of American journalism. At Knox, he made a circle of friends who later joined him in creating America's foremost magazine of the Progressive Era. Showing a talent for journalism, he served as editor-in-chief of *The Knox Student*, the college newspaper, during his senior year (1881–1882), with his close friends John Phillips as Literary Editor and Albert Brady as Business Manager. These three friends would later play the same roles at *McClure's Magazine*. In editing *McClure's Magazine*, McClure claimed he "followed exactly the same principles" he had learned as editor of the *Knox Student*." Whatever I know about editing I knew in the beginning."[26]

Reflecting on his experience as a college editor, McClure recalled, "We put out a very good college paper. John Phillips was easily the best read student in the college, a boy with a great natural aptitude for letters; and Albert Brady showed then the same unusual business ability that he afterward showed as Business Manager of *McClure's Magazine*. . . . It does not often happen that three boys, united in a college enterprise, keep in touch with one another and a few years after their graduation form a business partnership that lasts through a large part of their lives."[27]

McClure's editorials in the *Student* provide strong clues to his later career, especially founding his syndicate and *McClure's Magazine*. In an editorial on December 1881, McClure asked, "How can the College Press be elevated?" Answering his own question and anticipating his future syndicate, he urged the western colleges to form "An Associated College Press" service, which he offered to lead at Knox College. The participating college editors would send campus news items to him that he would collate and print in a bulletin. McClure's proposal received favorable responses from midwestern college editors at Carleton College in Minnesota; Lawrence in Wisconsin; Earlham and Franklin in Indiana; and Wheaton, Northwestern, the University of Illinois and Monmouth in Illinois.[28] In May 2, 1882, the college editors met in Indianapolis to organize the Western College Press Association. McClure, who had originated the idea for the association, worked with two other editors to draft the Association's Constitution. The Constitution stated the association's major goal was "to increase the efficiency and extend the influence of the college press."[29] The association's membership included the papers and editors of colleges in Illinois, Iowa, Wisconsin, Indiana, Missouri, and Minnesota. McClure was elected president of the association.

McClure's promotion of the association led him to edit *The History of College Journalism*, "an entirely new venture in an historico-literary point of view," which he predicted at twenty-five cents a copy "will we believe command a large and ready sale."[30] McClure's long-time associate John Phillips contributed the article on the history of student journals at Knox College.[31]

Anticipating the investigative reporting that would make *McClure's Magazine* a "muck-raking" journal two decades later, McClure, as a college editor, told his classmates, "It is necessary for us as students to keep pace with the events that are happening in our own land and across the sea. . . . We must comprehend the problems . . . which will demand solution in our generation." The young editor warned, "We see that grave question of monopolies slowly stalking in the issue. . . . We must keep step with the railroad, manufacturing and legislative news, to grasp all this problem. . . . We must understand today in order that we may understand to-morrow."[32]

After seven years as a student, S. S. McClure, third in a class of thirty, graduated from Knox College in June 1882. His choice of a topic for his commencement oration, "The Nature of Enthusiasm," revealed his personality.[33] Elevating his restlessness into a philosophy of life, McClure told his listeners, "There are men whom labor cannot weary, nor obstacles discourage, nor drudgery disgust, who do no blundering but with decision overcome any obstacle to attain their purposed end. The principle that animates these men is called enthusiasm. . . . It is that principle that renders man insensible to cold, hunger, disease, failure, ridicule, death; that lifts him above the dominion of circumstances, that renders defeat impossible. The enthusiast thinks only in deeds, finds his language in events, his credentials are victorious."[34]

As if describing his future intentions, McClure continued, "The men who start the great new movements in the world are enthusiasts whose eyes are fixed upon the end they wish to bring about—that to them the future becomes present. . . .

The enthusiast must always be considered impractical, because he ignores those difficulties of execution which make most men conservative; and his impracticality is his strength. . . . This kind of man would . . . get what he started out for."[35]

From his college graduation in 1882 until his death in 1949, McClure remained strongly attached to his alma mater. Knox College awarded him and his friend, John Phillips, honorary doctorates of literature in 1907. McClure served on the college's board of trustees from 1894 until his death. He attributed the "Greatness of Knox College" to its emphasis on the classical languages, Greek and Latin, and to the principles of self-government. He stated, "Of all the contributions of the English peoples to the advancement of civilization I regard as the greatest, their making the study of Greek and Latin the backbone of their education in school and college. . . . The colleges and universities and the preparatory schools of England and America, trained and educated the men who became leaders in public life and industry by study dominated by the languages and literature of Greece and Rome. . . . The Americans were the first Europeans to make on a vast scale the noblest experiment possible—the creation of self-government."[36]

Although he finally earned his college degree, McClure still found his "future was an absolute blank ahead of me. . . . I figured" that with "so many boys from so many colleges . . . going into regular lines of work . . . there might be room for one irregular."[37]

Now that he had his long-sought bachelor's degree, McClure pursued the other prize that had eluded him—Harriet Hurd. He had corresponded with Harriet, who was spending the summer of 1882 in Utica, New York. However, Harriet, who earlier agreed to his visit, was no longer answering his letters. Undeterred, McClure, at the end of June, arrived in Utica to visit Harriet but the couple's reunion did not go well. Even McClure, who rarely gave up, feared he had lost her, "My interview with Miss Hurd was almost too painful to describe . . . and more than justified the fears that the ceasing of her letters had aroused in me. When I left her, I carried away the conviction that she had absolutely ceased to care for me—that I in every way displeased her and fell short of her expectations. This dismissal I accepted as final."[38] Of course, for McClure, few things in life were ever final.

Without future plans, McClure impulsively took the next train departing Utica; it just happened to be going to Boston. McClure recalled, "I had never in my life thought of going to Boston before, and I had no reason for going there now. I was merely going wherever the next train went."[39]

In Boston without a job, McClure remembered a contact in that city. He had, as a college editor, sold advertising space to the Pope Manufacturing Company, the largest bicycle manufacturer in the United States.[40] On July 3, McClure had an interview with its president, Colonel Albert A. Pope, who hired him to teach cycling at his large rink, called the "riding academy." McClure, who did not know how to ride, rented a bike and quickly learned cycling.

Colonel Pope, an innovative entrepreneur, recognized that publicity would sell more of his bicycles. Seeking to capitalize on bicycling's wave of popularity in the country, Pope decided to start a cycling magazine, the *Wheelman*. Since McClure had experience as a college editor, Pope made him the *Wheelman*'s editor. Had it not been about bicycling, McClure's announcement about the new magazine could have been used as copy for *McClure's Magazine*. True to McClure's promotional style, the announcement read, "The *Wheelman* enters a hitherto unoccupied field in American periodical literature. It is to hold the same relation to bicycling weeklies that the literary magazine holds to the newspaper press. . . . Its readers and contributors will be cultured and intelligent people, its typographical and mechanical make-up will be equal to that of the best literary magazines."[41]

McClure, realizing that he needed a staff, persuaded Pope to hire his brother John and his Knox college friend John Phillips. The first number of the *Wheelman,* "an illustrated magazine of cycling literature and news," came out in October 1882. Among its far-ranging articles were the "Alps by Bicycle," "Bicycle for Physicians," "'The Poet's Tribute to Garfield," and "Art and Nature in Italy." McClure recalled, "I had never expected to be an editor, or planned to be one; but now that I found myself one, I was not surprised."[42]

In 1884, Colonel Pope bought William B. Howland's magazine, *Outing*, which he combined with the *Wheelman* as *Outing and the Wheelman: An Illustrated Monthly Magazine of Recreation*. Pope retained Howland, an experienced publisher, as the magazine's business manager. Howland was to share the editorship with McClure. McClure, who wanted to be the sole editor, balked and left the position that he had held for two years. His explanation for leaving signaled the attitude that marked his later career—that he should be the person in charge: "I could not edit a magazine where I shared the authority and responsibility with another man."[43]

McClure's job with Pope did not deter him from pursuing his quest for Harriet Hurd. After six years of a relationship frequently interrupted by parental objections, Harriet finally agreed to marry Sam. McClure often told the story of his long courtship of the Knox professor's daughter, "She had made every reasonable concession to her father's strong feeling; she had waited, as he besought her to, had gone away from Galesburg, formed new friends, and neither seen me nor written to me for four years. Our feeling for each other had endured through so much . . . that she at last felt that it would be right to marry me, even against her father's wishes. . . . Before the spring term of 1883 was over, Miss Hurd wrote her father that she intended to marry me."[44]

Sam McClure and Harriet Hurd were married at the Hurd family home in Galesburg on September 4, 1883. They honeymooned in Quebec and then rented a small house in Cambridge, Massachusetts. At the end of November, the couple moved to New York City, where McClure worked at the De Vinne Press and Harriet at the Century Company. McClure next worked at the Century Company, the publisher of *Century* magazine. The couple moved to East Orange, New Jersey, where their daughter Eleanor was born in July 1884. Sam took a two-week vacation to help with the baby. On November 16, 1884, the McClure's moved to a flat at 114 East Fifty-Third Street in New York.

Harriet and Samuel had three more children. Elizabeth was born in 1886; Robert Louis Stevenson in 1888, and Mary in 1890. Hattie McClure had a positive, if limited, influence on her husband, in that she loyally supported him even when his plans tended to be grandiose. In continual communication often by letter, Sam and Hattie shared insights about their children, their health, the changing fortunes of publishing, and the relationship with Maria Montessori. In 1895, Harriet, in response to an alumnae questionnaire from Knox College, filled in the line designated for "occupation," with "Wife of S. S. McClure (occupation enough for any woman)."[45] Her comment tells the story of their marriage and life together.

While McClure was on leave to help care for his first child, new ideas flashed through his fertile mind. What intrigued him the most was a plan for a syndicate to distribute stories to newspapers throughout the country. He proposed his plan to the Century Company, which owned many articles and short stories that could be syndicated to newspapers nationally. Roswell Smith, an officer at the Century Company, not only rejected McClure's idea but told him that he was unsuited to work in a large company and should go into business for himself.

Undeterred by Smith's rejection, McClure, obsessed with his syndicate idea, took Smith's advice to start his own business. "My plan, briefly," he said, "was this: I could get a short story from any of the best story-writers then for $150.00. I figured that I ought to be able to sell that story to 100 newspapers throughout the country, at $5 each. News was syndicated in this way, and I did not see why fiction should not be."[46]

In October 1884, twenty-seven-year-old Sam McClure, without financial resources or business experience, launched his McClure Newspaper Syndicate. When he approached potential clients for his service, he found editors skeptical and authors enthusiastic. McClure, with his usual persistence, eventually wore down the editors, who began subscribing to his service. He recalled that the *St. Paul Pioneer Press* and the *San Francisco Argonaut* were among the first subscribers, paying eight dollars a week for the service.[47]

McClure's syndicate began as a family business conducted from his flat in New York City. He was the salesman and acquisitions editor. Harriet, capable and versatile, handled the correspondence, translated stories from French and German authors, prepared copy for the printers, and mailed articles to newspapers.

Within a year, McClure's Syndicate was so successful that McClure hired a secretary and rented a New York office. He had turned the acquisition, sale, and distribution of short stories, serialized books, and comic strips into a profitable business.

McClure's search for promising authors enabled him to do what he enjoyed and needed to do—travel in the United States and Europe. Very generous in paying authors, he attracted such prominent writers as George Ade, Joel Chandler Harris, William Dean Howells, Jack London, Arthur Conan Doyle, Rudyard Kipling, and Robert Louis Stevenson as contributors to his syndicate. In London, McClure once found himself in a bidding war with his competitor, Charles Scribner, for the syndicate rights to publish Kipling's *Kim*. When Scribner offered $16,000 for the rights, McClure, who "couldn't see any sense in upping the bidding by easy stages" won the rights by offering "a flat $25,000 at once." When he heard that Robert Louis Stevenson wanted to live at sea on a yacht, McClure agreed to purchase one if Stevenson gave him the rights to syndicate his planned "South Sea Letters."[48]

In 1886, McClure's college friend, John S. Phillips, became the syndicate's business manager. Known for his organizational skill and careful financial accounting, Phillips was the opposite, but also the complement, of McClure, who claimed that he never kept books. McClure and Phillips later became partners in *McClure's Magazine*. McClure placed his brother Robert in charge of the syndicate's London office.

McClure's role as acquisitions editor enabled him to be on the road. He recalled spending "as many as seventeen successive nights in sleeping-cars" as he traveled to meet with editors and authors. He discovered "what people were writing and what people were reading, and in which of the happenings in the world people took the keenest interest." Often, he suggested topics to authors.

Just as he had turned his inherent need to keep moving into profit as a peddler during his college year, McClure did the same thing as editor of his syndicate. He wrote, "I never got ideas sitting still. I never saw so many possibilities for my business or had so many editorial ideas as when I was hurrying about from city to city, talking with editors and newspaper men. The restlessness which had mastered me as a boy always had the upper hand of me, and it was my good fortune that I could make it serve my ends. Whatever work I have done has been incidental to this foremost necessity to keep moving."[49]

McClure began a new pattern that would stay with him for the rest of his life—he became a frequent traveler to Europe on a quest to find and engage authors. In London in 1889, he read Arthur Conan Doyle's *A Study in Scarlet*. Intuitively recognizing Doyle's potential to be a best-selling mystery writer, McClure contracted with Doyle and bought the next twelve Sherlock Holmes stories for his syndicate.

As with his decision to publish Conan Doyle's stories, McClure had a keen, almost intuitive, sense in recognizing talented authors. He wrote "I had but one test for a story, and that was a wholly personal one—simply how much the story interested me. I always felt that I judged a story with my solar plexus rather than my brain; my only measure of it was the pull it exerted upon something inside of me. . . . I always made a rule of reading a story three times within seven days, before I published it, to see whether my interest kept up."[50]

After eight years of operating the syndicate, McClure, always eager to test new ideas, decided to inaugurate an inexpensive monthly national magazine. Intruding into a highly competitive arena, he would be challenging such nationally established magazines as *Harper's*, *Scribner's*, the *Atlantic*, and the *Century*, his former employer. McClure planned to finance his new venture, *McClure's Magazine*, with funds from his syndicate. He would begin its publication by reprinting in his new magazine the best of the two thousand short stories that his syndicate owned.[51]

Following his pattern of hiring friends from his student days at Knox College, he hired Albert Brady, who was then the publisher of the *Davenport (IA) Daily Times*, as the new magazine's advertising manager. Brady and John Phillips were solid, highly capable, and prudent businessmen who provided a balance to the creative and innovative but highly impulsive and erratic McClure.

Viola Roseboro', who McClure hired as a manuscript reader, became an indispensable addition to the magazine's staff in reviewing the unsolicited manuscripts sent to the publisher. McClure found Roseboro', like him, to have an instinctive skill in discovering talented, but unknown, writers. He assessed Roseboro' as having "a singularly open mind toward the manuscript bag, a natural attitude toward stories which is rare in professional readers." Roseboro' recommended the publications of the early stories of O. Henry, Jack London, Rex Beach, and Myra Kelley when these writers were unknown.[52]

The first issue of *McClure's Magazine* was published in May 1893. It sold for fifteen cents while the *Century*, *Harper's*, and the *Atlantic* cost thirty-five cents and *Scribner's*, the *Cosmopolitan*, and *Munsey's* cost twenty-five cents.[53] Of the first run of 20,000 copies, 12,000 were returned. The prospects for the magazine's success were dim in that its first issues came during the Panic of 1893, a deep financial recession that gripped the nation. Banks were wary of making loans to uncertain ventures like *McClure's*. Some syndicate subscribers, experiencing financial shortfalls, canceled their subscriptions. Advertising, too, was generating very little revenue. The magazine's expenses greatly strained McClure's assets. Stock in the magazine sold for $100.00 a share though there were few buyers. McClure reported that in the summer of 1894 the magazine was losing $1,000 a month."[54]

Each issue presented a financial crisis but, one way or another, it was published. Some authors, including Conan Doyle who invested $5,000 in the magazine, came to the rescue with loans.

Despite its earlier difficulties, *McClure's Magazine* rebounded and by 1896 had become the country's leading periodical. McClure reported its circulation was "far in excess of the *Century*, *Harper's*, or *Scribner's*, and soon to be greater than all three."[55] Though the magazine's sales soared, McClure, not known for his business acumen, was still in debt. Some profits went to buy a printing press and others were used to launch a second magazine, the *McClure's Quarterly*. McClure admitted that he "lost thousands of dollars" on the *Quarterly*, which "never got beyond the first two numbers." In January 1896, McClure, at age thirty-nine, assessed his financial status and found himself $287,000 in debt.[56]

McClure was able to keep his magazine in circulation, and it began to receive positive reviews and a promising public reaction. One of the magazine's unique features was the "Real Conversations" column, interviews by well-known writers with renowned public figures like Thomas Edison, Oliver Wendell Holmes, and Alexander Graham Bell. Making a determined effort to bring science to the public, the magazine featured articles on inventions such as Marconi's wireless telegraphy and the Wright Brothers' flying-machine.[57] When McClure promoted Montessori in 1911–1912, he presented the Italian educator as a genius who had successfully applied science to education.

The Human Document series published photo-biographies of noted individuals. Using the recently invented technology of photo-engraving which reduced the cost of images, *McClure's* articles were well illustrated. When the Montessori articles appeared in 1911–1912, they were copiously illustrated with photographs of children using the didactic apparatus in her schools.

Just as it had served him well in his syndicate, McClure's extraordinary ability to find and recognize talented writers served him as editor of *McClure's Magazine*. Not known for his humility, McClure recognized his literary acumen as an editor, stating that he was "open-minded, naturally enthusiastic, and not afraid to experiment with a new man. The men I tried did not always make good; but when they failed it never hurt anybody, and when they succeeded it helped every one concerned. A new writer gets to the people quickly enough, if he can once get by the editor. I was always easy to get by. If I believed in a man, I could give him a large audience at once; I could give him that gaze of the public which is the breath of life to a writer. . . . I could place him at once before a million families, the representative people who read the leading dailies in all parts of the country. The test of a writer's market value is, how many people will read him? I could give a new writer that test at once."[58]

Immersed in the literary world, McClure vigorously pursued good authors, acquiring their work for publication. Some were well-known while others were unknowns with a potential that McClure recognized. One of the unknowns was the British author Anthony Hope Hawkins, who wrote the popular *The Prisoner of Zenda* that was serialized in *McClure's Magazine*.

One of McClure's editorial coups was his agreement with Rudyard Kipling who, though well-known in England, was largely undiscovered in the United States. McClure predicted that Kipling would "be one of the great figures in English literature."[59] *McClure's* serialized the *Jungle Book* stories, *Kim*, and *Captains Courageous*. The loquacious McClure recalled that he once talked with Kipling for "eight solid hours" and that Kipling told him, "McClure, your business is dealing in brain futures."[60] In addition to Kipling, Conan Doyle, and Hawkins, *McClure's Magazine* featured such distinguished writers as Robert Louis Stevenson, Stephen Crane, O. Henry, and Jack London.

Attracting successful authors was costly but McClure pursued them, often recklessly promising them money he did not have. For the aspiring author who sought publication and the editor who acquired his work for a modest amount, it was a mutually beneficial arrangement.

While *McClure's Magazine* was a leader in serializing the work of great and promising European and American authors, it won its place in the history of American journalism by being the Progressive Era's groundbreaking journal. Despite his personal idiosyncrasies, McClure set the standards for authoritative journalism in the early twentieth century. He believed the modern industrial era needed a magazine whose writers would seek out the facts needed to accurately report the great economic, political, and social events of the time. Lagging behind the pace of industrial society's specialization, articles were still being written by reporters who, as generalists, were largely "uninformed in the subjects upon which they wrote."[61] McClure's standard required his reporters to thoroughly and accurately investigate an issue before writing about it. If his reporters could not write with the specialist's expertise, they were to consult with experts to accurately inform the public.[62] McClure recruited a staff of highly able investigative reporters that included such notable pioneer journalists as Ida Tarbell, William Allen White, Lincoln Steffens, and Ray Stannard Baker. A noted historian of the Progressive Era, J. Leonard Bates, wrote they succeeded as writers who "got their facts straight and wrote without undue sensationalism," and "some went another step with works that were perceptively interpretive and philosophic."[63]

Ida Tarbell (1857–1944) epitomized McClure's ideal of the thorough and accurate reporter.[64] A graduate of Allegheny College, Tarbell, who earlier had worked on the staff of the *Chautauquan*, was living in Paris when McClure met her in 1903. On one of his frequent European talent hunts, McClure interviewed Tarbell who was studying history at the Sorbonne and researching a biography of

Madame Roland, an opinion-maker of the French Revolution. Impressed by Tarbell, McClure hired her as a writer. Tarbell's first assignment was an illustrated "Life of Napoleon."[65] Her first installment on Napoleon appeared in November 1894. Tarbell's series on the French Emperor was so popular that *McClure's Magazine's* circulation doubled, from forty thousand to eighty thousand copies. Tarbell's next assignment, a twenty-part "Life of Lincoln," another success, boosted circulation from 120,000 in early 1895 to 250,000 at the year's end in December.[66]

Tarbell's investigation of the Standard Oil Company established *McClure's* Progressive credentials as a "muckraking" journal. McClure cited her "History of Standard Oil" as the *Magazine's* "first . . . work of importance." The Columbian Exposition, the World's Fair of l893, had stimulated McClure's idea for a series on "the greatest American business achievements." Rockefeller's Standard Oil Company was certainly in the category of a large and successful corporation. Standard Oil also was part of the contemporary issue of monopolies and trusts in American political and economic life. McClure's staff had decided on a strategy of deconstructing the complex issue by investigating a single trust's "history, its effects, and its tendencies." Standard Oil, the nation's largest and most powerful trust, was "the creature largely of one man . . . John D. Rockefeller. So that the history of this Trust would lend itself almost to the simplicity of biographical treatment."[67]

Tarbell, who had grown up in the oil region of western Pennsylvania, was ideally suited for the project. Her father, Frank Tarbell, a small operator in the oil business, had been squeezed out by the giant Standard Oil monopoly.[68] Tarbell did months of detailed documentary research in the records of Standard Oil, especially legislative hearings and court cases involving the company. She also interviewed businessmen and attorneys who had dealt with Standard Oil. According to McClure's accounting, Tarbell's painstaking research required "five years of labor" that cost the *Magazine* "over sixty thousand dollars."[69]

McClure's Magazine published Tarbell's "The History of the Standard Oil Company" as a series of nineteen installments from November 1902 through October 1904. Tarbell's articles won a highly favorable reception from readers. She had written an understandable and compelling narrative of a subject that could have been mired in complex and confusing details. Employing her talents as a biographer, she was able to personify the monopoly's manipulations in terms of one man—John D. Rockefeller. Her articles were later published as a book, *The History of the Standard Oil Company*, in 1904. Tarbell's articles were a factor in the US Supreme Court's decision to break up the Standard Oil monopoly in 1911.[70]

Lincoln Steffens (1866–1936) was another of *McClure's* famed investigative journalists.[71] His series of articles on corruption in municipal and state government became a driving force for reform during the Progressive Era. Each of Steffens's articles was a thorough investigation of the links between unscrupulous businessmen and corrupt politicians in a particular large city, as in his "The Shame of Minneapolis: The Rescue and Redemption of a City that was Sold Out."[72] His articles were published as a book, *The Shame of the Cities*, in 1904. McClure praised Steffens's articles as "the first accurate studies of this nature that had then appeared in a magazine in America."[73] He also recalled that Steffens averaged about four articles a year, each of which cost the magazine about two thousand dollars.[74]

Recounting how *McClure's Magazine* became known as a "muckraking" journal, McClure stated, "the January, 1903, number of *McClure's* which contained the third article of Miss Tarbell's Standard Oil series, also contained Mr. Steffens's Minneapolis article, and Mr. Baker's article on the anthracite coal strike of 1902. Thus the origin of what was later called the 'muck-raking' movement was accidental. It came from no formulated plan to attack existing institutions, but was the result of merely taking up in the magazine some of the problems that were beginning to interest the people."[75]

Theodore Roosevelt, though a Progressive, decried what he considered to be some journalists' excesses in their investigations as "muck-raking." McClure, disliking the sweeping brush of muck-raking, said they were investigations designed to bring reforms for good government. He said the articles "dealt with very serious questions, involving large property rights and large labor situations, and I believe that there was not an error of any importance in these articles. These articles were influential in causing activity on the part of the people and the government in relation to the system of rebates by the railroads and were regarded as having had a considerable influence on public opinion in carrying out the stringent reforms by President Roosevelt."[76]

S. S. McClure achieved personal and financial success, which included memberships in men's clubs, invitations to the White House, socializing with senators and ambassadors, and, in 1903, moving his family into a large imposing house at Ardsley, overlooking the Hudson River. He and his family, nurses, and friends traveled to Europe and Egypt for long periods of time. Heady with success, the enthusiastic McClure continually had ideas for new business ventures. In early 1896, the McClure Company bought its own printing plant and bindery so that the magazine could be printed in-house. He also cofounded a publishing house with Frank Doubleday. In June 1899, McClure bought the controlling interest in Harper & Brothers from J. P. Morgan. The Harper's acquisition included a syndicate service, five magazines, a lecture bureau, and two book companies. Harper's overwhelming debt and a host of other problems forced McClure to sell his interest in Harper's at a serious financial loss. Shortly thereafter, Doubleday announced that it was dissolving the publishing partnership with McClure. His effort to launch a new journal, *McClure's Quarterly*, failed after two issues. Despite these business failures, an ebullient McClure envisioned publishing an encyclopedia and starting a new magazine called *McClure's Review*.

Ellery Sedgwick, who worked on the *McClure's* staff in 1907, related his experiences in his memoir, *A Happy Profession*. Serving as the *Atlantic Monthly*'s editor from 1908 to 1938, Sedgwick, with a perspective into the world of publishing, provided keen insights into McClure's management style and professional expectations for journalists. Sedgwick remembered his time at *McClure's Magazine* as "an adventure of quality" where he observed "at close range a very remarkable man. Mr. McClure had genius, there was no doubt of that—genius with all its coruscations." Describing his chief as possessed by "a Napoleonic belief in his own star," McClure "would inflame the intelligence of his staff into molten excitement. The mood would be too hot to last but would bring results."[77]

Recounting McClure's management style, Sedgwick said; "A week in the McClure office was the precise reversal of the six busy days described in the first chapter of Genesis. It seemed to end in a world without form, and void. From Order came forth Chaos. . . . Never . . . in American business, was there a brighter talent than McClure's for disorganization. If the chief did not originate a design, he could at least obfuscate it. The chief was forever interrupting, cutting every sequence into a dozen parts." Sedgwick said the staff relished "the blessed quiet of those days when McClure was abroad. The dove of peace descended upon the office and every man took up his own life." But Sedgwick conceded that "the fires" McClure "kindled were brighter than any flames his staff could produce without him."[78]

While McClure as a manager was no model for Sedgwick, a future editor of a leading national journal, he was an exemplar for the high standard of journalism that he set. Praising McClure, Sedgwick said, "In journalism the standard is everything, and the standard was set by McClure himself. . . . Slipshod work, even in tiny details, he would not tolerate. . . . In *McClure's* accuracy was a moral force. . . . He demanded . . . expression in clear, logical, intelligible, hard-fitting form. He had also the artist's instinct against exaggeration. He reverenced the power of understatement."[79] Sedgwick, who would be the *Atlantic Monthly*'s editor for thirty years, summed up his apprenticeship, "The very name *McClure's Magazine* had an irresistible attraction for any young man who believed the American world susceptible of improvement and wished to be counted in as a 'helper' on the job of improving it."[80]

Following his own philosophy of enthusiasm, McClure was often frenetic, acting impulsively in his business as he did in his life. However, a darker side of his personality, episodes of mental depression, began to take hold of him. Sensitive to his psychological hills and valleys, McClure did some self-analysis of his condition. He recounted that in December 1882, he had contacted typhoid fever and was in the hospital for three weeks. He recalled: "My physical weakness showed itself in occasional fits of depression. Sometimes I got very far down indeed. . . . I used to be overwhelmed by the certainty of losing everything."[81] Despite his periodic depression, McClure, at other times, was vivacious, energetic, and determined to overcome all obstacles. He appraised himself, "When I had an idea, I pursued it; when I wanted anything, I went ahead and got it. My business associates, Albert Brady and Mr. Phillips, often counteracted the effects of my rashness in business, and saw to the ways and means of carrying out my plans. But I had squandered my strength more recklessly than I had squandered anything else, and nobody could help me to meet the overdraft I had made on my health."

Continuing his self-analysis, McClure said:

> When I was on the road, seeing editors, after my syndicate was well started, I used often to have to spend half the day in bed, in order to be strong enough to attend to business the other half. From 1890 on I was overcome more and more often by periods of complete nervous exhaustion, when I had to get out of my office and out of New York City, when I felt for my business the repulsion that a seasick man feels toward the food he most enjoys in health. Crossing the ocean seemed to relax this tension. New interests would take hold of me in London or Paris, and before I knew it I was picking up editorial ideas again. Good editorial work can only be done out of spontaneous personal interest; it cannot be forced. To lose his enthusiasm is the worst thing that can happen to an editor—next to having been born without any. In Europe I always got a renewal of the power to be interested; and that, for me, was simply the power to edit an interesting magazine.[82]

At the beginning of the twentieth century, psychiatry was in its infancy. McClure, who at times would be overwhelmed by what he called intense feelings of restlessness that he could alleviate only by being on the move, self-diagnosed his problems as physical exhaustion. McClure, to deal with his restlessness and depression, began to take frequent trips to Europe where he spent long periods of rehabilitation at European spas. When he was in the United States, he often retreated for a cure to the Kellogg Institute in Battle Creek, Michigan. His wife also followed the same pattern of seeking cures in Europe and at Battle Creek. It is interesting to speculate if Montessori, a medical doctor and a student of psychology, recognized any of McClure's psychological issues.

By 1900, McClure's success as a publisher was starting to fray as he began to lose control of his magazine in a decade-long process. The first stage occurred in the early 1900s, when McClure, a married man, engaged publicly in a number of affairs including one with Florence Wilkinson, a "tall, handsome, dark-haired young woman whose poems McClure had published in his magazine."[83] Florence was in the McClure party, as was Harriet McClure and their fifteen-year-old son Robbie, when they sailed to Europe in spring 1903. Hattie, who was ill, often stayed in her stateroom, while "Miss Wilkinson was much in evidence around McClure." When John Phillips, Ida Tarbell, and other staff members became aware, in 1904, of McClure's dalliance with Wilkinson, they feared that publicity about McClure's marital infidelity would damage the magazine's reputation as well as its staff members' finances and careers. Phillips pleaded with Miss Wilkinson to return McClure's love letters and to cease writing to him. Wilkinson's response was that in the future her letters to McClure would be sent in care of Mrs. McClure. Phillips wondered if there was an epidemic of lunacy.[84]

About S. S. McClure, Ida Tarbell "had the liveliest concern for his reputation as editor and chief figurehead of *McClure's Magazine*. . . . The magazine was approaching the zenith of its influence over national affairs." Dismayed by McClure's behavior, Tarbell called him "an uncivilized, unmoral untutored natural man with enough canniness to keep himself out of jail and asylums." She suggested telling Miss Wilkinson about McClure's other affairs, "to make her feel that far from her being the first and only one, there have been others, several of them."[85]

Phillips, Tarbell, and other staff members met with McClure and candidly expressed their serious concerns about his reckless behavior and their fears for the magazine's future. A chastened and penitent McClure agreed to their demands that he live abroad for an extended time and amend his behavior. In late May, McClure relinquished active control of the magazine; in June 1904 he, accompanied only by Harriet, departed for his exile in Europe. The public explanation was that McClure had taken a leave to recuperate from health problems.[86] During McClure's European exile, *McClure's Magazine* was managed by John Phillips and the staff.

The fear that McClure's infidelities would show up in the gossip columns of New York's newspapers were not over yet. In 1905, Edith Wherry, another young woman involved with S. S. McClure, wrote an exposé entitled "The Shame of S. S. McClure, Illustrated by Letters and Original Documents." Seeking to embarrass McClure, Wherry sent her exposé to Hattie McClure. Inexplicably, she hoped the injured wife would arrange for its publication in *McClure's Magazine*.[87] Happily for all concerned, Wherry's article was never published.

The second stage in S. S. McClure's downward slide occurred in late 1905 to early 1906, after McClure returned from his European exile bursting with a myriad of ideas for new projects. Rather than returning calm and relaxed from his leave, McClure, Tarbell observed, had grandiose dreams of building "a bigger, a more imposing house of McClure" on a grand scale."[88] Phillips and Tarbell discovered that McClure, without consulting them, had organized a new company whose charter provided "not only for a *McClure's Universal Journal*, but a McClure's

Bank, a McClure's Life Insurance Company, a McClure's School Book Publishing Company, and later a McClure's Ideal settlement."[89]

When they discovered the extent of McClure's plans, Phillips, Tarbell, and much of the magazine's staff were in a state of shock. While McClure optimistically predicted his new journal would be the greatest periodical ever published in America, his staff believed McClure's highly speculative and ill-conceived venture would ruin the company financially. Tarbell found it impossible to reason with McClure whose plans "possessed" and "obsessed" him "like a religious vision which was blasphemy to question."[90]

McClure planned to subsidize his new journal by using "the *McClure's* staff, the company presses at the new plant on Long Island, and accumulated literary material." He "was determined to support the whole financial structure with *McClure's* stock," estimated to have a value of one million dollars. McClure controlled six hundred shares, the majority of the stock. Phillips owned 146 shares and Ida Tarbell fifteen shares, valued at $1000 a share, which accounted for 16 percent of the company's stock. "In addition, Phillips owned 110 shares in the book company, worth $100 each, while Miss Tarbell owned 50, and D. A. McKinlay, an executive, owned 100. The total value of this stock was $187,000."[91] Phillips and Tarbell feared their stock could become worthless if McClure proceeded with his plans. "Both John Phillips and Miss Tarbell strongly argued against using the magazine's credit to finance a doubtful and expensive enterprise."[92]

Unable to dissuade McClure and fearing that he was jeopardizing their financial security, Phillips and Tarbell reluctantly led the magazine's staff in a revolt. Surprised by his staff's adverse reaction, McClure, in a long letter, tried to convince Phillips to accept his plan. The letter reveals McClure's state of mind—his insistence on moving forward with his plan—but also his desire to maintain his long friendship with Phillips.

McClure told Phillips that if they had discussed the issue privately, they could have averted the crisis. Now, he wrote, my "mind has become clarified" after I had "some time to find my bearings and reach a basic decision." McClure defended his one-man rule of the magazine and frequent European absences, saying,

> The idea that the magazine has become such an institution as to have gotten beyond the ability of one man . . . is utterly absurd. No institution can get beyond the ability of one man if it is properly organized. . . . My years abroad were not wasted. . . . I made such a study of comparative situations of different nations that I believe I am more competent to edit *McClure's* than if I had been here all the time. My facilities . . . to know public opinion and the opinion of able thinkers is vastly greater than it was ten years ago. . . . The management of this magazine is probably not one-thousandth as diffi-

> cult as Abraham Lincoln's job; but Lincoln could never have managed his job had it not been for the extraordinary facilities that went with his position for sensing public opinion. The more powerful *McClure's* becomes the more able we are to get at public opinion.

McClure then encouraged Phillips to take

> a long vacation on full salary and leave the country. . . . I love you, John, and I give you in the most serious fashion this advice. . . . Take your family and go to France. . . . Interest yourself . . . in study in connection with some university and in meeting the men who are making history. . . . You could stay away for a year, a year and a half or for two years. I am ready . . . at the end of that time, if you still insist upon it, to buy your stock, and this agreement will be signed by the principal people in the office. You would have your salary for a year and a half or for two years. . . . When you are well rested and return here you will find an office full of people eager to welcome you, to recognize your leadership and ability. You will find a prosperous business well established, a plant built and in good running order; the magazine pointed straight at the very heart of modern civilization. . . . You are not at present in a condition of mind to make the best decision. . . . Why, my dear John, I have never had any difficulty in this business in having my own way. My own way has generally been your way. And in regard to this new magazine, when I am fully decided to establish it and have the lines fully thought out and the facilities for doing, I should do it whether you were here or not. . . . You will come back to your work younger, stronger, [with] more courage and vigorous; . . .
>
> It is utterly impossible for me, John, to have a position in this business different from what I have had before. When you read history you find that kings who have come to the end of their tether, as a rule suffer death rather than give up part of their power. I would dispose of the entire business before I would give up part of my power. I can do the one but I cannot do the other. . . . I am ready and eager to resume relationships that began in college and to go on with you.[93]

John Phillips, McClure's partner and financial manager for twenty-five years, resigned on March 21, 1906. Other staffers who joined Phillips in the exodus included Ida Tarbell, John Siddall, Albert Boyden, Harry McClure (a cousin of S. S. McClure), Ed Phillips, and Lincoln Steffens. Phillips, Tarbell, and some of the others then purchased the *American Magazine*. Phillips's departure would prove to have serious consequences for McClure. Frederick L. Collins, a publisher very conversant of the world of publishing, wrote, "McClure was a great publisher—so long as he had John Phillips for a partner. . . . Patient, smiling, extremely able, [he] supplied both balance and understanding."[94] The events of 1906 began a downhill slide for McClure that led to his involuntary sale of his magazine in 1912.

To pay off Phillips and the other dissidents for their stock, McClure was forced to reorganize his company. He took Harold Roberts, a New York financier, as a partner. Roberts bought the insurgents' stock and paid an additional $130,000 for Brady's stock.[95] McClure's indebtedness had risen to $800,000. McClure, who had earlier stated that he alone would run the company, was forced to agree to a reorganization in its governance, with control lodged in a board of trustees, to which he had to yield his stock.

After the exodus of many of the key individuals from the staff and the financial restructuring, the future of *McClure's Magazine* was precarious. The situation was aggravated by the depression of 1907, which severely reduced revenues from advertising. When Roberts left the company, McClure turned to the West Virginia Pulp Wood and Paper Company for financing, agreeing to the exorbitant interest rate of 16 percent.[96]

In early 1911, undaunted by his financial reverses, McClure was in Europe acquiring new material for a fiction magazine he planned to launch when he returned to New York. Believing he had a financial plan for the new magazine, McClure wrote to his wife, "My month's work here has been very fruitful, and . . . has . . . put me back again inside of this business, where I was fifteen years ago, and has shown to me how easily I can edit the new magazine. I gave up the plan of raising the Capital as it would cost far too much. To get any adequate amount I should have to pay 7% interest, plus from 1/6 to 1/3 of the profits of the Fiction Magazine for all time to come. I believe that the ordinary credit from the Printer and the Paper manufacturer will found this Magazine."[97]

Despite his optimism, financial realities were closing in on McClure. Robert Mather, a Knox College classmate and fellow Knox College Trustee, was a corporate lawyer who, in 1906, handled "the financial details for separating Phillips, Tarbell, Boyden, and their supporters from the McClure enterprises."[98] In 1911, Mather, a director of the S. S. McClure Company, proposed still another financial reorganization designed to relieve the company's crushing debt. Mather, referring to the erosion of McClure's editorial and executive control, wrote. "I would like to get you freed from the disgrace as well as the expense of paying 16% on your borrowed capital. . . . There are elements of financial value in this plan, which . . . can be obtained without any further limitations than exist now upon your initiative and judgment in the editorial control of the magazine. . . . Such a plan as you now have . . . for the bringing out of a fiction magazine, would be more likely to receive intelligent and sympathetic consideration by Mr. Lamont and his associates than by the men who now control you financially."[99]

After McClure rejected Mather's proposal, Mather resigned. Sam wrote to Harriet, "I had a letter from Mather resigning. I fear that he regards me as foolish in refusing Lamont's offer."[100] Hattie responded optimistically. "I feel very sorry about Mr. Mather. . . . Tell him that more than money you and your family value your opportunity to do your work in the world at liberty. . . . I hope you'll be able to start your new Magazine."[101]

Cameron Mackenzie, McClure's son-in-law and company treasurer, submitted a counter refinancing proposal. Already, the McClure Company had sold its printing plant and book company and leased its building on Long Island. Clearly, *McClure's* administrators knew more needed to be done. "McClure retained control of a firm that was a half million dollars in debt and had little income."[102]

In his letter to McClure, Mackenzie advised: "In the first place, I believe that the time is fast coming, if it is not already here, when we will have to find some relief from our excessive interest charges. . . . I feel that I should have the first opportunity of putting the deal over as a matter of protection to you, to myself and to certain members of the organization who have given you great loyalty and affection."[103] Cabling his consent to Mackenzie, McClure had little choice but finally to face reality.

McClure's wife, Harriet, who usually supported her husband's decisions, now expressed her concern. She wrote to McClure. "Everything is at stake for me and the children as well as for you; and nobody has a shadow of a right to keep us in the dark and misrepresent the transactions of our own business. We have an absolute right to fully understand the tendency of everything that is being done. . . . I distrust these people completely."[104]

Harriet McClure's concerns about her husband were grounded in the reality that he was losing the magazine he had created. McClure, in 1912, signed a contract with the trustees of S. S. McClure Publications, Inc., that gave them control of the company that still carried his name. For a "period of twenty years," he was not "except with the consent in writing" of McClure Publications to "use in the United States, Canada or Great Britain or their territories . . . his name in . . . any periodical publication . . . nor contribute articles under his own name to any periodical publication (other than Ladies' World, McClure's Magazine or a daily newspaper)." He further agreed "to devote his time and energies to such editorial work in connection with its publications as McClure Publications, Incorporated, may from time to time prescribe, and to which he hereby agrees."[105]

Thus, McClure, who was always eager to launch a new magazine or found a new publishing company, was effectively prohibited until age 75 from functioning in the publishing world with the exception of those publications owned by McClure Publications, Incorporated. Even more limiting, McClure lost the rights to his own name in that the contract specified "his right to the use of the name 'McClure' in connection with publications shall belong exclusively to" McClure Publications, Inc. "for use by it in connection with any publication that it may at any time own or publish."[106]

No longer the publisher in charge, McClure was kept on as editor. Despite his severe setbacks, McClure, retaining some of his own optimism, wrote to Willa Cather: "I am enjoying my sense of irresponsible editorship more than I can tell you. . . . I am very happy and content and pleasantly situated here. . . . I am rather enjoying the new developments, the new body of jealousies that has sprung up against Cameron and Mr. Collins among their contemporaries. It amuses me and surprises Cameron. I am rather glad to be outside of it."[107] His wife, Harriet, more of a realist than her husband, wrote to her sister-in-law Helen McClure, admitting the unpleasant truth, "Sam has no longer any responsibility in the magazine office. He is full of plans and ideas for the future."[108]

From the time of his first publishing job as editor of *The Wheelman*, McClure knew he was unsuited to be, nor did he want to be, an employee. A man of many ideas, he wanted to be free to pursue his own initiatives. Thus, McClure's working as an employee of the new corporation that carried his name was doomed. Furthermore, his working on his own initiative in publishing was now closed to him. However, the young man who spoke about "enthusiasm" in his Commencement Oration at Knox College was undaunted. He would turn to the field of education and be the chief promoter of the Montessori Method in the United States.

In 1911 when the first Montessori articles appeared in *McClure's Magazine*, McClure still owned the magazine. He lost his magazine in May 1912 to a newly formed corporation, McClure Publications, Inc., which continued to publish the magazine. As editor, McClure, for a time, was still able to feature and promote topics like Montessori education. However, his hold on the editorship was tenuous. He saw the promotion of Montessori education as a way to keep public attention and to recoup some of his financial losses. Initially, because *McClure's Magazine* continued to be published, Montessori erroneously believed that McClure still owned the prominent magazine that had popularized her method in America. When he met with Montessori to negotiate her lecture tour in the United States, she was unaware of McClure's financial plight. She still regarded him as the famous American publisher and editor who had made her method known in the United States.

2

Maria Montessori

"An Educational Wonder-Worker"

Figure 2. This photograph of Maria Montessori at her desk was the frontispiece in Dorothy Canfield Fisher's *A Montessori Mother*, published by Henry Holt and Company in 1912.

Who was Maria Montessori and what did Americans know about her in the early twentieth century? At the time of her relationship with S. S. McClure from 1910–1915, biographical information about Montessori, in English, came to America in cameo pieces. The *McClure's Magazine* articles provided highly favorable glimpses into Montessori's life, career, and educational method. For example, Josephine Tozier in four of her nineteen pages in *McClure's* May 1911 issue portrayed the

Italian doctor as "an educational wonder-worker."[1] Montessori's own narrative in Anne George's English translation of *The Montessori Method* focused on her first educational endeavor with children at the Casa dei Bambini in Rome.

Comments by Americans Montessori had trained as teachers added more pieces to the mosaic of the Italian educator that was slowly taking shape. While Anne George was the best known of the Montessori-trained American directresses, others such as Zoe Bateman, Roberta Fletcher, Margaret Naumburg, Adelia Pyle, and Helen Parkhurst told parts of the Montessori story. Helen Parkhurst's detailed notes of Montessori's course at the Castel San Angelo in 1914 provided insights about Montessori and her method.

Extended biographies of Montessori in English such as E. M. Standing's *Maria Montessori: Her Life and Work* (1957) and Rita Kramer's definitive *Maria Montessori* (1976) would not appear until much later. Phyllis Povell's *Montessori Comes to America* was published in 2010.[2] To reconstruct what Americans knew about Montessori when McClure introduced her to the United States, this chapter deliberately relies on the earlier biographical accounts of Montessori and uses the later biographies to amplify and correct them.

Maria Montessori's biography stands in sharp contrast to S. S. McClure's life story. In addition to gender, there were differences in age, nationality, language, socio-economic class origins, careers, and education. Perhaps the strongest dissimilarities lie in their personalities, temperaments, and ambitions.

Thirteen years younger than McClure, Maria Montessori was born on August 31, 1870, in Chiaravalle, a hill town on the Adriatic Sea in Italy's Ancona province. She was the only child of Alessandro Montessori, a business manager in the state-run tobacco monopoly, and Renilde Stoppani, the well-educated daughter of a respected family.[3] A decorated veteran of the war for Italian unification in 1848, Signor Montessori was an imposing man, who, in the mode of *bella figura*, never lost his military bearing and style. He epitomized the attitudes and values of Victorian-era Italian middle-class respectability. Renilde, though from a traditional family, was less restricted by convention. Like her brother, Father Antonio Stoppani, a scholar-priest and natural scientist, Renilde enjoyed learning. She would be a strong influence on her daughter's education, even though it would diverge from the path followed by most Italian young women of Maria's generation. Because of Alessandro's secure position in the civil service, the Montessoris were comfortably situated in Italy's bourgeois middle class.

Unlike Maria Montessori's comfortable middle-class childhood, McClure was born to economically strapped Scots-Irish parents in Northern Ireland. After his father's untimely death, he was raised by his widowed mother who, with her four young sons, immigrated to the United States. Montessori, an only child, had the benefits but also the disadvantages of being the sole child in her family, while McClure was the eldest child of his family.

In 1875, Signor Montessori was reassigned to Rome and the family relocated to Italy's historic capital. Home of the Vatican and Italy's government, Rome was overladen by the monuments of Western civilization's major epochs and institutions—the Roman republic and empire symbolized by the Coliseum; Roman Catholicism by St. Peter's Basilica, the House of Savoy and the new Kingdom of Italy by the massive structure, dubbed the "wedding cake" by irreverent Romans, for the founding King, Victor Emmanuel. Walking through Rome's avenues, Maria saw evidence of the classical, medieval, renaissance, and modern periods of Western history. McClure's youth was spent in rural Indiana.

There was no doubt Alessandro and Renilde would provide their daughter, Maria, with an education appropriate to the family's standing. As a young woman, though, Maria was determined to make her own educational decisions. For McClure, the issue was not choosing what type of school to attend; instead, it was, could his family afford to have him attend any school?

Maria's formal education began at the state primary school on the Via di San Nicolo da Tolentino, which stressed the traditional instruction she would later rebel against. After Maria completed primary school, Alessandro and Renilde knew their precocious daughter, a government official's daughter and the noted Father Stoppani's niece, should continue her education. Italy's secondary school pattern was much like that of the rest of continental Europe. Many children, especially girls, ended their formal education with a certificate of completion from a primary school. A minority of adolescents, mostly males, went on to secondary school. The most prestigious secondary school was the highly academic university preparatory school, the *liceo*, with its curriculum of classical Latin and Greek languages and literatures. Since very few young women would go on to university, the *liceo* was not a viable option. Other secondary schools specialized in technology, engineering, art, agriculture, and commerce. But, again, these were attended by males. As a young woman from a middle-class family, Maria, like her peers, might attend a finishing school, generally conducted by a Catholic order of nuns, or a normal school to prepare to be an elementary school teacher. Choosing not to do what others expected of her, Maria decided to attend a technical school.

In 1883, thirteen-year-old Maria Montessori enrolled in the *Regia Scuola Tecnica Michelangelo Buonarroti*, a state technical school. Her teenage decision to chart her own course foreshadowed a pattern she would exhibit throughout her life; she, not others, would make her decisions. McClure, who had successfully worked with other strong-willed women such as Ida Tarbell and Willa Cather, assumed his persuasive powers would succeed with Maria Montessori. As we shall see, the McClure-Montessori relationship would be problematic.

Montessori would challenge many of the Victorian era's expectations about a young woman's proper role. How did her father, Alessandro, a traditional man in a traditional society, react to his strong-willed daughter's decisions? When he first heard of Maria's plan, Alessandro would say no. But Maria's persistence, usually abetted by his wife, would slowly win Alessandro's acquiesce and support for his daughter's efforts.

As a student in the *Scuola Tecnica,* Maria pursued a seven-year curriculum that was divided into a three-year segment followed by a four-year segment. Approved by the national ministry, the program emphasized mathematics such as algebra and geometry, and sciences such as chemistry and physics that had applications to technology. She also took courses in Italian literature, French, history, and geography. Instruction followed the conventional pattern of attending lectures, memorizing textbooks, and responding to instructors' questions with structured recitations.

Alessandro and Renilde Montessori were highly supportive of Maria's academic work. Her father, clearly perceiving Maria's academic abilities, encouraged her work in science and mathematics. Maria Montessori would make parental involvement a requirement for children attending her schools.

After three years of study, Maria graduated from the *Scuola Tecnica* in the spring of 1886 with a final cumulative grade of 137 out of a possible 150 points.[4] Continuing on to the four-year advanced course in applied technology, she enrolled in the *Regio Istituto Tecnico Leonardo da Vinci* which she completed in 1890. Then, at age twenty, Maria made a life-changing decision to leave engineering to become a physician. Dorothy Canfield Fisher, in *A Montessori Mother,* told her American readers in 1912 that Maria's decision came as a "bomb-shell" to her parents when they learned that their "singularly beautiful and singularly ardent" daughter had decided to become a doctor.[5] Margaret Naumburg, an American trained as a directress by Montessori, wrote in the *Outlook* about the "beautiful indomitable girl who fought her way inch by inch against the hidebound traditions of her country."[6]

When Maria Montessori applied to the University of Rome's School of Medicine, she faced strong gender bias and was rejected by the all-male medical faculty. Instead, she studied physics, mathematics, and natural science at the University of Rome for two years and earned the *Diploma di licenza,* which made her academically eligible to begin the study of medicine, to take courses in anatomy, pathology, and do clinical work. Showing the grit engrained in her personality, she reapplied and was admitted to study medicine.

Since medical education, like the profession, was completely male-dominated, Montessori faced regulations and practices designed for men but discriminatory against women. Described by Fisher as a "beautiful, gifted girl-student," Montessori was shunned and isolated by her male classmates.[7] She had to observe the rule that required her to wait to enter a classroom until all the male students were seated. Since dissection of a naked cadaver was regarded as improper for a woman in the company of men, her use of the anatomy laboratory was restricted to evenings when male students were absent. Surmounting these obstacles, Montessori achieved a distinguished academic record, earning commendations in surgery, pathology, and medicine.[8]

During her last two years of medical study, Montessori studied pediatrics at the Children's Hospital. Her clinical experience was at the women's hospital of *San Salvatore al Laterano* and the men's hospital of *Ospedale Santo Spirito* in Sassia. She learned the importance of clinical observation in diagnosing and treating illnesses. Later, she would emphasize the observation of children in her method of education.

Montessori next began research on "A Clinical Contribution to the Study of Delusions of Persecution," for her thesis requirement. Her extensive review of the literature on mental illnesses included findings about children's psychological disorders.[9] In 1896, Maria Montessori was awarded the degree of Doctor of Medicine. The twenty-six-year-old physician joined the staff of the university's *San Giovanni* Hospital and also began a private practice.

In their biographical sketches, the authors of the Montessori articles in *McClure's Magazine* claimed that as the first woman admitted to the University of Rome's Medical School, Montessori was also the first Italian woman to earn a medical degree.[10] Kramer's definitive biography, too, supports that claim.[11] However, Povell has identified two other women, Edvige Begnigni and Marcellina Corio Viola, who earned medical degrees at the University prior to Montessori.[12] In any event, Montessori's medical degree gave her entry into a very small circle of notable Italian women. For Americans, Montessori's medical degree added credibility to her educational method.

Montessori continued her research into psychology, a field that applied science to life. She wanted to know how children developed their thought processes and what environmental factors either promoted or retarded their learning. She especially wanted to use science to tear down the old, but persistent prescientific mind-body philosophical dualism.

Montessori's research in psychology and children's mental illnesses led her to take an appointment as an assistant physician at the University of Rome's *Clinica Psichiatrica* in 1897. Here, she worked with Dr. Clodomiro Bonfigli, an eminent specialist in children with mental disabilities. In 1899, Bonfigli established the National League for the Care and Education of Mentally Deficient Children. Montessori's responsibilities took her to Rome's insane asylums to identify patients for the clinic. Learning that many children, loosely labeled as "mentally deficient" or "idiotic," were confined in these asylums, Montessori wanted to diagnose their problems more precisely and to design a treatment that combined medicine, psychology, and pedagogy.[13]

As she gained recognition as an expert in children's mental illnesses, Dr. Guido

Bacelli, Italy's Minister of Education, arranged for Montessori to direct a training course for teachers who taught children with special needs. When a new educational institution, the *Scuola Magistrale Ortofrenica* (the Orthophrenic School), was opened to educate children with mental disabilities in 1900, Montessori and Dr. Giuseppe Ferruccio Montesano (1868–1961) were appointed as its codirectors. Like Montessori, Montesano, the chief physician at Rome's mental asylum, the *Manicomio di Roma*, was an expert in the field. Montessori's appointment at the Orthophrenic School deepened her insights into education but led to unanticipated consequences, as her relationship with Montesano became more personal and intimate.

In *Montessori Comes to America*, Phyllis Povell writes that Montessori and Montesano, who knew each other before their appointment as codirectors at the Orthophrenic School, most likely had met as early as 1895. In 1897, they were both assistant professors at the psychiatric clinic, where they conducted joint research and coauthored reports and articles.[14] They both were active members in the National League for the Care and Education of Mentally Deficient Children that Dr. Clodomiro Bonfigli had founded in 1899 and in *Per La Donna*, a society that encouraged women in science.[15] Montessori, at age thirty, was an attractive woman, with dark hair and fine features. Montesano, two years older, a scion of southern Italy's minor aristocracy, was a handsome well-styled gentleman. Their professional responsibilities and mutual interests became an intensely personal, intimate affair of the heart.[16]

Montessori became pregnant and bore Montesano's son, Mario, on March 31, 1898. The child's birth registration identified him as Mario Pipilli, born of unknown parents. He was placed in the care of Mancia Carlotta in the small town of Vicovaro, near Rome. Although Mario Montessori cites his birthdate as March 31, 1898, Kramer suggests that it might have been later. Montesano's family, especially his mother, strongly opposed a marriage to Montessori. Montessori's mother insisted that the child's birth be kept secret. The couple yielded to family demands to conceal their son's birth. Montessori, who seemed to have her way on so many other decisions, apparently acquiesced. Allegedly, Maria and Giuseppe pledged that neither would ever marry another. On September 28, 1901, when Mario was three years old, Giuseppe Montesano legally recognized Mario as his son, giving the boy the surname Montesano. Nearly a half century later, in 1950, Mario legally acquired his mother's surname, Montessori. Shortly after acknowledging paternity of his son, on October 6, 1901, Giuseppe Montesano did marry. His wife's name was Maria Aprile. Maria Montessori never married.[17]

No one can know what conflicts Maria Montessori experienced when, as an unwed mother, she placed her then-unacknowledged son with others. It is possible, however, to conjecture her feelings from the late Victorian, traditional, Catholic

Italian context. From the middle class, Montessori, a well-educated woman, unlike others of her gender, was a professional person, a medical doctor, with credentials in the emerging mental health and educational fields. Early in her career, she took a role in the women's movement. As an Italian delegate to the International Women's Congress in Berlin in September 1896, Montessori, supporting efforts to improve women's social and economic status, sponsored a resolution demanding equal pay for equal work for women.[18]

A year after her son's birth, Montessori, in February 1899, spoke about the "New Woman" of the twentieth century while on a lecture tour. She predicted that science and technology would liberate women from the traditional drudgery of domestic work, and free them to fulfill themselves as persons. She said, "Eventually, the woman of the future will have . . . a new self-awareness and will find her true strength in an emancipated maternity. . . . The new woman will marry and have children out of choice, not because matrimony and maternity are imposed on her, and she will exercise control over the health and well-being of the next generation . . . because when she can speak knowledgeably in the name of her children and in behalf of her own rights man will have to listen to her."[19]

Even for a self-determined woman like Maria Montessori such a future had not yet arrived. Her actions after the birth of her son were likely determined by the powerful traditional mores of the time. She fell into the role of the dutiful daughter who did not want to bring scandal upon her parents. To be an unwed, single mother would have made Montessori a social outcast. Even with her professional degree and credentials, her career would have ended.

When her son, Mario, was seven, he was sent to a boarding school near Florence.[20] Montessori saw Mario periodically, and at age fifteen he came to live with her after her mother's death. He was first presented as Montessori's nephew and then as her adopted son.[21] Then Maria Montessori acknowledged her son. In later years, Mario served as his mother's closest confidant in founding and administering the Association Montessori Internationale (AMI).

When McClure introduced Montessori to the American public, Americans read about Montessori's educational achievements but not her personal life. It was most unlikely that her American proponents—McClure, the Bells, and others—were aware that Montessori was an unwed mother. Although there was some liberalizing of attitudes, post-Victorian mores were still strong in the United States. If Montessori's personal situation had been known, it undoubtedly would have made her unwelcome to many Americans. When Montessori returned to the United States in 1915 to establish her demonstration school at the Panama-Pacific International Exposition in San Francisco, Mario accompanied his mother. Much later, biographers such as Kramer, in 1988, and Povell, in 2010, would tell the story of Montessori and Montesano.

What Americans knew about Montessori's work at the Orthophrenic School, where Montessori had been a codirector with Montesano, came to them from Josephine Tozier in *McClure's Magazine* in 1911, Anne George in *Good Housekeeping* in 1912, and Dorothy Canfield Fisher, in *A Montessori Mother*, in 1912. They recounted how Montessori had brought her medical expertise to education and had a "wondrous" success in training mentally deficient children. Acclaiming Montessori's work as "miraculous," Tozier told *McClure's* readers that Montessori taught children with cognitive disabilities (who at that time were referred to as "idiots") from Rome's "asylums . . . to read and write so well that they passed the same examinations" as "normal children" from the public schools. Tozier quoted Montessori who was planning to use her evolving method with all children: "I thought that if . . . the special education which had thus marvelously developed the idiots could be applied to . . . normal children, the miracle would vanish, and the gulf between the inferior and the normal mentality would reappear, never again to be bridged. While everyone was admiring the progress of my idiots, I was meditating on the reasons that could keep the happy and healthy common-school children on so low a level that my unhappy pupils were able to stand beside them."[22]

Anne George, like Tozier, informing American readers about Montessori's educational miracle, stressed its psychic causes. She quoted Montessori, "I felt sure that the boys from the asylum had equaled the normal children only because they had followed a different course. They had been helped in their psychic development, while the normal children had been suffocated and depressed."[23]

George then identified the overriding feature in Montessori's philosophy—the individual child's liberty to realize his or her own self-development.

Enlisting the heroic prose that colored many American accounts about Montessori, Fisher described her as "throwing herself into the work, heart and soul, with all the ardor of her race and her own temperament, she utilized her finely-tempered brain and indomitable will, in hand-to-hand struggle for the actual amelioration of existing conditions." By day, she worked lovingly with her children like a "devout sister of charity" but at night became the scientist "classifying and clarifying the results of the day's observations."[24]

After leaving the Orthophrenic School in 1901, Montessori returned to the University of Rome to study anthropology, psychology, educational history and philosophy, and pedagogy. She concentrated on physiological anthropology, which was being developed in Italy by Cesare Lombroso and Giuseppe Sergi. Lombroso lectured on forensic medicine, psychiatry, neurology, and anthropology. Montessori also studied with Sergi, who had established the University of Rome's Institute of Experimental Psychology.

From 1904 to 1908, Montessori lectured at the University of Rome's Pedagogic

School on the application of anthropology and biology to education. At the University of Rome, Montessori attracted students because of her highly motivated and energetic presentations. Drawing from disciplines ranging from medicine to anthropology and psychology, she presented a multidisciplinary approach that was unusual at the time. When she came to the United States in 1913, she was an experienced and confident public speaker, but a major problem was that Montessori lectured in Italian, not English.

Montessori published her lectures as *L'Antropolgia Pedagogica* (*Educational Anthropology*), a book that combined insights from pediatric medicine, child psychology, and cultural anthropology and applied them to children's development and education.[25] Her publications, which were establishing her scholarly credentials in Italy, had not yet appeared in English translations until Anne George's translation of *The Montessori Method* in 1912. The sources about Montessori for most Americans in the 1909–1914 period were *McClure's Magazine* and interpretive books about the Montessori Method by Fisher and Stevens. Montessori who fiercely guarded her ideas did not welcome secondary interpretations about her philosophy and method of education.

A crucially pivotal career change occurred in 1906 when Edouardo Talamo, director-general of the *Istituto Romano di Beni Stabili* (a real estate association called the Roman Good Building Association) asked Maria Montessori, at age thirty-six, to establish a school in the San Lorenzo district. Talamo, a civil engineer and the Association's Executive Director, was supervising its urban renewal program. Specifically, the association was remodeling substandard and overcrowded slum tenement buildings into livable and sanitary apartments for working-class families.

In post-*Resorgimento* Italy, large numbers of peasants, especially from the *mezzogiorno*, the South, had relocated to Milan and Rome, searching for jobs. In the 1880s, real estate speculators in Rome had hastily constructed a large number of apartment buildings. The over building was followed by a real estate crash. The buildings were converted into tenements in which speculators would rent a building and then sublease its rooms to many individuals crowded into a limited space.[26]

Tozier, skilled in establishing contexts as a travel writer, dramatically provided *McClure's* readers with the situation Montessori found in the San Lorenzo Quarter. Tozier described the district as "one of the most crowded, insanitary, and vicious warrens of the poor in which children grew up without light, without air, in precocious familiarity with every form of crime and degradation."[27] Montessori herself called the district a dim "world of shadows."[28]

In the San Lorenzo Quarter, Talamo wanted to solve a pressing problem. When their parents went to work, the children, especially those under school age, were left on their own, an early version of latchkey children. Unsupervised in the housing development, they wandered around, damaging the newly renovated buildings. Talamo saw Montessori's school as a day-care center to keep the children from damaging property. He did not anticipate sponsoring an experimental laboratory school.

Adept at seizing opportunities, Montessori accepted Talamo's offer. She would establish a school where she could implement and test her ideas on education. Just a few years earlier, from 1896 to 1904, John Dewey, too, had tested his educational ideas at the University of Chicago Laboratory School. These laboratory schools would establish Montessori and Dewey as the twentieth century's leading educators. In fact, Dewey would introduce Montessori at her lecture in New York City in 1913.

The San Lorenzo district was similar to depressed slums in the large cities of Europe and America. The pioneering American social worker Jane Addams had established Hull House, a settlement house for immigrants on Chicago's near west side. Hull House provided both a kindergarten and a Montessori school for the children in the area. The Casa dei Bambini and Hull House were but two of the philanthropic efforts to ameliorate the distress of the urban poor through educational means. Addams would introduce Montessori when she spoke in Chicago in 1913.

Signaling a new phase in her career, Montessori opened her first school on January 6, 1907. Called the Casa dei Bambini, or Children's House, it was located in a large apartment building at *Via dei Marsi* 58. Assisted by Candida Nuccitelli, a teacher she had trained, her first pupils were fifty children, from three to seven, whose families lived in the building.

Through her work at the Casa dei Bambini, Montessori developed the curriculum, the Montessori Method, which became the prototype for all future Montessori schools. Here she had tested and empirically verified her underlying educational theories. She implemented her principle of auto-education, in which the children educated or trained themselves, matching their needs and readiness with the materials and activities provided in Montessori's structured environment.

Montessori's success at the Casa dei Bambini led to the opening of a second school in the San Lorenzo district on April 7, 1907. A Montessori school was also established at the villa of the British ambassador to Italy. With the support of the *Societa Umanitaria*, the Humanitarian Society of Italy, a Montessori school was established on October 18, 1908, in Milan. The Society's House of Labor was also commissioned to manufacture Montessori's didactic apparatus and materials.

Montessori wrote about her work at the Casa dei Bambini in *The Method of*

Scientific Pedagogy Applied to Infant Education in the Children's Houses in 1910. *Scientific Pedagogy*, retitled *The Montessori Method* (1912), was published in eleven languages, including George's English translation in the United States.

Although those who told Montessori's story always highlighted her pioneering work at the first San Lorenzo Casa dei Bambini, Montessori, by 1910, was no longer associated with her original school. According to Fisher, a conflict with Talamo, who had initiated and supported the school as part of his urban renewal project, forced Montessori to leave the *Casa*. Fisher reassured readers that Montessori was "not to blame" for the argument.[29] According to Kramer, the dispute resulted from Talamo's resentment that Montessori's school, rather than his association's urban renewal project, had captured public attention. In an interview many years later, Montessori said that she had been locked out of the school by the porter, who had been "instructed by the contractors not to let me into the building." She said her educational work was "causing such a sensation that the businessmen who paid for the construction claimed she was using the project as a personal advertising campaign."[30] The dispute with Talamo would be one in a series of conflicts that Montessori would have with her male sponsors such as McClure and even Benito Mussolini, the dictator of Italy from 1922 to 1943.

Dorothy Canfield Fisher, a leading American source on Montessori in 1912, offered some advice to those traveling to Rome to observe Montessori's schools. Dr. Montessori, a very private person, she told them, has "neither money, time, or strength enough single handed to cope with the flood of inquiries about her ideas." They would find it difficult to meet with Dr. Montessori who is closely guarded and protected by a "little group of five devoted disciples, young Italian women who live with her, who call her 'mother,' and who exist in and for her and her ideas, as ardently and whole-heartedly as nuns about an adored Mother Superior."[31]

The Montessori schools that the Americans visited and which were featured in the articles in *McClure's Magazine* were the ones in the Convent of the Franciscan Missionary Sisters of Mary on *Via Giusti* established in 1910 and the School of San Angelo in the Pescheria Quarter that opened in 1911. Descriptions of the Convent and San Angelo schools, along with photographs of their happy students working with the didactic apparatus, rather than the well-known San Lorenzo *Casa*, shaped the impressions of most Americans about Montessori prior to her tour of the United States in 1913.

The Montessori school on *Via Giusti* was important as the site where Montessori conducted her international training courses. The sisters, a Roman Catholic religious order, operated orphanages and schools in foreign countries, especially China. At the time of the Montessori school, the sisters were caring for a hundred orphans who were victims of a massive earthquake on December 28, 1908, that had devastated Messina in Sicily and towns in Reggio Calabria. The children in the Montessori school were either these orphans or children from the neighborhood.

Tozier's "Montessori's Schools in Rome" in *McClure's* December 1911 issue featured a photograph with the caption, "Children in the Cloister School of the Franciscan Nuns in Rome, Playing a Game with Reels of Colored Silk." Anne George, who Tozier noted had been trained by Montessori, appeared in the photo.[32]

Describing the convent as "a beautiful old building with plenty of space and lovely gardens," Fisher, in her widely read book, *A Montessori Mother*, praised Montessori's work in the convent school as "an admirable example of the wonderful result of the Montessori ideas and is a revelation to all who visit it." Nevertheless, Fisher had a caveat about the school's location in a Roman Catholic convent: "though the good nuns make every effort to give a free hand . . . it can be imagined that the ecclesiastical atmosphere, which in its very essence is composed of unquestioning obedience to authority, is not the most congenial one for the growth of a system which uses every means possible to do away with dogma of any sort, and to foster self-dependence and first-hand ideas of things."[33]

Rome's municipal education authorities had allocated a room for a Montessori class at the San Angelo School in October 1911. The school, dubbed the "ghetto school" by *McClure's* authors, was located in a poverty-impacted area. Under the subhead, "The School of San Angelo in the Roman Slums," Tozier crafted a vivid narrative of Montessori's work at the school located in "dark, reeking streets," swarming with a "diseased, filthy, and degenerate" population" in the picturesque and foul quarter of the mediaeval Ghetto."[34] The support provided for the school by the educational officials was so meager that Montessori asked her friends and patrons for money to fit the classroom with furniture and equipment.

Tozier's article added more glowing prose brush strokes to the already highly positive portrait of Maria Montessori that Americans were getting. She called Montessori, "the great sympathetic soul" whose "genius discovered a method to broaden the outlook, lighten the drudgery, and assist the tender brain of the normal child."[35] A photograph showed Montessori being welcomed at the San Angelo School by a crowd of little girls who stretched out their hands to touch her.

Tozier then turned to Anne George, whom she identified as a "young American teacher . . . who had spent the entire winter studying the Montessori system," for her impressions of the San Angelo School. George, who would be a prominent and ever-present person in introducing Montessori to Americans, said: "These were children from the Ghetto, but, aside from the pallor that arises from inadequate nourishment, the faces before me had nothing in common with those of the poverty-stricken inhabitants of the streets along which I had picked my way. The happiness, the intelligence, and the ease with which the children welcomed me showed that some better force was at work within these natures. And, as I watched, my wonder grew."

George continued, "In this class for forty-five children I saw not one idler. Two little girls brought from its corner a square of carpet, old, cheap, and shabby, but absolutely clean, and this they spread in a narrow space in front of one of the desks; then, bringing a box containing the cut-out letters, began with joyous eagerness to form these letters into words and phrases. . . . I saw other children composing words with these same cut-out letters. . . . With all this activity there was no noise or disorder. Instead, there was everywhere joy in work. . . . In the attitude of the children toward their teacher and their directress, I observed the most beautiful reverence, the warmest affection, and the greatest respect."[36]

Though an experienced writer but not an educator like George, Fisher described her initial visit to the convent school where she saw twenty-five children, from three to six, "too busy with . . . their mysterious occupations even to talk." Fisher, at first, thought no teacher was present. Then, she noticed that a directress was quietly present, observing, but not interfering, as the children worked with the tying and buttoning frames, touched fabrics, and served lunch. Fisher told her readers that in visiting a Montessori school, "you can be sure of only one thing . . . that all the children will be happily absorbed in some profitable undertaking. It never fails."[37]

Fisher's comments on the almost-invisible teacher reflect Montessori's guiding directive that the directress needed to be a like a lady in waiting. In language that interwove the spiritual and the scientific, Montessori told her directresses to "be silent and keep still" so as not to "disturb" the children's activity. They needed, she said, to "acquire an attitude of patience. . . . It is a high virtue to wait—a virtue of genius . . . an attitude of saints."[38] As the teachers stood waiting, observing the children's actions, Montessori told them they were becoming like "scientists of life," waiting and observing because "the smallest phenomena has great value."[39]

By 1910, Montessori had earned recognition as a significant innovative educator in her native Italy. Her growing reputation attracted attention in educational circles in other European nations and in North America, especially in the United States and Canada. For Americans, Montessori was, depending on the source, the first Italian woman to earn a medical degree, a scientist who had developed a revolutionary method of education, and an "educational wonder- worker."

3
The Montessori Method

Figure 3. "Montessori children at dinner. The tables are set in the grounds of the school of the Franciscan Nuns, in Rome." (Maria Montessori, *The Montessori Method: Scientific Pedagogy, as Applied to Child Education in "The Children's Houses."* Translated by Anne E. George, Fifth Edition. New York: Frederick A. Stokes Company. 1912. p. 348.

When S. S. McClure decided to popularize Montessori education in the United States, his strategy was two pronged. He needed to introduce the great Italian educator, Maria Montessori, and her unique method of education. There were those, like Mabel Bell, who would come to prefer the method without having to deal with its difficult creator. McClure, himself, would learn that the method was inseparable from La Dottoressa. This chapter examines the method of instruction that Montessori put into practice at the Casa dei Bambini and which some eager Americans hoped to implement in their own country. In particular, the chapter includes sources on the Montessori Method that were available to American readers at the time.

Although Maria Montessori's early schooling was traditional, she would, in creating her own method, react decidedly against it. She would distinguish her scientific method of education from what she called the traditional old "ordinary schools" that had their students assimilate "content digested by others."[1] In these schools, Montessori said, "students learned by studying much—teachers explained much—the students' only labor was to accept the content of labor of those before them."[2] In contrast, Montessori told her trainees to use the "method of practical science" in their teaching. The new teacher "does not give ready made thoughts but allows the child to make his own."[3]

Maria's own formal education began at the state primary school on the Via di San Nicolo da Tolentino, which stressed the traditional instruction she would later rebel against. She watched her teacher, standing at the front of the classroom, attempting to transmit information, namely facts and dates, to her and her classmates, who were expected to store it in their minds and recall it later during examinations. Instruction in her primary school rigidly followed a syllabus and textbooks approved by the ministry of education. Contrary to the individualized learning that would characterize the Montessori Method, Maria's primary teacher was assessed as competent if she managed to teach all the children the same lesson at the same time. The only individualized part of the school day was the recitation, when a child was called upon to recite a previously memorized passage—able students, standing at attention, correctly responded to the teacher's questions with answers they had previously memorized from the textbook.

In Italian schools, the pupils typically used a single textbook that combined all the subjects taught—reading, writing, arithmetic, history, and geography. Italian schools, in particular, featured dictation in which students copied word for word statements made by the teacher. Each letter of the alphabet had to be placed squarely in a small box marked on a copy book. While providing basic literacy and arithmetic, children's spontaneity and creativity were not encouraged in syllabi approved by the minister of education.

As a university student, Montessori's research on cognitive disability and psychological disorders in children led her to Jean-Marc Gaspard Itard (1774–1838) and Edouard Seguin (1812–1880), two French physicians and psychologists. Her study of Itard and Seguin moved Montessori to hypothesize about creating a multidisciplinary approach to treating children's mental illnesses that integrated elements from physiology, neurology, psychology, anthropology, and pedagogy.

Josephine Tozier's lead article on Montessori in *McClure's Magazine*'s May 1911 issue featured a section on Itard, with the subhead, "The Wild Boy of Aveyron."[4] A specialist in Otiatria at the national French Institution for the Deaf and Dumb, Itard was famous for his well-publicized treatment of the "wild boy," an allegedly feral youth. According to Itard's case study, hunters came upon the boy in the forest in 1798. Apparently abandoned or lost as a child, the boy had lived with animals in the wild. Found at about age twelve, the boy uttered sounds but had no language or practical skills. After observing the boy, Itard devised a training plan to teach him a limited but essential vocabulary and some basic skills. Itard made some painstaking but slight progress in training the "wild boy."[5]

Adding the "wild boy" to his catalogue of cases with impaired children, Itard concluded that human beings, especially in their early years, go through necessary and specific stages of development. At each stage, they need to engage in activities for which they are physiologically and psychologically ready. These activities are the basis of subsequent development.

Itard's findings about the significance of stages of human development, especially in childhood, were not new. Quintilian, the Roman rhetorician, and the later theorists, Comenius, Rousseau, and Pestalozzi, had earlier commented on the educational importance of developmental stages. What was new about Itard's generalization and what captured Montessori's attention was his assertion that it was crucial that appropriate activities be performed at the right time in the child's developmental cycle. As in the case of the "wild boy," some children, due to physical or mental disabilities or to severely deprived environmental circumstances, who missed the activities specific to a particular stage, had a gap, a developmental deficit, that impeded their ongoing development.[6] While the "wild boy" showed signs of mental impairment, his environment also lacked the cultural and social occasions and materials needed for his development. Itard concluded that if children did not perform the activities needed in their developmental sequence at the right time, they suffered the consequences of continual and cumulative impairment.[7] Building on Itard's concept, Montessori would construct her method in which children learned in a "prepared environment" stocked with materials, such as the didactic apparatus that she later designed, that were suited to their particular stage of growth.

Itard's theory of the necessary stages of development, especially in terms of sensory and practical life skills, made a strong impact on Montessori, who saw his findings as "the first attempts at experimental psychology."[8] Itard, a physician, had used his clinical observations of children, not philosophical speculation, to construct his theory of education. But, according to Montessori, observation, though necessary in identifying a stage of development, was insufficient.

The child needed to be free to demonstrate what he or she wanted to do. Child freedom or children's liberty to choose their work became a compelling part of Montessori's method.

Montessori's research on Itard led her to another French medical doctor, Edouard Seguin (1812–1880). A student of Itard, his mentor, Seguin specialized in training cognitively impaired children. His treatment of mentally impaired children at the *Hospice de Bicetre* especially resonated with Montessori. Similar to her work in Rome, Seguin sought to transfer children who had been confined with adult inmates in the insane asylums of Paris to special environments appropriate to their age.[9] Seguin's *Traitement Moral, Hygiene, et Education des Idiots* (1846) (*The Moral Treatment, Hygiene, and Education of Idiots and Other Backward Children*) had established him as an early authority of the education of children with special needs.[10]

Anne George, the first American trained by Montessori as a directress, informed her readers in *Good Housekeeping Magazine* that Seguin's premise that sensory training was the necessary first step in children's intellectual and moral development profoundly shaped Montessori's educational theory.[11] Montessori would use some of Seguin's training materials as prototypes for her didactic apparatus.

Seguin's conviction that schools for handicapped children should be more than holding places became a foundational concept in Montessori's evolving method; they should combine training in practical life skills with more general education. Seguin's emphasis on developing practical skills that increased handicapped children's self-reliance shaped Montessori's curriculum design that emphasized the individual child's independent self-learning, which she called "auto-education."

Seguin's technique of diagnosing each student, as if he were treating a patient, was a further influence on Montessori, who as a medical doctor was already very familiar with the approach. In examining a child, Seguin took precise physiological measurements, recording height and weight, and detailed specific problems. He noted the child's behavior and skill level. Based on his diagnosis, Seguin designed a treatment plan for the child's education. In developing her own method, Montessori would incorporate the concept of developing a physiological and psychological profile for each child. Seguin and Montessori anticipated the contemporary Individualized Education Program (IEP) that is part of the education of children with special needs.

Montessori became especially intrigued with the didactic apparatus and materials Seguin had designed to train the sensory and physical skills of children with handicaps. For example, she readapted the apparatus Seguin used to train children to perform practical skills, such as buttoning coats or tying shoe laces, so they, despite their handicaps, could learn to do things on their own.[12] Improving on

Seguin's prototypes, she devised dressing frames, with durable and colorful fabrics, that not only incorporated Seguin's finger skills but added tying, hooking, and snapping. Montessori elaborated Seguin's simple nail board into a more refined geometrical series of wooden cylinders of varying heights and dimensions that fitted into corresponding holes.[13]

Both Seguin and Friedrich Froebel, founder of the kindergarten, had used building blocks in their systems. Montessori, too, used blocks, in her long stair exercise. For Seguin, the blocks were used to develop children's sense of dimension, especially sizing objects, going from small to large. In Seguin's tower-building exercise, children learned sizing by constructing a tower, with the larger blocks on the bottom as the foundation for the smaller ones on top.[14] Seguin and Montessori also used a similar approach to teach the alphabet. While Seguin used metal letters, Montessori's letters were cut from sandpaper and paper.

Both Montessori and Seguin emphasized sensory learning, especially developing the tactile sense, as necessary for other kinds of learning. Seguin developed his apparatus for children with serious cognitive disabilities, while Montessori would broaden the use of the apparatus to all children. Many, but not all, of the Montessori apparatuses were patterned after Seguin's earlier prototypes. Montessori's sound materials, such as the varied bells, used to develop children's ability to differentiate tone, were her original invention.

Montessori's didactic apparatus was a prominent feature in what Americans learned about the Montessori Method. The articles in *McClure's Magazine* were illustrated with photographs of children working with the didactic apparatus. Dorothy Canfield Fisher's *The Montessori Manual: For Teachers and Parents* (1913) featured sixteen photographs of the materials. Montessori's American lecture tour in 1913 included motion pictures of children using the didactic apparatus. These Montessori learning materials would play a key, and sometimes contentious, role in the introduction of the Montessori Method to the United States by McClure and others.

From her reading of Itard and Seguin, Montessori formulated four working hypotheses that would guide her later work in education. One, children need to perform activities appropriate to their readiness at a particular stage of development; two, the educator needs to observe children clinically to determine their particular readiness for learning at a given stage; three, children with disabilities, especially with mental handicaps, need a special kind of training and education that complements their medical treatment; four, specially designed learning apparatus and materials could be effective in training and educating children.[15] She would later conclude that these hypotheses could and should be applied to all children, not only those with handicaps. Tozier wrote that these principles formed "the starting-point of a process of thought and experiment that bids fair to revolutionize primary education by practically abolishing the difficulty of learning to read and write."[16]

Montessori saw herself as a scientist, striving to make education one of the sciences. "I wish to transform education into the experimental sciences," she said, and "make it a science in itself." Portraying the scientist in almost spiritual terms, Montessori saw him or her as "a great observer" who, willing to wait patiently for results, possesses "a great inner attitude in humility. . . . One who follows [the] path of experimental science must be self denying" and "must rid his mind of preconceptions which would otherwise obscure truth."[17]

When she began to train directresses, Montessori, drawing on her spiritually toned language, told her students that they had to become like scientists. Through "intensive study," like novices in a convent, they needed to rid their minds of "preconceived ideas," and by "spiritual exercise" needed to learn the practices of "denial" and "humility." The scientist experiences an "inner communication with truth" in which "inner attitudes are acquired" that bring "inner reward" and "internal satisfaction with each discovery."[18]

Montessori, in effect, told her students that to be true scientists in education they had to make an intellectual and psychic turn around, a conversion, from their previously held opinions. If they accepted the scientific truth she was offering, they would be converts, not unlike religious ones, to the truth. Her conception of scientific truth in education explains why Montessori regarded her directresses as disciples and why she regarded deviations or revisions of her method as heresies.

In September 1898, Montessori spoke on educating children with cognitive disabilities at the Pedagogical Congress in Turin. Still not categorically defined, at that time, "mental retardation" included not only mentally impaired children but those labeled loosely as "laggards" and delinquents. Disruptive and chronically truant or expelled from schools, these children roamed the streets, often exploited by adults. Children with severe cognitive disabilities, labeled "idiots," who were typically confined with adults in insane asylums, received little or no care to remediate their condition. Condemning these standard practices, Montessori urged placing these children in special schools, where skill training and education complemented their medical and psychological treatment. Teachers, collaborating with psychiatrists and pediatricians, would diagnose each child's specific problems and design an individualized learning prescription to meet the child's needs.[19]

Montessori emphasized the relationship of children's physiological development to their educational environment.[20] In her training lectures, she told her students to "make the anthropological study of the pupil precede his education."[21] Montessori directresses were told to accurately record each child's weight and height weekly. These measurements formed an individualized empirical record, "a biographical chart," that the team of teacher, pediatrician, and psychologist maintained for each child and shared with parents. Teachers needed to give attention to each child's diet, physical exercises, age of his parents, childhood illnesses, the date he cut his first tooth, began walking, began talking, and the family and home environment.[22] However, she cautioned that the scientific observation of children, though necessary, was not the same as educating them; it was rather a necessary guide to their education.[23]

In her medical training, Montessori had learned the importance of clinical observation in diagnosing patients' illnesses. For clinical observation to produce valid findings about children's development and behavior, it needed to be free from unnecessary adult constraints so children could act to achieve their own growth and development.[24] The educator could then prepare a structured learning space (the Montessori school) with the materials (the didactic apparatus), opportunities, occasions, and encouragement for children to interact with the environment in an educative way.

Montessori emphasized the connection between the child's freedom and the educational environment. The individual's "intellect," she said "draws nourishment from the environment," and the "work of education" is to provide the "correct" environmental conditions so that "life may develop freely." In the correct educational environment, the child has physical freedom to move that in turn nourishes "inner liberty."[25] "By liberty in the development of life," she said, "I mean . . . that children must be free to develop in the best way possible according to the potentiality of their life." Liberty can be observed in the actions of children "we have left free to develop."[26]

Biological liberty, Montessori said, is the liberty of "living beings" to "grow by themselves and reach a determined finality, to go through human life's physical or biological stages. Living beings" exist only in their "close communion with" their "external environment." While the stages of human development are fixed, the environmental conditions in which individuals develop are varied. Teachers can provide the optimum conditions for life by compensating for "the deficiencies" in the environment.[27]

Montessori's application of anthropology and biology to education foreshadowed her philosophy—the five underlying principles of which would become the Montessori Method: (1) each child, as an individual, needs to be free to work at her or his self-development; (2) children experience major stages of development for which there are appropriate educational activities; (3) the methods and materials used to train children with mental disabilities could be applied effectively to normal, indeed to all, children, throughout the world; (4) the clinical observation and diagnosis of children was a necessary prelude to planning their education; and (5) instruction needed to be calibrated carefully to the major developmental stage a child was undergoing at a particular time.

Americans first became aware of the Montessori Method as an innovative approach to early childhood education. Montessori called this first stage the period of the "absorbent mind," from birth to age six. She later identified two subsequent stages of human growth and development: from six to twelve and from twelve to eighteen years of age. By 1910, Montessori had developed educational strategies for the first stage when children, exploring their immediate environment of home and neighborhood, absorbed information and constructed their initial concepts about reality. Beginning to use language, they were entering the larger social and cultural world.

What children absorbed depended on what their environment offered them. If the home and neighborhood were impoverished culturally and materially, the information children absorbed would likewise be poor. If the environment was rich in materials and activities, the information children absorbed would also be enriched. Montessori came to envision a structured learning environment, a school that was rich in the apparatus, materials, and activities children needed in the highly formative stage of the absorbent mind. Montessori's stages were not rigidly discrete. For example, the six and seven year old, moving from the first to the next stage, from six to twelve, exercised the skills and ideas acquired in the first stage, making them more precise, reinforced, polished, and expanded.[28]

Montessori's concept of the absorbent mind included the "sensitive period," a time of developmental readiness when a child was especially ready to learn something. Learning began with the child's sensory explorations of the objects and materials in his environment. Based on her study of physiology and anatomy in medicine, Montessori saw learning as having a neurological connection between touching, seeing, hearing, smelling, and the brain. Her didactic apparatus would make this sensory neurological learning efficient, effective, and rewarding for the child.

Montessori reasoned that the information that children absorbed was clustered in their minds at points of sensitivity that related to powers such as judging distances, making comparisons, and developing language. This sensitivity, or readiness, spurred children to find a challenging task that interested them and to work at it until they had mastered it.[29] Importantly, a challenging task became interesting for the child because it was appropriate to her or his particular stage of development. It was the child's interest that was paramount, not the teacher's or the parent's.

Around age three to six, children experienced the later stage of the absorbent mind as they used their native language and absorbed their culture. Montessori called this a time of "constructive perfectionment," when children through their own self-activity are consciously and deliberately involved with the culture.[30] What Montessori called "perfectionment" comes from the child's need to master a task with a sense of precision. Children are especially attracted to manipulative tasks—with how to do something and how to arrange objects—which satisfies their need to coordinate and control their movements. The child, involved in a piece of work, will repeat the same series of movements over and over until it is mastered. This repetition, Montessori asserted, established a neurological control that related mind and body, bringing about muscle coordination with the mental goal of completing the task. The repetition fixed the power of knowing that something is being done correctly which, in turn, leads to the empowerment of independent performance. The repertoire of skills and the world that the child constructs lays the foundation for future learning.[31]

The period of the "absorbent mind" is highly important for children's entry into their culture and society in that they are absorbing the distinctive language and beliefs and values of their cultural group. As an individual matures, he or she will make cultural and social adaptations and revisions to the patterns acquired in early childhood. However, any changes will take place in the network of cultural patterns already absorbed during early childhood.[32]

Initially Montessori had worked with children with mental disabilities but later concluded that her method of education was applicable to normal children as well. At the San Lorenzo school, Montessori emphasized her method's applicability for the uplifting of working-class children. However, she did not want her method referenced to specific categories or socioeconomic classes of children but claimed it was applicable for all children everywhere in the world. She saw all children as being, by their nature, essentially the same, regardless of socioeconomic class, ethnicity, nationality, or race.

At her San Lorenzo school, Montessori envisioned the Children's House as a school-home, a learning center in the same building where the children lived. She stated, "We have placed the school within the house . . . as the property of the collectivity." The school, through the children, would lead their families to education and to a better life.[33]

Montessori was responding to the needs of working mothers who, in the emerging industrial economy, were employed outside of their homes. She believed that in the future women of all classes would face this problem. Schools, like the Casa dei Bambini, would make it possible for mothers to leave their children safely and "proceed with a feeling of great relief and freedom to their own work." The school Montessori designed would assist working mothers in providing the physical and moral care their children needed.[34]

In constructing their biographical image of Montessori, American writers, though emphasizing her self-sacrificing heroism in the San Lorenzo district, focused on the method's general themes rather than its application to poor children. Anne George told her American readers that at the Casa dei Bambini, Montessori, "for the first time . . . applied her system of liberty, and her ideas of a broad, practical sense-training, to normal children. It was her object to provide an environment in which the child might be free to manifest those happy and useful instincts natural to him, and true to this ideal."[35]

Neither the articles in *McClure's Magazine* in 1911–1912 nor Montessori's lecture tour in 1913 emphasized the role the Montessori school might play for working mothers. Neither did they emphasize the method as an educational strategy to improve the conditions of the working poor. Rather, the American interpreters of Montessori framed their message to correspond to the educational aspirations of progressive middle-class parents who read *McClure's Magazine*.

The story of Montessori's first school, the Casa dei Bambini, became well-known to middle-class American parents. Montessori herself told her story in *The Montessori Method*. George, Tozier, Fisher, and Stevens retold the revolutionary effort made by the heroic doctor turned educator. However, although Anne George may have visited the school in 1909, most American writers had never visited Montessori's San Lorenzo Casa dei Bambini (Casa), as Montessori had left the school in 1910. The schools the writers visited and the children they observed were at the convent on Via Giusti or the school of San Angelo. However, these schools, too, tended to be class referenced. The children at the convent school at Via Giusti were mainly orphans; those at the school of San Angelo were from an economically disadvantaged area of Rome.

Montessori believed her schools' success depended, at least in part, on the expectations the children and their parents had for education. Admission to her first school in the San Lorenzo district was not selective; admission was open to all children between the ages of three and seven who lived in the building block. Furthermore, the parents paid no tuition or fees. Montessori understood that many parents, especially the mothers, who were largely uneducated, had little understanding of the function of schools, especially one dedicated to early childhood education. To generate a positive climate, Montessori established rules to govern the parents' relationship to the school and encourage their respect for education.

Devoting a large section to the rules for the Casa, Tozier's article in *McClure's* quoted Montessori on the parents' imperative obligations: "To send their children to the school-room at the specified hours, clean in person and clothes, and wearing a suitable pinafore" and "to show the greatest respect and deference toward the directress and staff of the House of Childhood, and to cooperate with the directress in promoting the education of the children."[36] Mothers were advised that, at least once a week, they could meet with the directress and receive her recommendations for improving their children's behavior at home and in school. Tozier proceeded to Montessori's warning that pupils would be expelled who came to school "in an unwashed and slovenly condition; who are not amenable to discipline; whose parents fail to respect . . . the persons in charge of the House of Childhood, or in any way threaten to counteract by bad conduct the aims and the educative work of the institution."[37]

In a class-referenced comment about Montessori's rules, Tozier reassured *McClure's* readers that these regulations did not apply to their own children. She advised them, "It is possible that the benevolent despotism of these regulations would not everywhere be appreciated, but there is no doubt that the Houses of Childhood are, and are felt to be, an immense boon to the class of people for whom they are intended."[38] Tozier's comment expressed the prevailing American middle-class attitudes to the education of the working class, especially immigrant children, in contrast to their own children. Children from the lower socioeconomic class, especially those of foreign-born parents, needed to learn basic middle-class behaviors and values about punctuality, respect for property, and cleanliness and hygiene. Since their own children had already learned these attitudes at home, they had higher educational aspirations for them.

With her rules in place, Montessori turned to setting up the first Montessori structured learning environment. Talamo's Association had provided a large room in the apartment building for the school. Montessori knew that a room, however, was not a school; neither was the school she envisioned like a traditional classroom. The school's physical layout needed to complement, not interfere, with the implementation of her ideas. She set about creating a child-friendly environment in which the tables, chairs, and apparatus were suited to children's needs rather than adult preferences. She did not want the classroom furniture to limit the children's freedom of movement as in traditional schools.

Later, when Montessori described her ideal school in her training classes, she said that it should have "plenty of space—a garden," and a "well ventilated, sunny . . . large work room . . . that contains all the tables and chairs." Ideally, the school should have a "dining room," a "room for sleeping," a "parlor with pictures & papers," a "cloak room," and a "toilet room." It should be adorned with "beautiful plants and pictures" that, like the art in a church, should nurture the child's spiritual life.[39] Montessori specified that a school should be furnished like a home, with tables, chairs, and cupboards. Unlike the standardized desks placed in rows in an ordinary school, a Montessori school's furniture need not be uniform in design but in its accessibility to children. Cupboards should be low so that children can easily reach them. Tables and chairs should be light enough to be easily moved. Since children enjoy working on the ground, there should be mats that can be easily folded and spread.[40]

Montessori turned to creating what became her distinctive curriculum and method. Her four years at the San Lorenzo Casa was a work in progress, as she observed her children and implemented and then refined and improved her ideas. Once Montessori was satisfied that her ideas were verified by the children's successful learning, they were in place to be refined and made more precise but not drastically altered. She believed that her method was based on the unchanging nature of the child's mind, which like the human body did not change in its necessary essentials.

Montessori's children in the Casa, from poor working-class families, were often making the transition from village to urban life. She found that many of them had not learned the standard habits of hygiene and cleanliness; they did not know how to brush their teeth, comb their hair, or clean their fingernails; they did not know the proper way to serve and eat meals. So, Montessori set about teaching them what she called the "Exercises of Practical Life," which became a standard part of the Montessori school curriculum for all children. The children were trained to perform the skills needed in everyday life such as washing their hands and face, brushing teeth, tying shoe laces, buttoning a shirt or blouse, setting tables and serving meals, sweeping floors, gardening, and caring for small animals.

Montessori applied what she learned about training children with mental handicaps to all children—their need to be as independent as possible. All children needed to perform these skills without help from adults. Thus, the Montessori's principle of child independence was implemented in practice. In addition to their practicality, Montessori believed the skills had a moral and cultural significance. Children who were independent could become their own moral agents. Furthermore, the skills of health, hygiene, and manners were the necessary features of a civilized society.

School materials included ordinary items and utensils found in typical middle-class households. There were plates, cups, glasses, saucers, knives, forks, spoons, tablecloths, and napkins so the children could learn to set tables, serve meals, and pass food properly. Dorothy Canfield Fisher described how children served food in a Montessori school: "the little girls . . . stood before . . . tables set for twenty little people, set neatly and regularly, without an item missing." After the children had taken their places at the table, "four little waitresses enter the room, each carrying a big tureen full of hot soup. I would not have trusted a child of that age to carry a glass of water across a room. The little girls advanced slowly, their eyes fixed on the contents of their tureens, their attention concentrated on their all important enterprise that they seemed entirely oblivious to the outer world." They ladled the soup out as "deftly as any adult could have done."[41]

Montessori's didactic apparatus included framed pieces of cloth with buttons, laces, and hooks that the children could use to practice fastening, buttoning, zipping, lacing, and tying skills, so that they could transfer to buttoning and hooking their own clothing and tying their shoes. Designed to develop and exercise motor, muscular, and coordination skills, the successful performance of everyday skills gave children a sense of independence and self-confidence.

The children, eager to learn new skills, would stay with a task, repeating it, until they had mastered it. Montessori concluded that children did not have to be forced to learn; if permitted to choose between work and play, they would choose work. Montessori concluded that when a "child fixes intense attention" on an activity and "pursues and repeats [it] many times—this is [the] basis for auto-education."[42]

Montessori's second major curriculum area, based on her concept of "sensitive periods" when a child exhibited a high degree of readiness for a particular kind of learning, was the activities and apparatus designed to promote children's sensory and motor development. Especially important in sensory and motor development were the didactic apparatus and materials that included:

- a series of solid insets—wooden cylinders of different sizes to be inserted in holes of the same size in a wooden block
- ten pink wooden cubes of graduated size with which the child built a tower, then knocked it down, and rebuilt it
- ten brown wooden prisms and ten red rods with which the child built a broad and long stair
- geometric solids (pyramid, sphere, cone)
- little boards with rough and smooth surfaces and others of different weights and colors, and pieces of fabric of different textures
- a little cabinet of drawers, each containing framed geometrical figures—blue triangles, circles, squares of different sizes—to be taken out and replaced correctly in their frames
- cards with paper geometrical shapes pasted on them
- a series of cylindrical boxes filled with different materials that produced different sounds when shaken
- sixty-three little tables in nine different shades from light to dark of seven different colors
- a series of musical tone bells used with a wooden board that had musical staff lines and a set of wooden disks to represent the notes
- sensory boxes filled with spices with distinctive odors

Each child was free to choose the apparatus on which she or he wanted to work. The apparatuses were self-correcting, in that the child could proceed only if she was using it correctly. For example, the cylinders could only be inserted in holes of the same size in the wooden block. Montessori observed that the children would repeat the same activity until they did it correctly. Since the child was free to choose the particular apparatus, her choice reflected her interest and was appropriate to her stage of development. The self-correcting aspect of the apparatus was based on Montessori's belief that children would acquire self-discipline and self-reliance by becoming aware of their own mistakes and repeating a particular task until they had mastered it. Teachers, though guiding the process, were not to interfere with it.

Montessori's emphasis on children's sensory development was especially attractive to Alexander Graham Bell, the telephone's inventor, who would join McClure in promoting Montessori education. The origin of Montessori's method in the ideas of Itard, a teacher of the deaf, had a special meaning for Alexander Graham Bell, who, like his father, had been a teacher of the deaf. Bell's wife, Mabel, who was profoundly deaf, developed an intense interest in the Montessori Method. Enlisted by McClure into the Montessori movement, the Bells took a leadership role in the Montessori Educational Association in the United States. Though their motives differed from McClure's, the Bells were highly visible in the circle of prominent Americans who allied with him in promoting Montessori.

Visitors to Montessori's school were impressed with the sight of children working independently with a didactic apparatus. Some left thinking that the apparatus was the core of Montessori's method. This was especially true of some of the Americans who wrote about the Montessori Method.

Visitors to the Casa were most excited by the children's rapid and apparently easy "explosion" into writing and reading. Convinced that children possessed the power of self- or auto-education, Montessori did not believe that reading and writing needed to be forced on children. When they were ready, children would do what was necessary in learning these skills. While Montessori's claim that children of four and five years "burst spontaneously into writing" awed her devotees, it drew strong skepticism from her more traditional critics.

Montessori had designed materials to stimulate children's readiness for writing and reading, two skills she believed developed in tandem. She devised cardboard letters covered with sandpaper. As the children touched and traced these letters, the directress voiced the letter's sound. Thus, as they were being prepared to write the letter by tracing its shape, they also learned the sound it represented. Children discovered reading when they understood that the sounds of the letters they were tracing, and then writing, formed words. When the children knew all of the vowels and some of the consonants, they were ready to form simple words. Using the vowels, the directress showed the children how to compose three-letter words and to pronounce them clearly. In the next step, the children wrote the words dictated by the directress. After enough practice, the children were able to compose words without assistance.

Readiness for arithmetic began with counting exercises in which the children arranged objects according to their number. They learned to count by using rods of different units and lengths and by arranging strings of beads of various lengths.[43]

Montessori's curriculum informally connected physical exercises and nature study with the exercises for practical life. Arguing that children's activities should be purposeful and meaningful, she criticized the gymnastic programs in some schools that broke movements down into very small specific exercises such as repeatedly raising the right or left arms. Unlike gardening, caring for small animals, serving meals, or sweeping a floor, these specific physical exercises did not solve a practical problem of life. Purposeful activity, according to Montessori, united mind and body to accomplish a task.[44]

Montessori told her students in training that "movements are complex" in that "psychic factors enter into performing any action directed and followed to completion." By carrying out "intelligent movements" to their end, children "acquire a practical idea of order" and learn to distinguish "chaos from order." The sense of ordering leads to the concept of "reordering" or rearranging the environment. For example, reordering can mean actions such as rearranging the furniture, transplanting plants in a garden, or even sweeping a floor. Reordering activities lead children to greater independence in that they do these things for themselves.[45]

Children learned about the natural environment by planting and cultivating gardens, which Montessori believed established the intellectual connection between sprouting of seeds and the growth of plants with the larger world of nature. Caring for small animals introduced children to zoology and developed a sense of responsibility.

The children at San Angelo followed the Montessori curriculum of practical life skills. Impressed with how the children learned personal cleanliness and orderliness, Tozier wrote, "All the little girls were taught to brush and comb one another's hair, and to dress and undress themselves in an orderly and intelligent fashion. They were taught to move safely and quietly in the cramped spaces between the desks and chairs, to carry about breakable objects of various shapes securely, to place them in order upon the desk and to put them back again in the cupboards. They were taught to open and close doors quietly, to make the room tidy, and to walk with secure confidence up and down long flights of stairs leading to the courtyard."[46]

Ellen Yale Stevens, an American educator, who had observed Montessori's schools in Italy, highlighted Montessori's credentials as an educational theorist. Steven's article, "The Montessori Method and the American Kindergarten," in

McClure's Magazine and her book, *A Guide to the Montessori Method* (1913), distinguished Montessori's scientific method of education from the earlier philosophical theories of Jean-Jacques Rousseau, Johann Heinrich Pestalozzi, and especially Friedrich Froebel.[47]

The articles in *McClure's Magazine* on Montessori focused on the early years of education, the period of the absorbent mind. Although Montessori was constructing a rather profound philosophy, the articles in *McClure's Magazine* did not probe or analyze her philosophy of education. Written to attract the widest possible audience, they focused on the method's more concrete features: the Montessori school as a structured environment; children's freedom of movement and choice; the didactic apparatus; and especially the success in teaching very early reading and writing. Although she wanted her method disseminated to the widest possible audience, Montessori resented its popularization and often attempted to correct the more popular accounts. McClure's tendency to popularize her method and Montessori's desire to philosophize it would create tensions during the method's introduction to the United States.

Montessori's university lectures were organized on the themes of: (1) applying the scientific method to pedagogy; (2) using the correct techniques to clinically observe both deficient and normal children; (3) using empirical techniques to record, collect, and interpret data; (4) generalizing this anthropological and clinical information into replicable and usable educational practices; and (5) designing and using didactic apparatus and materials that developed children's skills and abilities at sensitive periods in their development.[48] The early American interpreters of Montessori, such as George, Tozier, Fisher, and Stevens, reiterated these themes in their articles.

4

Creating a Favorable Climate of Opinion for the Montessori Method in the United States

By 1909, Montessori was recognized as an educational innovator in Europe while in the United States her work was not yet widely known. The four years between 1909 and 1913 were important in introducing Montessori to Americans and in creating a favorable climate of opinion for the Montessori Method. Used by the renowned historian Carl Becker in his analysis of the eighteenth-century Enlightenment, the concept of a climate of opinion is useful to describe and analyze the dramatic and rapid rise of interest in Montessori education in the twentieth century's first two decades in the United States. It is especially instructive in examining the relationship between the publicist, S. S. McClure, and the pedagogue, Maria Montessori. McClure, particularly *McClure's Magazine*, played a key role in creating this climate, which he would use as a launching pad for his concerted campaign to promote Montessori from 1911 through 1914. The publication of an English translation of *The Montessori Method* in 1912 was also important.

The Montessori climate of opinion in the United States was created by Americans who voyaged to Italy to meet Montessori, interviewed her, attended her lectures, and observed her method of education. They can be sorted into three major groups: One: writers and journalists who, like McClure, were generalists, not professional educators, who had met interesting famous individuals before. Montessori, the woman, was their focus. They wanted to construct a prose portrait of Montessori and tell an interesting story that would attract readers. Two: professional educators, mainly professors of education, who wanted to analyze Montessori's philosophy and wanted to question her about the philosophy and psychology behind her method. Three: young women who wanted to be trained by La Dottoressa so they could become authentic Montessori directresses, the name Montessori gave to teachers she had prepared. Many of these young women looked to Montessori as their mentor.

When these educational explorers reached Rome, they wanted to meet and talk with Montessori and visit her schools, but not all succeeded. A visitor fortunate enough to visit a Montessori classroom saw children busily engaged in individual and independent work with didactic materials. While all the visitors had attended some kind of school and some of them had taught in a school, many asked, was this Montessori learning situation still a school, or was it something very different? Visitors were familiar with the narrative of how Dr. Montessori had established a school in the slums of Rome where three- to five-year-old children from impoverished families had rapidly developed their sensory and muscular skills, learned basic life skills, and had almost miraculously burst into reading and writing.

How did the perceptions of the three major groups of visitors construct the Montessori climate of opinion? In answering this question, chapter 4 focuses on a significant individual who is representative of each of the three groups: Dorothy Canfield Fisher for the writers and journalists; Henry W. Holmes of Harvard University for the professors; and Anne George for Americans who Montessori trained as directresses.

Writers such as Dorothy Canfield Fisher and Josephine Tozier were important in moving Montessori and her method from the more limited circle of professional educators into the popular mainstream. They knew that Montessori's interesting story would appeal to general readers, especially to parents looking for new ways to educate their children. Some, like Fisher, crafted a dramatic and appealing narrative about one of the first woman to earn a degree in medicine in Italy, about her dedication to the poor children of Rome, and about her wonderful new method of education that promised great results for all children. Fisher, a novelist and biographer, did not have the scholarly distance of the professors. She knew that the story, like Montessori herself, was of contemporary interest and needed to be told while interest was high.

Dorothy Canfield Fisher (1879–1958) joined the pilgrimage to Rome in 1911 to meet Montessori and observe her schools. The thirty-two-year-old Fisher had already established herself as a best-selling American writer. Fisher's doctorate in Romance Languages, awarded by Columbia University in 1904, gave her insights into the Italian culture and language that many other Montessori advocates, such as McClure, lacked. Fisher met with Montessori and visited the Montessori school at the Franciscan Convent on the Via Giusti in Rome. Returning to the United States, she quickly wrote *A Montessori Mother*, published in 1912, which enthusiastically endorsed the Montessori Method. Fisher went so far as to call Montessori's philosophy a "new religion" on which she was giving "Americanized meditations."[1]

Building the favorable climate of opinion for Montessori, Fisher wrote, "Over there in Rome, in a tenement house, a woman doctor begins observations in an experimental laboratory of children, and in five years' time, which is nothing to a real scientist, her laboratory doors are stormed by inquirers from Australia, from Norway, from Mexico, and, most of all from the United States. Teachers of district schools in the Carolinas write their cousins touring Europe to be sure to go to Rome to see the Montessori schools. Mothers from Oregon and Maine write, addressing their letters, "'Montessori, Rome.'"[2]

Fisher, a progressive, was a proponent of educational reform and women's rights, but she advised her readers that she was not a professional educator. She wrote *A Montessori Mother*, she said, for general readers, especially mothers. Her readers were "no more scientific than I am, an audience of ordinary, fairly well-educated American parents."[3]

Fisher told mothers of young children that they, like American women in the past, had long been leaders in the vanguard of educational reform. She wrote, "It is a universally accepted description of American women (sometimes intended as a compliment, sometimes as quite the reverse) that, whatever else they are, they are less negative, more forceful, more direct, endowed with more positive personalities than the women of other countries."[4]

Dedicated with permission to Maria Montessori, in the preface to *A Montessori Mother*, Fisher wrote that she constantly encountered questions about Montessori's schools in Rome. "Now, you've been to Rome: you've seen the Montessori schools. You saw a great deal of Montessori herself and were in close personal relations with her. Tell us all about it. Is it really so wonderful? Or is it just a fad? Is it true that the children are free to do exactly as they please? . . . Do they really learn to read and write so young? And isn't it very bad to stimulate them so unnaturally?" These questions led inevitably to, "What is there in it for our children, situated as we are?"[5]

To answer the question about children's freedom, Fisher gave Montessori's philosophical principle of liberty and independence a practical application. Telling parents to avoid interfering with their children's efforts to do things for themselves, she advised "help that is not positively necessary is a hindrance to a growing organism." Allow the child to wash his face and hands, brush his teeth, put on and button his clothes, carry his own toys and books, regardless of the time it takes.

Placing Montessori's concept of liberty into an American ideological context, Fisher wrote: "The principle . . . of the Montessori school is the ideal principle of democracy . . . that human beings reach their highest development (and hence are of most use to society) only when for the growth of their individuality they have the utmost possible liberty which can be granted them without interfering with the rights of others."[6] Exalting it as a new phase in "the religion of humanity," Fisher gave Montessori's concept of child liberty a broad interpretation that extended from the school, to the home, and reached into society. It meant freedom from any kind of despotism, including that of parents and teachers, that kept individuals dependent. It did not mean anarchy in which children did as they pleased nor did it mean that children should not be protected from danger. A feminist, Fisher told mothers, "We must take care that we mothers do not treat our children as we reproach men for having treated women, with patronizing enfeebling protection."[7]

Fisher explained Montessori's concept of discipline—doing what is necessary to complete a task and staying with the process until the task is accomplished—in practical terms. Fisher said that she had to unlearn the Puritan rules she had acquired as a child, that children became disciplined by being forced by adults to do what they did not like. She had to reject the traditional attitude that adult-imposed prescriptions and proscriptions make a good boy or girl. A child develops his own will power to complete a freely chosen activity when adults refrain from intervening with misguided help.

Fisher's efforts to put Montessori education into an American context led her to an informal network of Montessori advocates. When McClure and the Bells organized the Montessori Educational Association, Fisher served on its original Board of Trustees. When any new political, philosophical, or educational movement comes into being, its proponents give themselves creditability by citing each other as authorities. Fisher did this when she referred to the work of Anne George. When she visited the Tarrytown school, Fisher was impressed with how well George had replicated what she had learned from Montessori in Rome.[8] Her comments about George's school strongly suggested that Montessori's method would work well in the American context. Fisher wrote, "The notable success of Miss George's Tarrytown school disposes once and for all of the theory that 'it may work for Italians, but not with our naturally self-indulgent, spoiled American children."

Fisher turned to the feature of the Montessori Method that most excited parents: the early transition of the children from the sensory activities to reading and writing. She wrote, "For of all the profound, searching, and regenerating effects of the Montessori system, none seems to have made an impression on the public like the fact, almost a by-product of the method, that Montessori children learn to write and read more easily than others."[9]

Though the "way Montessori children learn to write is very spectacular," Fisher promised her readers "a short-cut, unscientific explanation of the process." Devoting fourteen pages to reading and writing, Fisher moved her readers from the sensory activities in which children used their fingers to touch, feel, and trace the form and shape of objects, to use the movable alphabet, and to the "burst" into writing and reading. (Montessori's process of learning to read and write is treated in detail in chapter 5, "*McClure's Magazine* Publicizes Montessori.")

Fisher commented on what would be a continuing debate over the kindergarten and Montessori approaches. Though she found much common ground in the two early childhood education methods, Fisher found the sharpest difference in the "moral atmosphere" of the two approaches, which "is actually and fundamentally opposed to the other." In the kindergarten, she wrote, "the teacher teaches," while in the Montessori school, "the emphasis is all on the fact that the child learns." Fisher contrasted the "pretty, smiling, ever-active, always beckoning, nervously conscientious kindergarten teacher, always on exhibition" with the "calm, unhurried tranquility of the Montessori directress, always unobtrusively in the background."[10]

Like many Americans, Fisher was intrigued with the Montessori didactic apparatus. She was impressed when she first visited the Casa dei Bambini where she saw children busily working on their own, using Montessori's didactic apparatus with little supervision by a teacher. Emphasizing the importance of the apparatus in the Montessori Method, Fisher said, "The central idea of the Montessori system, on which every smallest bit of apparatus, *every detail of technic rests solidly, is a full recognition of the fact that no human being is educated by anyone else. He must do it himself, or it is never done.*"[11] The Montessori apparatus, Fisher continued, is intended, "*first to stimulate the little child's natural desire to act and learn through action; second, to persuade him with action which shall give him a better control of his own body and will power; and third, which shall lead him naturally from a simple action to a more difficult one.*"[12]

Fisher devoted seven of her sixteen chapters in *A Montessori Mother* to descriptions of the apparatus. Only one year later, in 1913, she wrote a follow-up volume, *The Montessori Manual for Teachers and Parents*. Illustrated with sixteen photographs, Fisher's *Manual* provided specific instructions on how mothers should use Montessori's didactic apparatus in teaching their children. In her foreword Fisher said she wrote the *Manual* to meet the needs of mothers "untrained in educational methods, of a more concrete and definite and less philosophical presentation of the ideas of the great Italian teacher." Also, she wanted to provide teachers with "valuable hints . . . which their . . . greater experience and professional training will enable them to expand into school-room exercises."[13]

Fisher warned, "Any attempt to use the Montessori apparatus or system by anyone who does not fully grasp or is not wholly in sympathy with its bed-rock idea, results inevitably in a grotesque, tragic, caricature of the method."[14] This fundamental principle is that the child is his own teacher; that all genuine learning is done by the learner who is guided by his interior need for self-development. Fisher described the purpose and use of the various Montessori apparatus. Her narrative was illustrated with photographs provided by Carl Byoir, President of the House of Childhood in the United States, which manufactured and sold the didactic apparatus and materials. The photographs showed children in Montessori's school using the apparatus to perform sensory skill exercises, often blindfolded, such as building a block tower, tracing sand paper letters, tracing geometrical designs, and working with a cut out alphabet. There were also photographs, similar to catalogue pictures, of some of the apparatus such as the buttoning and lacing frames, the geometrical inserts, and the long and broad stairs. Fisher's prose and photographs were both a warning that the apparatus had to be used carefully in conformity to Montessori's underlying principles and an enticement to parents to obtain the apparatus for their children's education.

Throughout the introduction of the Montessori Method in the United States, in books like Fisher's and in the articles in *McClure's Magazine*, didactic apparatus was prominently featured. This fascination with and promotion of the apparatus carried with it a contradiction. According to Montessori, only directresses whom she had trained possessed the requisite skills needed to use the apparatus properly; however, parents were also encouraged, at least by some Montessori promoters such as Fisher, to purchase the apparatus for their children to use at home. She told her readers, "We in America who have children between the ages of two and seven can not as yet send our children to a Casa dei Bambini. Therefore, if we wish our children to profit by the great work of Dr. Montessori, we must do the next best thing and give them the Montessori training in our own homes."[15] Fisher's books led potential buyers to Byoir's House of Childhood.

Fisher fell into the contradiction, which would imperil her relationship with Montessori, when she advised her readers, "The first thing to do, if you can manage it, is to secure a set of the Montessori apparatus. It is the result of the ripest thought, ingenuity, and practical experience of a gifted specialist who has concentrated all her forces on the invention of the different devices of her apparatus."[16] Fisher provided parents with practical guidelines for using the apparatus: (1) observe your children as individuals to know their stage of development; (2) do not push your children to use a particular apparatus; just have it there so they can choose when it interests them; (3) use the apparatus only for the purpose and in the way for which it was designed.

An example of Fisher's clear style of presentation is found in her instructions on how to use Montessori's Buttoning Frame, called the "frame with hooks and eyes." She advised mothers to explain "the method of fastening and unfastening . . . in the usual Montessori way; that is, as briefly as possible. It is often best not to say anything, but merely to go through the exercises one's self, unbuttoning or unhooking the cloth, buttoning or hooking it up again, and handing the frame to the child. In most cases he at once sets to work, and even though his first efforts seem to the observing mother incredibly clumsy and slow, she must keep her hands off, and let him work out his own problems. The only rule should be that if he does not wish to play with the apparatus, or when he grows tired of its use, he should put it away; and for that purpose it is very essential that there should be a well-defined place, which the child can easily reach—not only for the Montessori apparatus, but for his other toys and for his clothing." Fisher concluded her description of this exercise with "one of the incidents of this work is that he learns to dress and undress himself. This, it should be remembered, is not the primary factor that Dr. Montessori has in mind. It is incidental to the general muscular co-ordination that is effected."[17]

Fisher then entered a region that would cause severe consternation to Montessori. Might Americans adapt or add to the Montessori apparatus? Since Montessori said that her method was still incomplete, Fisher reasoned that others could add to the method. After all, Montessori, herself, had added to and revised the apparatus that Seguin had originally developed. Fisher, to her peril, misread Montessori. Only Montessori would complete her method and others, trained by her, were to replicate, not change it.

Not understanding how Montessori jealously and zealously guarded her method, Fisher predicted that Montessori would find "all over the world, a multitude of ingenious co-partners in her enterprise." Seeing herself as a co-partner Fisher wrote it "would not be presumptuous for us . . . to attempt to apply her main principles in ways which she has not happened to hit upon."[18] Fisher went on to describe a need in the Montessori Method: "There are in it none of the devices for gymnastic exercises of the whole body which she recommends so highly, but which as yet she has been able to introduce but little into her schools. Here, too, what she would wish us to do is to make an effort to comprehend intelligently what her general ideas are and then to use our own invention to adapt them to our own conditions."[19]

Books such as Fisher's *Manual* and Tozier's articles in *McClure's Magazine* left Americans with the impression that the didactic apparatus was at the core of the Montessori Method. Montessori adamantly rejected Fisher's *Manual*, along with all other unauthorized versions of her method. She published *Dr. Montessori's Own Handbook* in 1914 as the official guide to her method to distinguish it from others, such as Fisher, who were writing about Montessori education.[20] Montessori wrote a letter that was published in the London *Educational Times Supplement* that pointedly disassociated her work from Fisher's book: "I have taken the pains to prepare myself a handbook to fulfill exactly the task which Mrs. D. Canfield Fisher's book has the pretension of fulfilling. I should be very glad if you would give me the opportunity of saying that I have not deputed—and do not propose to depute—to others the work of a practical popular explanation of my method, as I have taken great pains to do this myself. I hope my system will not be held responsible for any want of success that may arise out of the use of other books than my own in connection with the Montessori apparatus."[21] Her two-volume work, *The Advanced Montessori Method*, appeared in 1918–1919.[22]

Montessori's repudiation of Fisher's attempt to popularize her method was revealing of Montessori's personality and prophetic of issues that would arise with McClure. Montessori adamantly believed that she alone had ownership of the method that she had created. She resented and would block those who might try to share this ownership. Although Fisher had made some effort to explain the philosophy behind the apparatus, her attempt was inadequate in Montessori's judgment. Montessori believed that she had developed a profound and deep philosophy of education that others needed to understand but not simplify. Further, Fisher had broken a fundamental Montessori rule: the method was not to be implemented by following instructions in a simple manual, like Fisher's; it could be implemented only by directresses that Montessori herself had trained. Finally, there were financial considerations. As a self-supporting woman, Montessori needed the income that the sale of the apparatus and her books and lectures might generate. She saw no reason why others should appropriate her work for their own profit. All of these issues, especially ownership and profit from the apparatus, would resurface when Montessori's method was first introduced to the United States.

While writers like Fisher were taking a general, often dramatic, view of Montessori and her method, the educational professionals, especially professors of education, were more cautious and critical, even skeptical about the latest innovation in education coming from Italy. Among the professors who went to Rome to witness the Montessori Method were: Howard Warren of Princeton; Arthur Norton of Harvard; Lightner Witmer of the University of Pennsylvania; Theodate Smith of Clark University; Anna Logan of Miami University; and William Heard Kilpatrick of Columbia University's Teachers College.[23]

Immediately critical of Montessori, Professor Witmer described his frustration in failing to gain access to Montessori and her school. Like professors generally, many filtered their perceptions through lenses of academic objectivity, allowing scholarly time to elapse before they put their impressions of Montessori into articles and books. The response of the professors, even when favorable, did not match the enthusiasm of would-be Montessori directresses. Some professors came to support the new method radiating out of Rome. Others became critics, often identifying points of disagreement with Montessori but not rejecting the whole system. Later, some of these academic critics, like William H. Kilpatrick, would become adversaries.

A key event in generating the favorable climate of opinion for Montessori occurred in 1912 when the Frederick A. Stokes Company published *The Montessori Method*, an English language translation by Anne E. George of Montessori's

Il Metodo Pedagogica Scientifica. Professor Henry Wyman Holmes (1880–1960), chair of the Division of Education at Harvard University, wrote the book's introduction. The acknowledgements included a thank you to Mrs. John R. Fisher (Dorothy Canfield) "for translating a large part of the new work by Dr. Montessori of the American edition," most likely the two new chapters written for the American edition.[24] Recognizing McClure's role in popularizing her method in the United States, Montessori wrote, "I know that my method has been widely spoken of in America, thanks to Mr. S. S. McClure, who has presented it through the pages of his well-known magazine. Indeed, many Americans have already come to Rome for the purpose of observing personally the practical application of the method in my little schools. If, encouraged by this movement, I may express a hope for the future, it is that my work in Rome shall become the centre of an efficient and helpful collaboration."[25] The book's publication brought together leading individuals from the main groups involved in constructing the favorable climate of opinion for Montessori education: Fisher, the popular writer; McClure, the publicist; Holmes, the professor of education; and George, the Montessori-trained directress.

Blending autobiography, educational philosophy, and teaching methods, *The Montessori Method* told Montessori's story of how she constructed her theory and implemented it at the first Casa dei Bambini. The book described her work, explained her philosophy, and was a guide to her method. It also provided Montessori's commentary on the social and economic changes impacting women, children, and families in the early twentieth century.

The book's publication in 1912, concurrent with the articles in *McClure's Magazine* and a year before Montessori's tour of the United States, was pivotal in developing the atmosphere that McClure needed to attract a receptive audience to Montessori. The translation was readable enough to appeal to a general audience and scholarly enough to attract professional educators.

An illustration of the wide interest in Montessori education is provided by its reception at the Chautauqua Institute in western New York. The Institute and the many local Chautauquas across the United States were significant adult education agencies that provided information, inspiration, and entertainment in the period from 1890 to 1920. Foremost of the Chautauqua activities were lectures by prominent national figures such as Theodore Roosevelt and William Jennings Bryan. S. S. McClure spoke at Chautauqua in 1909 on "The Making of a Magazine." Ida Tarbell, *McClure's Magazine*'s star investigative reporter and author, began her journalism career as a writer and editor of *The Chautauquan*, the Institute's magazine. It was not surprising that articles about Montessori education appeared in *The Chautauquan*.

The Chautauquan's "Talk About Books" column in September 1912 featured a favorable review of the recently published English-language translation of *The Montessori Method*, saying it should "be of interest to all who teach little children." The reviewer praised the method for its insistence "on the liberty of the child, and on the development of its individuality; it prescribes a course for training of sensory, motor and mental capacities; and it leads to wonderful results in early reading, writing and arithmetic as well as in poise, self-control and accuracy."[26]

Reviewing Montessori's *Educational Anthropology* in the December 1913 issue of *The Chautauquan*, Earl Barnes added to the growing Montessori climate of opinion. He wrote, "All students of education must have been impressed by the rapidity with which Dr. Montessori's educational ideas have taken hold upon the public mind during the past five years. In this short period, an Italian woman has become the most widely known figure in the educational world. Her books have been translated into all languages and widely read. Her special pedagogical apparatus has been sold . . . even to those who knew her only as a name. Hundreds of students have flocked to Rome to see her "Children's Houses" and Montessori schools have been opened everywhere in the country." As a reviewer, Barnes found that Montessori's *Educational Anthropology* presented a well-balanced explanation of the relationship of science, especially biology and anthropology, to education. Of particular interest was Montessori's injunction that teachers should maintain a biological and anthropological record of each child's mental and physical development.[27]

Reflecting the popular interest in the use of Montessori's didactic apparatus in stimulating children's sensory learning and skills, *The Chautauquan*, in December 1913, carried an article on applying the Montessori Method to children in their homes. According to Montessori, the article reported, children feel an instinctive urge to learn through their direct sense impressions of shape, color, and texture. Underlying Montessori's strategy of sensory learning is the child's freedom to choose the activity that the stage of development demands. Acting on this instinctive need, the child develops a sense that he or she is engaged in purposeful activity. The child will persevere in the task, learn it, and enjoy his independent accomplishment.[28]

Montessori was delighted with her book's favorable reviews and its sales in the United States. In a letter to the editor of the *New York Times*, she wrote that "the English translation . . . was exhausted in four days, a first edition of 5000 copies, and at the end of five months a sixth edition was in circulation."[29] The book stimulated the founding of the national Montessori Educational Association by McClure and Alexander and Mabel Bell and the establishment of Montessori schools in the United States. It was instrumental in promoting Montessori's American lecture tour.

Professor Holmes's twenty-five page introduction sought to situate and suggest the future of the Montessori Method in the American context. Holmes attributed the widespread interest in the Montessori Method to the "enthusiastic and ingenious articles in *McClure's Magazine*." Holmes called *The Montessori Method* a "remarkable book . . . eagerly expected by" a large audience, but showed academic caution, stating, "The astonishing welcome accorded to the first popular expositions of the Montessori system may mean much or little for its future in England and America." It remains for those in education to "decide upon its value, interpret its technicalities to the country at large, and adapt it to English and American conditions."[30]

Like many of the Montessori Method's commentators, advocate and critic alike, Holmes focused on the method's creator, Maria Montessori, calling Montessori's work "remarkable, if for no other reason, because it represents the constructive effort of a woman." He continued, "We have no . . . other educational system . . . inaugurated by the feminine mind."[31] Professor Holmes's comments, complimentary in the early twentieth century, would be judged sexist in the twenty-first century. Holmes found the Montessori Method remarkable "because it springs from a combination of womanly sympathy and intuition, broad social outlook, scientific training, intensive and long continued study of educational problems, and, to crown all, varied and unusual experience as a teacher and educational leader." He then identified the significant features of the Montessori Method: the adaptation of methods developed for training deficient children to the education of normal children; a "radical" conception of child liberty; the training of separate sensory, motor, and mental skills; and "the rapid, easy, and substantial mastery of reading, writing, and arithmetic."[32] These features would be major themes in the *McClure Magazine* articles and the forthcoming lecture tour.

Then Holmes, resuming his professorial role, advised that Montessori's materials, used in the education of children with handicaps, were not original to her. They had been developed by Seguin, once head of the Massachusetts Institution for the Feeble-Minded at Waverly; further, Dr. Walter S. Fernald, a later Waverly Superintendent, had, before Montessori, maintained that they could be used effectively with normal children. Despite this borrowing from others, Holmes praised Montessori for "the crystallization of these experiments" into a system of education.

Holmes then entered an area that would bring conflict into the introduction and implementation of the Montessori Method in the United States. Montessori, herself, had said that her method was not yet complete and was still being developed. What Holmes, like Fisher, did not understand was that Montessori intended that she would be the one who would complete her work; it could be disseminated, but only as she had designed it. Holmes, taking the experimental attitude generally found among professors of education, said "a system of education does not have to attain perfection in order to merit study, investigation, and experimental use. Dr. Montessori is too large-minded to claim infallibility, and too thoroughly scientific in her attitude to object to careful scrutiny of her scheme and the thorough testing of its results."

Although not obvious at the time, Montessori and Holmes, like other professors of education, held different conceptions of the scientific method applied to education. Believing her method of education to be scientifically rather than metaphysically based, Montessori meant that it was derived from her clinical observation of children at their work. These observations could be organized into a method much like one used by physicians in diagnosing and treating illness. Successful learning activities in children, like successful treatments in medicine, could be replicated if the teacher was properly trained. Holmes and many other professors of education saw observation as a first step in using the experimental method in education. These observations needed to be rendered into hypotheses that could be tested empirically to arrive at predictable outcomes. Variables could be introduced into the formula that might change and improve outcomes. For the professors, science generated hypotheses to be tested further and revised when necessary. For Montessori, however, scientific outcomes could be replicated by using the exact method that had caused them.

In introducing Montessori's book, Holmes assumed an eclectic perspective, saying "An all or nothing policy for a single system inevitably courts defeat." Warning against adopting one program to the exclusion of others, Holmes advised, "We must try out several combinations, watch and record the results, compare them, and proceed cautiously to new experiments." Again Holmes's eclecticism was not what Montessori had in mind. She did not want her method tampered with by combining it with other methods.

Holmes made a considered effort to compare and contrast the Montessori Method and the kindergarten. Both the Montessori and the kindergarten approaches were directed to early childhood education. Some kindergarten educators, especially purists who adhered closely to Friedrich Froebel's original philosophy, saw the Montessori Method as a rival approach. The Montessori-kindergarten issue surfaced in the early introduction of the Montessori Method, in the articles in *McClure's Magazine*, and during and after Montessori's lecture tour.

Holmes believed the issue could be resolved by an educational compromise that eclectically combined complementary elements from both the Montessori and the kindergarten systems.[33] Holmes emphasized that both Montessori and Froebel had agreed on the principle of child freedom and the need for a structured educational environment. From this concurrence, it would be possible to resolve some of the differences between the two early childhood education approaches. Holmes carefully identified the differences that needed compromise and synthesis. While children in the kindergarten participate in group activities designed to socialize them, each child worked individually and independently in the Montessori classroom. While both Froebel and Montessori agreed on the need to develop children's sensory and muscular skills, Montessori's didactic apparatuses were specific to a particular sensory or physical skill while Froebel's gifts, such as the building blocks, to overall skill development. Montessori's sensory training is specific, developing one sense at a time, while the kindergarten's approach is more generalized to deal with all the senses simultaneously. While both methods featured free body activity and rhythmic exercises, the kindergarten used imaginative group games, while Montessori stressed specific individual exercises to develop physical skills and functions. While the kindergarten's group games were highly imaginative and symbolic, the Montessori school's activities were geared to performing the work of real life.[34]

A charge raised repeatedly against the Montessori Method was that it failed to encourage children's imagination and creativity. Froebel's kindergarten philosophy emphasized encouraging children to learn by freeing their imagination through play, stories, and arts and crafts. Rejecting fantasy for reality, Montessori stressed the need for children to learn the practical skills needed in real life.

Still another divergence between Montessori and the kindergarten was when and how to teach reading and writing. The kindergarten philosophy opposed rushing or pushing children into reading and writing, but rather built readiness for these skills in preparation for the primary grades. In the Montessori system, too, readiness was emphasized as the children worked with the didactic apparatus in developing their sensory skills. A much-publicized feature of the Montessori Method was that reading and writing were not delayed but encouraged as children "exploded" into reading and writing.

After identifying the similarities and differences between the kindergarten and the Montessori Method, Holmes proposed a reconciliation of the two systems. This fusion of the two early childhood education approaches could take place in a public school kindergarten that offered a two-year program to children from ages of three and a half to five. The Montessori materials, especially the didactic apparatus, would be used extensively in the program's first year. In the second year, Froebel's gifts, stories, songs, and arts and crafts would be emphasized. Then, near the end of the second year, the Montessori exercises, preparatory to reading and writing, would be introduced.[35] Holmes underestimated the strong loyalties and the dogmatic purity of kindergarten and Montessori educators. He certainly did not understand that Montessori would regard methodological compromises as an anathema that would dilute her principles.

Holmes next turned to the Montessori Method's strong appeal to lay persons, especially parents who read *McClure's Magazine*. The greatest appeal for many parents was the didactic apparatus—the devices and materials that Montessori had designed to develop sensory, muscular, and mental skills. Since each child worked with the apparatus individually in the Montessori school, parents believed that they could do this work at home. Advising them to read *The Montessori Method* for a more complete rendition of the method and its principles, Holmes admonished parents that the mere possession of the didactic apparatus would not work "an educational miracle." For the method to be effective, there needed to be the trained and skilled directress, who knew when and how to intervene in the learning process. To be educationally effective, the materials needed to be used with the proper guidance.[36]

Holmes's discussion of the Montessori apparatus was insightful. The promotion, distribution, and sale of the Montessori materials would erupt into a highly contentious issue between Montessori and McClure. Except for Montessori's repudiation of Fisher, this issue lay submerged under the pervasive climate of opinion that welcomed the Italian educator and her method in the United States.

The American women who went to Rome to be trained by Montessori as directresses formed the most direct and also the most emotional connection between Montessori and her public in the United States. Among them were those who would promote the Montessori Method, establish Montessori schools, and write articles and books about the Montessori Method. Ellen Yale Stevens, Helen Parkhurst, Margaret Naumburg, Anne George, and others would win a place in the history of American education as either pioneer Montessori educators or as creators of their own methods of education.

Margaret Naumburg, who studied with Montessori in 1913, was typical of the young women who created a highly lyrical and romanticized image of their mentor. When she met Montessori for the first time, Naumburg wrote that "a soft light came into her eyes, a deep smile to her lips. In that smile lay all the haunting enigma of the 'Mona Lisa,' and yet a richer, deeper tenderness. In her smile was mirrored the secret conflict of her own personality. I had expected to find a hard, efficient scientist, and here was a soft and tender woman of intense personal charm. There she sat beside me, the symbol of all the womanly woman has ever been." Naumburg continued, "She has the mind of a keen and critical observer, but it is ever in conflict, with her warm and intuitive sympathies. When roused to fight for a principle, her courage is boundless. When called upon to meet social duties, her courage often fails her. . . . It is curious that a woman who has achieved such sure distinction and is well aware of her strong personality should still have moments of embarrassing shyness."[37]

Ruth French, another American acolyte, ecstatically praised Montessori as a "magical personality that makes her words seem winged messengers of light and the mighty fever of enthusiasm is amazing to the beholder."[38] This reverent language created a mysterious and romantic aura surrounding Montessori's personality. It would also pervade the articles in *McClure's Magazine* and accounts of Montessori's lecture tour in 1913.

It was most likely their first encounter with Montessori, with her powerful personality and presence, that initiated her students' loyalty, dedication, and commitment. Then, Montessori's training courses reinforced the power of her personality as she moved them into her philosophy. They would need to be more than ordinary teachers; they, like her, would need to become, as she was, a scientist who clinically observed children. But the Montessori kind of scientist was a quiet observer who, as a patient, almost contemplative observer, was able to penetrate into the child's internal life and psyche. She told them they would be agents in the child's developing personality and ability who would not interfere but quietly guide the child's self-development. In demonstration classes, they learned how the apparatus was to be used in schools. They left the training courses not just as teachers in the usual sense but as disciples, trained by a gifted mentor, who were doing the most important work of all—bringing children to achieve the fullness of their human nature.[39]

Of the young women Montessori trained as directresses, Anne Everett George, who became Montessori's leading early disciple in the United States, had a leading role in the unfolding McClure-Montessori story. As a personal friend of McClure and his wife, Hattie, and as the directress in the Washington, DC, school established by Alexander Graham Bell and his wife, Mabel, Anne E. George (1878–1973), who left no autobiography and whose biography is still unwritten, was born in Columbia, Missouri, the daughter of Benjamin Y. George, a Presbyterian minister, and his wife, Adeline Gilman George.[40] George's experience as a teacher was in private rather than public schools. She taught at the New York Military Academy at Cornwall and the Roland Park School in Baltimore. From 1905 until 1909, she was an elementary teacher at the prestigious Chicago Latin School.

The title of George's article in *Good Housekeeping Magazine*, "Dr. Maria Montessori: The Achievement and Personality of an Italian Woman Whose Discovery Is Revolutionizing Educational Methods," illustrates the major features of the Montessori climate of opinion: Montessori's personality, her scientific discoveries, and her revolutionary educational method. The editor's introduction to the article established George's credentials: "Dr. Montessori's influence upon educational methods promises to be more fundamental and far-reaching than any other educator since Froebel. Miss George is, we believe, best qualified of all American students of Montessori to write concerning the woman and her work. This new and very effective method of teaching young boys and girls proceeds by stimulating learning through natural appeal to the five senses of the individual."[41]

A letter in May 1909 from Elizabeth Risser, a friend living in Italy, started

George on her path to become a Montessori directress. Risser told George that her visit to a "remarkable" school in a social settlement in Milan that used the Montessori Method had made a very strong impression on her. Observing children working happily and independently, Risser said, "The idea of the method is to train the senses first, and reach the mind through them. Not to present any direct abstract information, but to lead the child to reach a fact for himself through the training of his fingers, his eyes, his perceptions generally."[42]

George, who had been searching for a method in which children were free to learn by acting on their own interests and needs, was so intrigued by Risser's letter that she decided to go to Italy to see for herself. In the summer of 1909, George, age 31, met Montessori for the first time. Since George did not speak Italian and Montessori did not speak English, the women communicated in French. While Montessori was fluent in French, George's skill in the language was quite limited. Recalling her first meeting with Montessori, George said "I managed to say that I was a teacher, then we sat and mutely looked at each other for what seemed to me an endless age. I have since learned that the Dottoressa is always unresponsive if she suspects a visitor of being interested only in the fact that her children read and write at an early age. To take a superficial attitude toward her methods is to place a wall between your mind and hers. I think I divined something of this as I met the quiet, questioning look from her dark eyes. I know few other people whose personality is so untrammeled and makes itself so frankly and strongly felt." George, the young American teacher, perceptively discerned the complexity of Montessori's personality—a complexity that would intrigue, baffle, and dismay McClure, the Bells, and many of her American supporters.

Describing her impressions of Montessori, George fell into emotional romanticized language. "I knew that this woman dealt with the real soul of things, and her work was big, sincere, and reverent. . . . I shall never forget the smile with which she welcomed me then; nor the beautiful sincerity with which she talked to me of her work and her hopes. . . . Busy as she was, she gave up several mornings to me, taking me to the various schools, giving lessons herself, and in every way trying to show me the spirit of the work she was doing."[43]

For George, "the impression made by those mornings has stayed with me and has been my guide in all my work since. Dr. Montessori's simplicity was a revelation. Whenever we entered a class-room, I distinctly felt that a new and sweeter spirit pervaded the place, and that the children were, in an indescribable way, set free."[44]

George found that "there was order in everything. With a straightforwardness often stripped entirely of words, Maria Montessori taught, or to use her own word, 'directed,' her children. She treated her children, not as automatons, but as individual human beings. She never forced her personality, or her will upon them, and made none of the efforts to attract and interest which I had often made use of."[45]

George, like other young women who met Montessori, underwent an educational conversion experience. She became a "true believer" in Montessori and her method. George exalted the Italian educator, elevating her to extraordinary heights as a "genius," a "miracle worker," a scientific saint.

George, searching for an approach to teaching that stressed children's freedom, found it in the Montessori Method. When she returned to Chicago, George tried to implement in her classes what she had seen in Rome but she knew she needed to be trained by La Dottoressa. George resigned her position at the Chicago Latin School and returned to Italy in the summer of 1910. After studying Italian in Siena, she enrolled in Montessori's eight-month training course.[46]

Montessori's approach to training teachers is an important chapter in the McClure-Montessori story, and in the subsequent efforts to implement Montessori education in the United States. Prior to her work with Montessori, George had been a teacher at a military academy, known for its discipline, and the Chicago Latin School, a prestigious highly academic institution.

Like George, Montessori trainees were generally young women, often talented in art and music, and attracted to teaching careers. Some of them had taught in kindergartens or primary schools. In the early twentieth century, elementary teaching was highly feminized in the United States and other western countries. The propensity of Montessori education to attract women to its ranks was to be expected since Montessori schools, like kindergartens and primary schools, generally employed women as teachers. However, George and other Montessori directresses had to unlearn what they had earlier studied about schools and teaching. They had to abandon their conventional role of cramming information into children's heads; of controlling what and when they learned; and of doing their work for them. While teachers in conventional elementary schools took center stage in their classrooms, Montessori's directresses were to quietly guide children to teach themselves.[47] George stated, "The degree of success, then, of a teacher using Dr. Montessori's method depends on the extent to which she is prepared by temperament and experience to accept the scientific attitude. Certainly no one who comprehends the high task to which Dr. Montessori calls the teacher could possibly see in her 'method' an immediate and simple substitute for existing methods."[48]

George and the other young women in training heard Montessori lecture on the philosophy underlying her method. George wrote that her philosophy resulted from "years of preparation, of scientific training, of extensive experimentation, deep and earnest thought, reverent, unprejudiced observation. Perhaps no educator has ever approached a pedagogical experiment through such broad . . .

training. It is characteristic of Maria Montessori's peculiar genius that her gifts as a scientist, a physician, and a psychologist have always been but means through which she might help more vitally the lives of those about her. It is the human being, the individual, that interests her, and to be interested means to help."[49]

George then dealt with Montessori's philosophy, which was fundamental to understanding her method. For Montessori, children, by their very human nature, possess a spiritual and physical need to develop themselves. This self-development came as they worked to develop their sensory, motor, practical, and mental skills. Grounded in Montessori's emphasis on the clinical observation of children and scientific pedagogy, the directress needed to be sensitive to children's readiness and stages of development.

To truly understand the Montessori school, the directress needed to appreciate it as a pre-structured learning environment that contained the didactic apparatus and materials that interested and engaged children in their self-development. Through observation and practice, the directress learned to arrange the environment and to set the didactic apparatus in places easily accessible to the children. They were to guide the children but not to interfere with their self-learning and self-development.

Montessori's relationship to her trainees was that of the mother-leader and her students were her disciples. The word disciple is deliberately used here since that is exactly what Montessori expected—directresses who would be devoted to her and to her method.

The mother-leader and student-disciple relationship was not a comfortable fit for some of the trainees, especially those like Margaret Naumburg and Helen Parkhurst who wanted to be professional educators rather than acolytes. Because of Montessori's commanding personality and controlling attitude, there would be a cadre of loyal disciples but also, in almost religious terms, occasional heretics who deviated from her true system or who tried to alter or revise her method; she regarded them as disloyal revisionists. Montessori's controlling attitude would prove to be a problem with some Americans including some directresses and professors of education, and with S. S. McClure.

For Montessori, trained as a medical doctor, successful surgeries and other medical procedures followed techniques that had been clinically tested. Montessori's thinking about education paralleled her medical training. Montessori was the great educational innovator; she had based her method on clinical scientific observation. Those whom she trained as directresses were to replicate, not change her method. She would control the training of Montessori educators to prevent any deviation from her method. However, it would prove very difficult to protect the purity of her method from writers such as Fisher and especially from professors who saw their role as critical agents of educational interpretation and change.

George, who gained notoriety as the pioneer American Montessori educator, established the country's first Montessori school at the home of Edward Harden in Tarrytown, New York, in October 1911.[50] Her school, supported by Frank A. Vanderlip, exemplified the patronage of Montessori schools by wealthy individuals who supported the method.

George, trying to be a "pure Montessorian," believed the method, which Montessori said was applicable to children universally, would be effective with American children.[51] Although George tried to follow her training by Montessori as closely as possible, she found she had to make some cultural adjustments for her American students, which held portents for the future. Montessori claimed that she had discovered the universal laws of childhood development. George had observed that cultural and socioeconomic differences also had an impact on how children learned. The major questions that Montessori education would encounter in the United States were: Should the Montessori Method be adapted to meet cultural and socio-economic differences? If it was adapted, would it still be the Montessori Method?

In the fall of 1912, Alexander Graham Bell and his wife, Mabel, asked George to establish a Montessori school in Washington, DC. Placing her assistant, Miss Bagnell, in charge of the Tarrytown school, George established a Montessori school in the Bells' large house that enrolled twenty children.[52] Like at her school at Tarrytown, George sought to make her second school into an accurate reproduction of Montessori's schools in Rome so that the method would be a "pure application of Dr. Montessori's principles."[53]

Recognized as the foremost Montessori educator in the United States, George, who had learned Italian three years earlier, did the English language translation for *The Montessori Method*, published by the New York company of Frederick A. Stokes in 1912.

George, along with McClure and the Bells, organized the Montessori American Committee in the spring of 1912. The committee was instrumental in organizing Montessori's first international training course in 1913. The course attracted over a hundred students of whom seventy were Americans.[54] The committee was the spark for the establishment of the larger Montessori Educational Association in which George was Director of Work. During Montessori's lecture tour in the United States in 1913, George served as her translator.

Present at each stage in the introduction of Montessori in America, George recognized that a popular public momentum for Montessori was building in the country. She attributed that momentum to the readiness for the method generated by *McClure's Magazine* that spoke to a popular audience rather than to professional educators. Just as she sought to remain loyal to Montessori's principles, George tried to walk a careful line between the popularization of the method by

McClure and the scientific approach insisted on by Montessori. With a sense of caution that was absent in the enthusiastic McClure, George wrote: "A popular article can only give a superficial presentation of any scientific achievement and is almost certain to overemphasize nonessentials, or even weaknesses, and thus for serious students and fellow scientists such a presentation often amounts to a condemnation of the achievement itself. For this reason the peculiar publicity given to the movement, with the consequent rapid manufacture and sale of its material, has been unfortunate in that it has obscured its essential principles."

Though a directress seeking to be scientific in her teaching, George was associated with McClure and others who were vigorously popularizing Montessori's method. Just as Fisher had been caught up in contradictions about the use of the Montessori apparatus, George, too, was beset by contradictions between purity and popularity. While questioning the popularization of the Montessori Method, she also endorsed it. She wrote, "It must be considered that mothers and fathers *everywhere*, the teachers of all the children, are the educators whose experiments, whose pedagogical activities are going on constantly; theirs is the action which takes direct and persistent effect upon the children of the country; they are, therefore, the persons most in need of inspiration and information. After more than four years of daily contact with this twofold situation, I am convinced that while scientific recognition and investigation of Dr. Montessori's work have been retarded by the unusual form of presentation to the world at large, the actual progress of the world toward a recognition of the need of serious study and observation of man in the period of development has been given tremendous impetus."[55] Striving to be loyal to Montessori and a compatriot of McClure, George's situation would not be easy.

Building on the favorable climate of opinion for Montessori, McClure was ready to use his magazine to promote both her method and himself.

5

McClure's Magazine Publicizes Montessori

Samuel S. McClure used his magazine to become Maria Montessori's leading publicist and promoter in the United States. Although he had lost financial control of the magazine he had founded, McClure, still editor of *McClure's Magazine*, mounted a concerted publicity campaign to promote Montessori education in the United States. Enthusiastic and an opportunist, McClure's motives in promoting Montessori education were mixed. A Progressive, he sincerely believed that Montessori's revolutionary new method would bring unprecedented improvement to education. McClure, because of his reckless business practices, was facing a largely self-inflicted bankruptcy. At the time he publicized the Montessori Method, he was certain that his promotion of Montessori education would generate the profits that would return him to financial solvency. McClure did not see any contradiction in his motives. While doing a public service to advance American education, his leadership role in the Montessori movement would bring him financial profits. He would share in tuition from Montessori training classes, from the revenue generated by his lectures on the Montessori Method and from Montessori's 1913 lecture tour.

Despite his erratic personality, McClure, a highly innovative and creative publisher and editor, had made *McClure's Magazine* a widely read and influential progressive monthly periodical. An "idea man" who disregarded conventional business practices, McClure's strategy involved identifying highly talented new writers and engaging them to write for his magazine. *McClure's Magazine*, known as the country's leading progressive journal, featured articles based on the investigative reporting of skilled reporters including Ida Tarbell and Upton Sinclair. Wherever there was political or financial corruption a reporter from *McClure's* would be there to investigate and write about it. This style of reporting and writing made *McClure's Magazine* a journalistic herald of the Progressive Era.

McClure, not known for his humility, attributed his journalistic success to what he called the "McClure Ideal" of "portraying in close, personal studies the character and achievements of the great men of the day; by reporting . . . the new discoveries, tendencies or principles in science and their application in new inventions."[1] Montessori, a great woman of the day with a new scientific method of education certainly fitted the McClure ideal.

Always enthusiastic about promoting original "breakthrough" ideas, McClure was especially optimistic about the promise and prospects of Montessori education in the United States. He planned to use the same strategy in promoting Montessori education that had made his magazine a success. He judged Maria Montessori to be an educator of exceptional talent whose innovative scientific method of education would appeal to American readers—especially to parents and teachers. He would keep his readers attention by serializing the descriptions of Montessori's schools and methods into installments. On-site observers of Montessori's schools in Rome would provide first-hand accounts of how the revolutionary new method of education actually worked and how it might be implemented in the United States. A large and receptive American audience for Maria Montessori would grow into the movement that he would lead.

Although innovative as a journalist, McClure was an enthusiastic doer, not a reflective planner. With McClure, one idea gave birth to myriad other ones—all of which had to be acted on as quickly as possible. He would personally introduce Montessori to the American public; he would use his magazine to launch a concerted campaign to publicize the Montessori Method; he would sponsor a Montessori lecture tour; he would establish an educational institute to train Montessori teachers (directresses) in the United States; he would be Montessori's American spokesman; and very importantly, he expected to make a considerable profit from his leadership of an educational movement that was sure to sweep the country.

Although an often erratic man, McClure had achieved a noted reputation as a publisher and editor. He had developed *McClure's Magazine* into a leading and popular monthly publication by following his own rules for success in the highly competitive arena of journalism in early twentieth-century America. McClure hypothesized that American readers, emerging from their country's cultural isolation, wanted to be enlightened about the world. He reasoned that popularly-written biographies of great men and women would appeal to his largely middle-class progressive readers. His hypothesis about how to increase circulation was proven by the popularity of Ida Tarbell's serialized biographies of Napoleon, Lincoln, and John D. Rockefeller. Maria Montessori's life, if correctly publicized, would, he believed, have a similar impact on his readers.

An innovator in journalism, McClure sought out advances in other fields, especially science and technology. The twentieth century's early decade witnessed

Marconi's experiments with the cable, Bell's with the telephone, Edison's with electric lighting, and Ford's with the automobile. McClure believed that Montessori was an innovator who would bring revolutionary changes to the staid field of education. His readers, many of them parents, looking for ways to improve their children's education, would be eager to read about the Italian "wonder-worker." McClure understood that he needed to continually expand his readership. Magazines with large readerships would attract the advertisers that made them profitable and kept magazines like *McClure's* in operation.

Planning for McClure meant immediate action on an idea as it surfaced in his mind. McClure, however, did not fully share his plans with Maria Montessori, the star of his ambitious publicity campaign. McClure and Montessori had radically different personalities. While McClure was enthusiastic but erratic, Montessori stayed on her own self-determined course with a steel-like steadfast determination. She was keen to seize opportunities to promote her method. Just as Signor Talamo had given her the opportunity to create her first school in Rome, McClure would give her an even larger opening in the United States.

Honored to have the famous American publisher at her door, Montessori was eager for her method to gain a wider audience, especially in the United States. Who would not appreciate the publicity? In her preface to the English translation of *Montessori Method*, Montessori acknowledged her debt to McClure, writing: "I know that my method has been widely spoken of in America, thanks to Mr. S. S. McClure, who has presented it through the pages of his well-known magazine. Indeed, many Americans have already come to Rome for the purpose of observing personally the practical application of the method in my little schools." Like McClure, Montessori hoped that their alliance would advance her cause. She wrote, "If, encouraged by this movement, I may express a hope for the future, it is that my work in Rome shall become the centre of an efficient and helpful collaboration."[2] However, she had much to learn about the publisher and the publisher had much to learn about the pedagogue.

McClure and Montessori entered their relationship from two very different personal perspectives. For McClure, Montessori was a highly talented woman. Just as he had earlier discovered and developed the highly talented writers Ida Tarbell and Willa Cather, he had now discovered a new internationally talented woman, Maria Montessori. He thought he knew how to develop a gifted person's talents. From his beginning as a student editor at Knox College in Galesburg, Illinois, to his rise as a prominent New York publisher, McClure followed his philosophy of enthusiasm—if you had an idea, act decisively on it; don't be afraid to take a risk. However, for McClure, enthusiasm was more than a philosophy; it was part of his psychological makeup. Propelled by his enthusiasm, McClure had grandiose plans for Montessori.

Montessori was a totally different personality. As a scientist and a trained physician, she carefully observed reality, gathered evidence, and came to conclusions slowly, cautiously, and thoroughly, not by random and scattered bursts of enthusiasm, but through a structured and methodological empirical process. With a steel-like determination, Montessori alone would direct her own career. Only she would control the educational method that she was still creating when she met McClure. She had learned to be a deliberate person, especially as she defined her own career in medicine, running against traditional male-generated conventions. Further, she was suspicious of enthusiasts, especially those who only knew her method superficially. Such people, skimming like minnows on the surface, lived in the shallows of life; seeing only the obvious, they were unable to penetrate to and understand the deep spiritual and psychological foundations of her method. She had to be on guard against superficial enthusiasts and opportunists. She would protect the scientific purity of the method that carried her name from distortion by well-meaning enthusiasts and cunning exploiters.

McClure's campaign to popularize Montessori was most unusual for an educator and an educational method. Articles about educational methods typically appeared in educational journals, not popular magazines. Written by professional educators and professors, these articles were descriptive, evaluative, and cautious, not rave reviews. Further, they made their way into print rather slowly, going through a process of peer review. Patently laudatory, McClure's promotion of Montessori was not a cautious scholarly exposition and evaluation; it was an enthusiastic, often emotional and romanticized, endorsement of an "educational wonder-worker." The educator Ellen Yale Stevens, principal of the Brooklyn Heights Seminary, noted how McClure's coverage of Montessori moved a popular magazine in a new direction. She wrote, "For the first time, I believe, in the history of educational thought, a new movement has come to the front through the medium of a popular magazine, instead of by means of a scientific treatise by a specialist in education, which would naturally have a limited appeal. The result of this is that the interest of the whole country has been aroused, not only in the work of Dr. Montessori in Italy, but in the present state of education in this country."[3]

Tozier's trial article, "An Educational Wonder-Worker: The Methods of Maria Montessori," published in May 1911, received a greater response from readers than McClure had anticipated. Sensing that he had come upon a very popular topic, McClure launched a full-scale publicity campaign to promote Montessori education.[4] Tozier followed her lead article with "The Montessori Schools in Rome," which appeared in the December 1911 issue and described Montessori's "revolutionary educational work" in her schools, and a third article, "The Montessori Apparatus," appeared in the January 1912 issue. The Tozier articles established who Montessori was and how her method had produced startling achievements. Montessori's article "Disciplining Children," published in *McClure's* May 1912 issue, and the great Italian educator's first article in an American magazine, described her educational principles. Next came Anne George's article, "The First Montessori School in American," in June 1912, that assured parents that the Montessori Method could be used successfully with American children. In the last article in the Montessori series, Ellen Yale Stevens's "The Montessori Method and the American Kindergarten," in the November 1912 issue, sought to resolve the kindergarten issue.

The Montessori articles in *McClure's Magazine* had a somewhat ordinary, perhaps accidental beginning. McClure, in his autobiography, recalled their origin. In the winter of 1910, McClure, on one of his frequent trips to Europe, met with Mary L. Bisland, his magazine's London agent. Bisland mentioned that she had reviewed some material submitted by Josephine Tozier, a travel writer, about the Montessori Method.

While researching her book, *Susan in Sicily*, Tozier, traveling through Italy, had spent some time in Rome.[5] Alert for new material, Tozier, hearing about Maria Montessori's educational method, arranged an interview with Montessori and then observed children at her schools at the convent on Via Giusti and San Angelo. Exploring the possibility of writing an account of her observations, Tozier told Bisland about Montessori's remarkable new approach to education.[6]

McClure was immediately interested and decided to publish an article on Montessori. When he presented his plan to feature an article on Montessori education, his editorial staff in New York disagreed, believing that an article on an obscure Italian educator and her school would bore their readers. Relying on his own intuition, McClure, however, commissioned Tozier to write her article on the Montessori Method.

McClure's decision to publish Tozier's article on Montessori proved to be a sound one. Tozier had established a reputation as a travel writer with her *Among English Inns* (1904), *The Traveler's Handbook* (1905), and *A Spring Fortnight in France* ((1907).[7] Writing when it was customary for young women from well-established families to take the "grand tour" of Europe before they married, Tozier's prose, though occasionally florid, was clear and engaging. Her style was especially well-suited for general readers like those who read *McClure's Magazine*.

Tozier was a well-known popular writer rather than a professional educator. In his autobiography, McClure noted that important articles such as Tozier's were reviewed by subject area experts prior to publication. William Archer (1856–1914), a noted British literary and dramatic critic, read and approved Tozier's submission. Archer was familiar with Montessori's book, *Il Metodo della Pedagogia Scientifia*, which had not yet been translated into English, but, like Tozier, was not a professional educator.

McClure sent Tozier's submission to "several authorities on kindergartening and pedagogy in the United States." Prophetic of future events, McClure found, "These experts . . . greatly differed in their estimates of Montessori's methods. Some . . . were very antagonistic in their attitude, and declared that, because Mme. Montessori recognized and valued the work of great educators of the past, there was nothing new about her method."[8]

Beginning her article with a highly flattering six-page biography, Tozier introduced Montessori as a great woman, a scientist, and an innovator who was bringing revolutionary improvement to education. In 1911, when Tozier's article appeared, accounts of Montessori's life, in English, were still rare, including the fact that Montessori, one of the first women to earn a degree in medicine from the University of Rome, became a specialist in treating children with mental disabilities. She applied her scientific findings to the education of normal children. Tozier told the story of Montessori's founding of her first school, the Casa dei Bambini, in Rome in 1907, where she developed her scientifically based method of education.

Tozier presented Montessori's philosophy and methods in nontechnical language for *McClure's* readers. Skirting the abstract nuances in Montessori's philosophy, Tozier deliberately highlighted the principles that would most appeal to middle-class, educated, progressive American parents: auto-education, children's liberty, the use of didactic apparatus, and the almost spontaneous development of reading and writing. Many parents wanted something better for their children than the rote recitations, drills, rules, regulations, and discipline that they themselves had experienced in late–Victorian era schools.

Montessori's principle of auto-education was very different from the school experience of many readers of *McClure's Magazine* where the teacher controlled what they were taught. Presenting Montessori's alternative to teacher-dominated learning, Tozier told her readers that auto-education meant that the children were their own instructors, with teachers present to guide but not control the learning process. Children needed to be in a preorganized structured learning environment, a Montessori school, stocked with the apparatus and materials that motivated them to learn. Remembering their own education, the progressive parent saw auto-education as a way in which their children could learn without being prodded or coerced. The photographs illustrating Tozier's article depicted highly engrossed children who appeared to be enjoying their work with the Montessori apparatus and materials.

Montessori's principle of children's liberty, like auto-education, resonated well with *McClure's* readers. While Montessori saw the child's freedom emanating from an inner psychic need to become independent of others, Tozier simplified it as meaning a child, not confined for hours at a desk, was free to move about the school. This freedom of movement gave children the liberty to search the classroom for apparatus and materials that most interested them. Tozier did not emphasize that the learning environment was prestructed in that it specifically contained the materials that led the child to do what Montessori wanted them to do.

Twelve pages of Tozier's article focused on Montessori's didactic apparatus designed to develop the children's physical, sensory, motor, and practical skills. The apparatus included framed pieces of cloth with buttons, laces, and hooks for practicing fastening, buttoning, zipping, lacing, and tying skills; wooden cubes, prisms, and rods to develop the sense of size, depth, and quantity; little boards with rough and smooth surfaces to develop the sense of touch and feeling; musical tone bells; sandpaper and cardboard letters and numbers to develop reading and writing readiness.[9] Thirteen photographs showed children working busily and happily with the apparatus.[10] Tozier wrote, "the apparatus enables, or rather compels, the child to correct his own errors—to see at a glance whether his work 'comes out' right or wrong."[11]

After laying out the general principles of Montessori education, Tozier then discussed some of its specific features. Under the subhead "Maria Montessori Rediscovers the Ten Fingers," she illustrated how the apparatus developed sensory skills. She wrote, "At the very root of her method lies . . . rediscovery of the ten fingers. . . . She realized that the sense of touch, the basis of all the other senses, was the great interpreter of vision and guide to accuracy of perception. It was at the same time the earliest developed of the faculties and the first to be dulled if left uncultivated. She found that the fingertips of young children are almost unbelievably sensitive, but that, in the absence of careful training, they begin to lose this sensitiveness after the age of six. The first step in her method, then, is to teach children to 'see with their fingers' and thus to cultivate a delicately retentive muscular memory."[12]

Tozier described how Montessori used "rough" sand paper and "smooth" satin covered cards to develop children's sense of touch. While the child touches the sand paper card, the directress says, "rough" and with the satin card "smooth." This sensory learning is reinforced as the directress asks the child to give her either a smooth or rough card. If the task is performed correctly, the teacher thanks the child. If the child's response is incorrect, the directress does not correct the child but leaves the table. She and the child will return to the task at another time.

Under the subhead "Children Correct Their Own Mistakes," Tozier informed her readers of Montessori's general rule that the directress is not to correct a child's mistakes. A "mistake" simply means the child is unready at that time to perform a particular task. When the child is ready, he or she will try again. The task is to be performed for its own intrinsic value in the child's growth and development; there should be no prodding with external rewards, nor punishment. The sole reward, which reinforces the correct performance of a task, is that the child experiences a sense of self-competence and growing independence. For Montessori, the movement to independence not only means that the child has acquired a skill but also develops the moral value of staying with a challenge until it is mastered. With rhapsodic prose, Tozier exclaimed, "The bambini are so perfectly under control that they can be swayed by a gesture as an orchestra is swayed by the baton of the conductor. When I said to Maria Montessori, 'How do you manage to keep them so quiet and good?' she replied, 'Because they are doing what they like to do. '"[13]

Tozier moved to the development of practical skills with the subhead, "Children of Three Learn to Tie Bow Knots and to Fasten Buttons and Clasps." Learning to tie one's shoes certainly resonated with *McClure's* readers, many of whom undoubtedly recalled their own difficulty as children in learning this skill. Personifying the process, she described how Lorenzo, "a chubby little boy," learned to tie. The boy worked at "fastening together two strips of cloth, attached to the opposite sides of a light embroidery frame, by tying them with bows of ribbon.... Working unremittingly at these bows for some days ... and ... only three years old, he has come to tie them so creditably that I, watching, could almost blush with shame to think of the hard knots that were all I could tie at the age of seven."[14]

Aware that the magazine's readers, especially parents, wanted to know more about how the Montessori Method taught children to almost spontaneously "burst" or "explode" into reading and writing, Tozier wrote, "There can be no doubt that the teaching of young children to write, without the slightest strain or effort, is the most striking and impressive of Maria Montessori's achievements."[15] Montessori's ease in accomplishing these vital cultural skills could be contrasted with the laborious drills of the traditional school. While progressive parents wanted their children to enjoy their promised freedom to learn, they also wanted them to acquire the literacy synonymous with middle-class economic and social success, the mastery of reading and writing.

Tozier gave a full account of the process of learning to write and read in the Montessori system. After the San Lorenzo school had been operating for six months, some mothers asked Montessori to teach their children to write and read. Unsure that four- and five-year-old children were ready for writing and reading, Montessori, herself, was not ready to begin instruction in these skills. However, the children, asking her to teach them to write and read, really initiated the process.

Montessori rejected the traditional method, based on Pestalozzi's idea of breaking objects into their parts, as a boring waste of children's time and energy. In traditional classes, children repeatedly practiced drawing the parts of letters until they had mastered each part and then finally put the parts into the whole letter. Rather than the traditional method, Montessori believed that the didactic apparatus that had been so effective in developing children's sensory skills could be used in writing instruction. Tozier quoted Montessori, who, herself, was surprised with how easily and rapidly the children learned to write: "I was on the terrace roof, and the children were playing about or standing near me. I was sitting beside a chimney, which rose above the tiled pavement, when it occurred to me to say to a little boy of five, who was standing by, 'Draw this chimney.' And I handed him a piece of chalk. He threw himself at once on the ground, and began to draw the chimney quite recognizably; wherefore, as was my practice, I praised him warmly. The little fellow looked up at me, smiled, was evidently on the point of bursting into some ebullition of delight and then cried, 'Scrivo! Io scrivo!' (I can write! I am writing!) Lying on the ground, he wrote on the pavement mano (hand), then with new enthusiasm, he wrote camino (chimney), and as he wrote, he continued to call out 'I am writing!' so that other children came running to see the sight, and surrounding them staring in amazement. Then two or three of them, trembling with excitement, said to me. 'Please, please, a piece of chalk. I want to write too!' and in fact they set a work to write various words."[16]

Acclaiming Montessori's results in teaching writing, Tozier wrote that four year olds learned to write in only six weeks and five year olds in a month. Further, the Montessori children's handwriting was just as skilled as that of third graders in public schools.[17] She then went on to a shorter description of a reading exercise, "The Game of Learning to Read." Describing the game, she wrote that words, in cursive, on pieces of cardboard are placed by the objects they name around the room. Then, the names of the objects are placed in a bag; each child draws a name from the bag; if the child can pronounce the name of the object, particularly the toys, she or he gets to play with it for the rest of the day. This is followed by papers with short phrases, with questions or activities. The child then answers the question or performs the activity.

Tozier concluded her laudatory article: "For the present, she has more than enough to do in recruiting a corps of teachers, of disciples, or missionaries. There can be little doubt that, when this is done, the influence of her ideas, will spread far beyond Rome and Italy, to 'regions Caesar never knew.' It may not be long before, in her own words, 'the figure of the old schoolmistress, who labors to preserve the discipline of immobility, and wears out her lungs in a shrill and continuous flow of talk, shall have disappeared. For the mistress will be substituted a *didactic apparatus* which itself controls errors and places the child on the path of auto-education. The function of the mistress will then be simply to direct, *patiently* and *silently*, spontaneous efforts of the children.'"[18]

In the December 1911 issue, McClure announced that *McClure's Magazine* would act as the clearing house for the Montessori movement in the United States. The editor's note stated that "Four years ago Maria Montessori, an Italian physician and educator, opened the first "House of Childhood" (Casa dei Bambini) in Rome, and began to apply her revolutionary methods of education to the teaching of little children. Her work has set forth a new educational movement that is not only transforming the schools of Italy, but is making rapid progress in other countries. In June 1911, Switzerland passed a law establishing the Montessori system in all its public schools. Two model schools were opened in Paris this September, one of them under the direction of the daughter of the French minister to Italy, who has studied with Montessori in Rome. Preparations are being made to establish Montessori schools this year in England, India, China, Mexico, Corea [*sic*], Argentine Republic, and Honolulu. In the United States schools have already been started in New York and Boston, and Montessori has received applications from teachers in nearly every state in the Union who wish to study with her in order to apply her methods. To meet the demand for instruction, Montessori will open a training class in Rome this winter for teachers from England and America."[19]

The magazine also reported the support of a prominent Italian nobleman and his American wife for the Montessori movement. Baroness Franchetti (Alice Hallgarten) was encouraging publication of Montessori's *Il Metodo della Pedagogia Scientifica*, and her husband, Baron Franchetti, had arranged for the international patent of Montessori's didactic apparatus. As the movement developed in the United States, prominent individuals such as Alexander Graham Bell and Margaret Wilson would be featured in accounts about Montessori education.

Tozier's lead article had presented Montessori's guiding pedagogical principles and described her didactic apparatus, which enabled children to educate themselves, even to the point of learning to read and write. Imitating the tone and style that had made her first article so successful, Tozier's second article, "The Montessori Schools in Rome: The Revolutionary Educational Work of Maria Montessori as Carried Out in Her Schools in Rome" appeared in *McClure's Magazine*'s December 1911 issue.[20] Fifteen pages long with illustrative photographs, Tozier's article sought to show how Montessori's principles were implemented at her schools at the Convent on Via Giusti and at San Angelo.

Tozier, whose first article had emphasized the practical application of Montessori's method, veered into its underlying philosophy. Beginning with the sweeping assertion that the method would improve humanity, Tozier wrote "The Montessori system of education is more than a mere method of teaching young children: it is a branch of applied modern science—directed toward the development of a new race of men." She backed up her claim with Montessori's own words, "The external world transformed by the tremendous development of experimental science in the last century, must have as its master a transformed man. If the progress of the human individual does not keep pace with the progress of science, civilization will find itself 'checked.'"[21]

Although questionable if Tozier's entry into philosophy was what parents, seeking to improve their children's reading and writing, were looking for in *McClure's Magazine*, it may have served other purposes. Tozier's emphasis on the Montessori Method being based on empirical observations of children fit well with the scientific method's growing credibility among the educated public. The claim that Montessori education would improve the human condition resonated well with those readers who supported the Progressive ideology. These Progressives believed that the application of the scientific method to government, society, health care, and education could and would make life easier, more efficient, and better. McClure, himself, who saw science as the key to social improvement, featured scientists, especially those who applied their findings to life, in his magazine. Montessori, herself, who believed that her method could regenerate humanity, reiterated this claim in her writings and in her American speaking tour in 1913.

Tozier turned to the Montessori's principle of child freedom, writing "Madame Montessori tries to give the child an environment that liberates his personality; she places him in an atmosphere where there are no restraints . . . no opposition, nothing to make him perverse or self-conscious, or to put him on the defensive. His personality is thus liberated into free action, and the thing he is expresses itself."[22] Again, she used Montessori's own words, "We can not know the consequences of suffocating a *spontaneous action* when the child is just beginning to act; . . . it is necessary rigorously to avoid the *arrest of spontaneous movements* and the imposition of *purely arbitrary acts* . . . .We do not refer to useless or dangerous actions."[23]

Continuing the theme of sensory training from her first article, Tozier, illustrating its positive effects on children's growth, wrote, "By her system of sense training, she develops in the child a sense of his relation to his material surroundings and a facility in accommodating himself to them. . . . He learns to manage his body deftly, to walk without stumbling, to carry without dropping, to touch objects delicately and surely—in short, to move among the material things that surround him . . . with ease and freedom, and with the least possible fret and wear to his spirit and to his body."[24]

Tozier discussed the training of directresses, highlighting the differences between them and traditional teachers. This contrast was especially useful in McClure's efforts to attract students to Montessori's teacher-training program in Rome and in laying the groundwork for his envisioned Montessori training institute in the United States. Using the subhead "The Old-Fashioned Teacher Suffocated the Activity of Her Pupils," Tozier described the new Montessori directress. The new teacher, like a physician observing a patient, was to be trained to observe children, their environment, and their activities in a clinical fashion. The directress, unlike the traditional teacher, would not be the classroom's central figure. The child, never the teacher, was the center of the classroom.[25]

Tozier reminded her readers that Montessori had found that even intelligent teachers who comprehended her principle of children's self-active learning had difficulty in implementing it. The concept of the teacher they had acquired in their own school experience interfered with the Montessori admonition that the teacher needed to be a noninterfering passive onlooker in the new school. They needed to unlearn the old rules of instruction that forced children to be silent and still while teachers tried to pack their minds with information. To make the point, Tozier again quoted Montessori, "In those first days of training my teachers, I saw the dangers of blind intervention in the children's activities. These teachers almost involuntarily, recalled the children to immobility, without *observing* and *distinguishing* the nature of the movements they repressed."[26]

Illustrating Montessori's principle of active children and passive teachers, Tozier, with the subhead "The Ordinary Teacher's Mistaken Notion of Helpfulness," provided the following example: "Madame Montessori . . . gives an illustration of a little girl of two and a half who, finding that she could not see either under the legs of or over the heads of the other children, who were crowded about a basin of floating toys, stood for a moment in deep thought; then, with her face alight with interest, ran toward a little chair, with the evident intention of placing it so that she might see over the heads of her friends. Just at this moment she was spied by a young teacher, who, before Montessori could prevent, seized the baby and, lifting her up so that she could see above the heads of the others, cried: "Come dear, come, poor little one, you shall see, too."

Montessori, assessing the incident, said, "Certainly, the child, seeing the toys, experienced no such joy as she felt in overcoming the obstacle with her own powers. The teacher prevented the child from educating itself without bringing any compensating good. She had been about to feel herself a victor, and instead she found herself held fast in two imprisoning arms, so impotent."[27]

Tozier took on the difficult challenge of explaining the principle of the child's freedom to learn within a prestructured educational environment, the Montessori school. Directresses were to learn how to replicate Montessori's structured environment at her first Casa dei Bambini. This structure, rather than the teacher, indirectly set the boundaries of child freedom.

Tozier explained the importance of a structured school: "Nothing in the Casa dei Bambini is accidental. . . . Everything . . . has been carefully planned." She described features of the school environment, "The squares of carpet upon which the children work are so small that they can conveniently brush and fold them and carry them about. The tables are so light that babies of two and three can easily move them. When the children are taught to wash their faces and hands, they use little basins and pitchers which they can handle easily and safely. The cupboards in which the children keep the apparatus are low and open easily."[28]

Liberty in this setting meant that the child was free to select the apparatus and materials that the directress had deliberately placed there.

Tozier then explained how the child's freedom in the structured school led to moral as well as to sensory and skill development. She quoted Montessori, "The first idea that the child must acquire, . . . to be actively disciplined, is . . . the difference between *good* and *evil*; and the task of the educator lies in seeing that the child does not confound *good* with *immobility*, and *evil* with *activity*, as often happens in the case of the old-time discipline. . . . Our aim is to discipline for *activity*, for work, for *good*; not for *immobility*, not for *passivity*, not for *obedience*. A room in which all the children move about usefully, intelligently, and voluntarily, without committing any rough or rude act, would seem to me a class-room disciplined very well indeed."[29]

The relationship of the individual child to the group was a controversial issue. Some progressive and kindergarten educators criticized Montessori's emphasis on the child's individualized self-learning, which neglected participation and socialization in the group. This issue was especially meaningful for *McClure's* progressive readers who valued individual liberty but placed in the context of social welfare.

In traditional schools, the teacher's challenge was to force individual children to behave as a group so that she could give all of them the same lesson at the same time. Where learning was highly individualized, the Montessori directress did not need to enforce group conformity. In American graded schools, typically a class of children of the same age worked simultaneously on the same lesson under the teacher's direction, often with the same textbooks. The teacher's challenge was to motivate and control the children so that they worked together. A good portion of teacher preparation in American normal schools and colleges dealt with the problems related to group motivation, control, and discipline.

Montessori addressed the issue of the individual child's relationship to the group, which she called "collective education." Montessori used the analogy that collective order in the classroom was like the music of a well-trained orchestra. Each musician individually played her or his own instrument. But, following the director's baton, the individual musicians became an orchestra that produced harmonious music. Realizing that Montessori's concept of "collective education" was not an easy one to understand, Tozier's article was illustrated with photographs that showed children working side by side but individually on their particular activity. One photograph showed three children, each facing in a different direction, working separately on the joint task of sweeping the school's courtyard. Another showed children, seated together at a table, but with each working individually with reels of colored silk.

Tozier noted that visitors to Montessori's schools were impressed by the children's earnest and quiet activities. She told readers about her observation of how a group of students at the San Angelo school had moved from the building to its courtyard: "One morning, sitting among the children in their school-room, I heard Signora Galli's assistant say quietly: 'Let's have school in the court now.' That was all she said. Yet I have seen many teachers fail, with a dozen explicit commands to achieve the result that I witnessed after this simple sentence. The effect was immediate. There was no scrambling, no confusion . . . forty-five little girls put themselves to work getting ready to go down into the court. . . . There was a hall to cross, two doors to open, and three flights of narrow, awkward stone steps to descend. . . . I saw the security and patience displayed in the movements of these children, that the sense training exercises had given them a control that I had never attained with children and have seldom seen in grown people."[30]

An editor's note at the end of the article announced: "In her January article Miss Tozier will describe in detail the Montessori educational apparatus, and will show what is accomplished with each toy. Arrangements have been completed for the manufacture and sale of this apparatus by the House of Childhood, 606 Flatiron Building, New York City, under the management of Mr. Carl Byoir. The manufacturers of the apparatus hope to place the material within the reach of parents and educators by the first of January. Dr. Montessori's representative in this country will collaborate in the preparation of a book of instructions and suggestions which will be sold with each set of apparatus."[31]

Tozier's third article, "The Montessori Apparatus: A Description of the Material and Apparatus Used in Teaching by the Montessori Method," appeared in the January 1912 issue of *McClure's Magazine*.[32] Readers wanted to learn the secret to the success of the Montessori Method, which seemed to be the didactic apparatus that Montessori had designed. In 1913, Dorothy Canfield Fisher's *The Montessori Manual: For Teachers and Parents* gave another detailed account of the apparatus.[33] (See chapter 4, "Creating a Favorable Climate of Opinion for the Montessori Method in the United States," for more on Fisher's book and Montessori's rejection of Fisher's commentary.)

Tozier's third article reiterated the ease with which children learned to write and read in the Montessori Method. Immediately capturing her readers, especially the parents, attention, she enthusiastically acclaimed: "The most conspicuous of Montessori's achievements has undoubtedly been her discovery of a process by which children spontaneously break forth into reading and writing—'an explosion into writing,' as Montessori herself graphically puts it."[34] The explosion to writing and reading came, Tozier said, "spontaneously, from an impulse within the child," sparked by exercises with the didactic apparatus.

Tozier gave detailed descriptions of the didactic materials and their use. The first apparatus were cylinders, arranged into three sets of ten each. Each set was fitted into a case from which the children took and returned a particular cylinder.

In the first set, the cylinders were of equal length but graduated in diameter; in the second, of the same diameter, but graduated in length; in the third, both length and diameter varied with the cylindrical shape constant. Each cylinder had a small brass button at the top so the child could easily remove and return it to its correct place in the case. In performing the exercise, the children removed the cylinders from their case, mixed them on the table, and then replaced them into their correct hole. Since a particular cylinder would fit only one hole, the process was self-correcting. The child, through trial and error, learned to place the correct cylinder in its appropriate place.

In the Big Stair, the Long Stair, and the Tower, the children used rectangular blocks of various sizes. In constructing the Tower, the children learned to make the tower's base with the larger blocks. The exercise developed the child's skill in discriminating between long and short, thick and thin, and big and small blocks. Personalizing the work with the Long Stair, in her section "How Pietro Learns to Make the Long Stair," Tozier wrote:

> When little Pietro came into the school he was very active and intelligent, but disordered in his manner of play. When he began to play with these various sets of blocks, he mixed them up together and ran confusedly from one to another. He could not make the Stair in an orderly and well-graded fashion. His power of attention was too unstable, his mind too volatile. A lesson was given him. The rectangular blocks were placed without any order upon one of the little carpets upon which the children love to play these games, and he was asked to pick out the largest block. Having done this, he was asked to place it on a table some distance from the square of carpet. He was then asked to select the largest of all those left, and was shown how to place it close against the block already on the table. So, little by little, he was brought to understand that the Stair descended gradually, and that had no connection with the blocks of the Tower or the Long Stair. When, finally by his own efforts, the Stair was made, his delight was unbounded. He destroyed it at once and set about reconstructing it. So intense was his pleasure that he showed his joy by kissing each block as he put it in place. For nearly an hour, he could not be enticed from his bewitching occupation.[35]

Tozier described the tactile exercises, in which children used a set of tablets and cards mounted on strips of rough and smooth paper. She wrote about how she had observed a four-year-old boy performing the rough-smooth exercises:

> The teacher put down in front of him two square cards, one smooth and white, the other black and rough. She then took the first two fingers of

> the child's hand and drew them over the surface of his smooth card, saying distinctly, slowly, and quietly: "Smooth, smooth, smooth." After his fingers were released . . . he continued . . . to rub his finger-tips up and down the shiny surface of the card. . . . When his fingers were brought into contact with the sandpaper surface he promptly jerked them away, showing his displeasure. . . . At the teacher's request, "Give me the rough," . . . the child showed by frowning severely as he handed up the objectionable card, how unlikely he was to forget the sensation. When asked to name the quality of each of these cards, he imitated the accent and voice of his teacher, saying "'liscio' . . . (smooth) but . . . with a frown" when he said, "ruvido" (rough).[36]

Tozier described the didactic apparatus for training the sense of touch—a box with little drawers that hold two squares of cloth such as velvet, silk, wool, tweed, flannel, cotton, linen, and so forth. The exercise began with the child blindfolded as he was given squares of two sharply contrasting textures. After feeling the difference between them, he picked their duplicates from a mixed pile of squares. Many of the photographs showed children working with the apparatus with blindfolds.

The children's favorite apparatus, Tozier reported, was a series of wooden tablets whose weight varied by one-fifth of an ounce. The child balanced two tablets on the palms of his hand and determined which one was heavier and which was lighter. Then, he performed the exercise blindfolded, placing the heavier on one side of the table and the lighter one on the other side.

Tozier then turned to children's spontaneous "explosion" into writing and reading. In contrast to American schools where children learned to write at age six, she wrote that the Montessori child, ready to write at age four, learns the process quickly, usually in a month or six weeks. She explained that the term "explosion into writing" needed elaboration in that the children learned to write by following a sequence of exercises with the didactic apparatus. After a child's sensory readiness and skills had developed, she or he was provided with a set of metal geometrical forms that are placed on paper. After tracing each form with a colored pencil, she filled its outline in color. This exercise is repeated so the child can develop muscular control in holding and using the pencil, which is the mechanical part of writing. The children then apply their earlier learned skill in tracing geometrical shapes—triangles, ovals, and squares—to tracing the letters, all placed on a table. The children were free to select any letter from the table that they wished to trace, first with their fingers, then with crayons, and finally with pencils.

Children learn the alphabet by working with sandpaper letters. Tozier described a lesson in using large sandpaper letters, in clear script, mounted on glazed cardboard. For example, the directress takes the "O" card and gives it to the child while slowly and distinctly pronouncing the sound for "O." Taking the child's hand, she shows her how to use her forefinger in tracing the letter, as if she were writing it. While tracing the letter, the child pronounces its sound. In these first lessons, the child learns the letter's sound but not its name. The same process is repeated with all the letters of the alphabet. According to Tozier, "The sound of each letter is indelibly associated in his mind with the muscular movements necessary to reproduce it; and thus, when he hears clearly spoken a single letter, or a word of which all the letters are perfectly clear to him, his fingers instinctively make the motion that they have so often made in tracing the sandpaper letter; and if he has in his fingers a piece of chalk, this record becomes visible."[37]

After learning the sandpaper letters, the child is introduced to the "movable alphabet" made of stiff paper letters, with vowels pink and consonants blue. The letters are contained in boxes with a particular letter placed in a specific compartment. At the bottom of the compartment is pasted a copy of the particular letter with the duplicates of the letter on top. Tozier quoted Montessori on the use of the movable alphabet: "When the child has learned to trace and distinguish sandpaper letters, he undoubtedly knows the movable paper letters. When he can make the syllables with the sandpaper letters, he can do so with the movable letters; the one difference is that he no longer touches, but recognizes the form instantly. So the making of words is not difficult. . . . When he knows how to compose, he knows how to read. . . . This form of composition is akin to both reading and writing."[38]

Montessori drew a close relationship between learning to write with reading. Devoting a section to "How Children Learn to Read," Tozier described how the method of teaching of reading came suddenly, like a "revelation," to Montessori. In the school garden, on a sunny spring day, Montessori was listening to a group of children talking about their interests. Suddenly four children got up and went to the blackboard and wrote sentences about the garden, such as "How glad I am that our garden is beginning to bloom." Surprised that the children had arrived as spontaneously at composition as they had at writing, Montessori understood that they were ready for reading. She recalled, "Going to the blackboard, I wrote, '*Mi volte bene?*' (Do you wish me well? The children read slowly and mechanically aloud, were silent for a moment, as if thinking, and then cried delightedly, 'Yes, yes!' . . . Thus began between me and the children communication by means of written language, and little by little, they discovered the great quality of written language: . . . that it transmits thought."[39]

Building on Montessori's experience in the garden, Tozier described the first exercise in teaching reading. She wrote, "The names of familiar objects are written on . . . a card. . . . The teacher shows the card and lets the child translate slowly the sounds of the word written on it. If he interprets these sounds correctly," she has him say the word more quickly, repeating it until he masters it. "Through this exercise the children gradually master the mechanism of the words until the word, instead of being a succession of sounds, becomes . . . the instantaneous symbol of an idea."[40]

Anticipating objections that Montessori's method of teaching writing was more suited to Italian than English-speaking American children, Tozier wrote, "In Italian, spelling is an art that requires no effort. When a word in that language is properly and distinctly spoken, it has really spelled itself. But English spelling is a much more erratic and distracting proposition. In Italian, the vowel sound never changes, nor, in fact, does that of the consonant. In English, the capricious vowels upset every known rule of spelling or pronunciation. Nevertheless, English teachers who have used the Montessori Method have found that, by presenting the letter sounds according to the system of phonetics usually taught in our schools, the ability to read and write is quite as remarkable as when Italian is the language used."[41]

After discussing the Montessori apparatus, Tozier, under the subhead "Montessori Does Not Encourage Imagination in Young Children," addressed imagination, a controversial topic with kindergarten educators. She wrote, "Montessori does not encourage imagination, because she feels that the strength of imagination is so great that it will fulfill its own work, and her business as an educator is to eliminate those thousands of false impressions which children get from being too fanciful, as well as from being insufficiently instructed concerning the objects that constitute their daily environment." In the Montessori school, children's "attention wandered when a fairy tale was read to them, and they showed a decided preference for writing or reading single words or simple phrases that sprang from some thought in their own minds. . . . Reading and writing interested them as a means of expressing their own practical interests and activities, rather than as a key to an imaginative world outside of their own."[42]

Tozier's articles, which generated wide reader interest in the Montessori Method, emphasized two points that appealed to middle-class progressive parents: (1) children, liberated from Victorian restrictions, would be free to learn on their own; (2) the specially designed Montessori apparatus would efficiently give their children the keys to literacy and numeracy. The articles came close to being a very readable textbook on Montessori education that: (1) introduced Montessori as a great educator; (2) told how she had based her principles on scientifically based findings; (3) portrayed how children were free to learn in the structured Montessori school; (4) highlighted Montessori's achievement of early writing and reading in four year olds; (5) illustrated how the didactic apparatus provided an effective and efficient way to learn for children in the United States.

Tozier, the travel writer turned educational commentator, set the stage for McClure's national promotion of Montessori. Anne George credited the great response to Tozier's articles as the catalyst that launched the Montessori movement in America.[43] Four months after Tozier's last article, *McClure Magazine* brought La Dottoressa's words directly to its readers. In *McClure's* May 1912 issue, Montessori's "Disciplining Children," heralded as her first article in an American magazine, was featured as her "latest word on education." The editors introduced Montessori's article as "a remarkable expression of the principles that govern the new system of teaching children developed by this great educational genius."[44]

Montessori's article began with the claim that her philosophy of discipline, based on liberty, produced better results, even in large classes of forty to fifty children, than found in ordinary schools. She described the Montessori school in Rome conducted by Anna Maccheroni, a directress she had trained: "There are forty little beings, from three to seven years old, each one content on his own work; one going through an exercise for the senses, one an arithmetical exercise; one is handling the letters, one is drawing, one is lacing together the pieces of cloth upon one of the little frames, one is dusting. Some are seated at a table, some on a rug on the floor. There are muffled sounds of objects lightly moved about, of children tiptoeing. Once in a while comes a sound of joy only partly expressed: 'Teacher! Teacher!' an eager call: 'Look! See what I have done.' But, as a rule, there is entire absorption in their work. The teacher moves about slowly and silently, goes to any child who calls her, supervising operations in such a way that any one who needs her finds her at his elbow, and whoever does not need her is not reminded of her existence. Sometimes hours go by without a word."[45]

Montessori elaborated on her system of classroom management. First, the usual exhortations, orders, commands, or reprimands by teachers in conventional classrooms had only short-term effects on children in that they were imposed from without. Second, teachers could not impose genuine discipline that came from the inner depths of the child's mind and spirit. Third, the child's work generates the first impulse of internal discipline. By connecting the impulse to work with instruction, Montessori stated that her method encouraged children to choose their work and the apparatus that exercised it independently, individually, and spontaneously. Thus, the sense of discipline came from an internal source within the child who then externalized it by staying with the task until it was done correctly and completely.[46] Montessori wrote, "To have learned something is, for the child, only a point of departure. When he has learned something, then he enjoys repeating the exercise, and he does repeat it a great number of times, with the most apparent satisfaction."[47] Children turned their self-discipline into a habitual moral response. In Montessori's words, "it is necessary not only to wish to obey, but also to know how to do it. . . . When the child completes coordinated actions directed toward a given end, when he achieves something he set out to do, when he repeats patiently his exercises, he is training his positive will power."[48]

In the early twentieth century, when the Montessori articles appeared in *McClure's Magazine,* American public schools, especially in urban areas, had been reorganized into graded schools, in which children of the same age were streamed into the same class. The graded school, heralded as an educational innovation, had replaced the one-room multiage school where instruction tended to be by individual recitations. Group learning, according to educational administrators, was more efficient and effective in that a group, using standardized textbooks, could be taught the same skill or subject at the same time.

Montessori emphasized that children in her schools became self-disciplined because they were self-motivated and free to do what interested them. In contrast, a major and ongoing problem for teachers in conventional schools, especially graded ones, was how to motivate and engage a group of students, each with their own interests and needs, in a simultaneous classroom activity. By individualizing learning, Montessori limited the group's educational role. Montessori directresses did not have to motivate an entire class of students. Montessori deliberately minimized "collective" or group lessons. An over reliance on group instruction forced the teacher to act as a drill sergeant who had to use commands to get the children to follow her orders as a unit.

Montessori, whose method originated in her work with the impoverished children in Rome's San Lorenzo district, gave special attention to developing manners and civility that were complementary to the life skills that gave children their independence. Under the subhead "Faultless Table Manners of the Children," she wrote: "Little four-year-old waiters take the knives and forks and spoons and distribute them to the different places; they carry trays that hold five water glasses; and finally, they go from table to table carrying big tureens full of hot soup. Not a mistake is made, not a glass is broken, not a drop of soup spilled."[49]

Montessori's example of children performing such life skills illustrated her principle that children have an unconscious desire for their own independence and self-development. Independence meant they could accomplish a task or surmount a challenge without the help, aid, or interference of an adult. Being able to perform the tasks and master the skills needed in everyday life were necessary steps in their own self-development. According to Montessori: the child "prefers the action of dressing himself to the state of being dressed, even finely dressed; he prefers the act of washing himself to the satisfaction of being clean;"[50]

Montessori then connected her method's sensory learning activities to the development of self-discipline. The aim of the sensory activities is "not that the child shall know colors, forms, and the different qualities of objects, but that he shall refine his senses in an exercise of attention, of comparison, of judgment." She continued, "The child who trains his various senses separately, by means of external stimuli, concentrates his attention and develops, piece by piece his mental faculties, just as with separately prepared movements he trains his muscular activities."[51]

Montessori's article in *McClure's Magazine* confirmed the famed educator's interest in a wider audience and her acceptance of McClure's efforts to bring her educational method to the American public.

Anne E. George's "The First Montessori School in America" was a companion piece to Montessori's article in *McClure's Magazine*. George had established her credentials as a Montessori educator in the United States with several important "firsts." She was the first American trained by Montessori as a directress and the first to establish a Montessori school in the United States. She had translated Montessori's book, *Il Metodo della Pedagogia Scientifica*, into its English version, *The Montessori Method*. She would be the directress at the Bells' Montessori school in Washington, DC, a member of the Montessori American Committee and director of work for the Montessori Educational Association. Accompanying Montessori and McClure on their tour in 1913, George would be at Montessori's side to translate her lectures into English.

Coming after Tozier's articles on the Montessori Method and Montessori's article on discipline, George's "The First Montessori School in America" had a strategically pivotal role in creating the Montessori movement in the United States.[52] So far *McClure's* readers had read about an Italian educator's method in schools in Rome. Even though Montessori was hyped as an "educational wonder-worker," could her revolutionary method work with American children? George, citing her experience with American children in Montessori schools, answered the question with a resounding yes. (George's training as a directress by Montessori is discussed in chapter 4, "Creating a Favorable Climate of Opinion for the Montessori Method in the United States.")

George, who Montessori had trained as a directress in 1910, established a Montessori school in 1911, enrolling twelve children in a school held in the home of Edward W. Harden in Tarrytown, New York.[53] The school attracted the attention and support of the banker Frank A. Vanderlip, a noted authority on international finance. Vanderlip, a trustee of the Carnegie Foundation for the Advancement of Teaching, was especially interested in the Montessori Method's potential for American education.

George's twelve-page article, with sixteen illustrations, highlighted her school at Tarrytown to demonstrate that Montessori's method was well suited to American children. George was guided by Montessori's philosophical assertion that children everywhere in the world are basically alike, regardless of race or ethnicity, in that they share the same universal human nature, internal spiritual impulses, and need for independence and self-development. George accepted Montessori's premise that, though children would bring cultural and language differences with them to school, the essential method could be used with all of them—poor or wealthy, Italian and American alike.

George anticipated concerns that the Montessori Method was better suited to economically disadvantaged children rather than to middle- and upper-class children. Indeed, the early Montessori schools in the United States, at Tarrytown and in Washington, DC, supported by wealthy parents, served children from economically affluent families. George wrote that Montessori's first Casa dei Bambini, in Rome's impoverished San Lorenzo slums, stood in sharp contrast to her American House of Children in a "beautiful house overlooking the Hudson. My children all came from cultured families, whose greatest ambition it was to give their children everything possible in the way of education and rational enjoyment. We recognized, however, that these external differences had no especial bearing upon the Montessori idea."[54] They were "only on the surface. The fundamental impulses and aspirations of childhood are the same in the San Lorenzo Quarter of Rome as on the Hudson." George assured her readers that the Montessori Method's genesis in a slum district in no way impaired its transference to children of all socioeconomic classes. George emphatically told *McClure's Magazine* middle-class readers that their children would benefit by being educated in a Montessori school.

George was insightful about her mentor, especially regarding the loyalty Montessori demanded of her directresses. Aware that Montessori did not want her method revised by others, George made it patently clear that she was implementing, not adapting, the method. She wrote, "I had observed Montessori work from day to day in Rome, and my only ambition was to do for American children precisely what she had done for Italians."[55] George's declaration that she was following the method as she had learned it was meant to reassure Montessori and enabled George to serve as a bridge between Americans, like McClure and the Bells, and Montessori herself.

There would be tension between Maria Montessori and Americans who felt that the method had to be adjusted for their children. These revisionists assumed that the method would also need to be modernized to meet changing times. Montessori strenuously opposed those she regarded as deviationists; indeed, they might be classified as heretics who had fallen away from the truth. Montessori feared that the more her method was changed, the less it would be her method. Her insistence that her method be applied as she had originally designed it would be a point of conflict between Montessori and American Montessorians in the 1910–1915 introduction and then again in the Montessori revival in the 1950s.

Believing she had addressed matters of ethnicity and economic class, George described her work with the "odd dozen" Tarrytown children. Her students, all under age five, were in school for the first time. As a Montessori-trained directress, she had arranged a structured environment and was guiding them, with the least possible direction, "through the development of the senses, into the knowledge and the use of their intellectual powers as well as to normal physical control."[56]

Despite her training, George confessed that the first two weeks of school were challenging. She and her assistant, Miss Meda Bagnell, had to struggle against what they had learned earlier as teachers in conventional schools.

At first, the children's "movements were entirely aimless." They stumbled against tables, overturned chairs, and grabbed several apparatus at a time. Then, a sudden change occurred. The children began to orient themselves to the Montessori prepared environment and discovered their genuine individualized interests. The change, quick and unexpected, occurs when a child discovers something that spontaneously arouses his interest. George told about a boy who showed little interest in anything. "Then, I casually showed him the red and blue spools and called his attention to the difference in color. He at once seized upon them with a kind of hunger. He learned five different colors in a single lesson; in the next few days he took up the articles he had previously scorned and mastered them all."[57] As other children discovered their interests, the disorder was replaced by children occupied, with serious concentration, in their own work.

Although she had earlier emphasized the Montessori Method's applicability to all children, George, acknowledging the impact of culture on education, contrasted the differences between Italian and American children in sensory learning. She wrote,

> The Italian children are more sensitive to form, and indeed to all sense impressions; they will recognize a circle, a square, an ellipse by the sense of touch more quickly than Americans. On the other hand, they do not have the ability to discriminate, to note differences and to make comparisons that American children have. This is only another way of saying, of course, that American children have more initiative, greater reasoning power, or, in other words, more originality. The . . . geometrical insets served as a useful test. There are wooden pieces of different shapes—circles, squares, and triangles— which . . . fit exactly in corresponding wooden frames. The game consists in taking up one of these insets by a small button, following its contour with the finger tips, and fitting it into its appropriate place. The Italian children learned to do this more quickly than the Americans; but having accomplished the task, they were content. My American pupils, however, made certain independent alterations. 'Look here!' one little boy cried, with all the excitement of discovery. 'I can fit this triangle in three different ways. The circle goes in any way you put it. The square goes in four ways. The el-

> lipse fits in two ways. But there is only one way you can put the oval in!' . . . I have never seen Italian children do anything like that. Simple as the operation seemed, it really indicated the budding of certain of the highest qualities of the human mind—inventiveness, originality, the logical faculty, the ability to deduce general conclusions from carefully observed facts.[58]

George had recognized the importance of cultural relativism in education. If American children learned some things differently from their Italian peers, did it not follow that certain aspects of the Montessori Method would need to be adjusted for the Americans? Would George become a revisionist?

George then turned to the "explosion into writing." She introduced the children in her Tarrytown school to Montessori's sandpaper letters. They learned to trace them with their index finger. In this way, they exercised and coordinated their small muscle movements and also learned to form the letters. George and her assistant would sound the letter out and the child would repeat it. George had to make a necessary adaptation to the English language, which unlike Italian, was unphonetic. In a very short time, her students had mastered the entire alphabet. Next, the children literally "burst" or "exploded" into writing words. Since they knew the words they were writing, they simultaneously exploded into reading

Again, George commented on a cultural difference. The Italian children, less familiar with writing, showed greater enthusiasm when they learned to write than the Americans who, accustomed to seeing their parents and siblings writing at home, were more matter-of-fact about their achievement.[59]

George, like Tozier, came to Montessori's defense on the imagination issue raised by kindergarten educators. When the Montessori Method was first introduced to the United States, some of its proponents saw it replacing the kindergarten and others saw it as reconstructing the kindergarten along Montessorian lines. For the orthodox kindergarten educators who followed Friedrich Froebel's Idealist philosophy, Montessori had seriously minimized the educational potency of the child's imagination.

George wrote, "I have been able . . . to dispose of this criticism which has been brought against the Montessori system. The Italian educator, it is said, makes the mistake of bringing the children too closely to the earth, as distinguished from other methods which encourage the imagination and deal in fairies and knights and imaginative games. Dr. Montessori makes the children see the world as it really is. To her a block is a block, not a castle; the hands and fingers are anatomical structures, not pigeons; the children learn real geometrical forms by their right names—triangles, squares, circles, ovals—and not as symbolic abstractions. Does this not destroy the imaginative instinct, it is asked and destroy one of the qualities most essential to moral and intellectual growth?"[60]

Answering her own question, George stated, "My Montessori children still have their imaginative faculties unimpaired. They are just as much interested in birds, trees, flowers, snow, and in people as the children of the kindergarten."[61]

George concluded with an unusual comparison of the imaginations of Americans and Italians: "The imagination plays little part in the Montessori schools in Italy, simply because imagination is not the predominant quality of the Italian mind and never has been. The basic purpose of the Montessori Method is to bring out whatever is in the child, and, since the Italian child is not naturally imaginative, that quality does not appear. On the other hand, the American child is highly imaginative, and according to its very genius, the Montessori system does not destroy this quality, but causes it to flower."[62]

George's claims on the superior imaginative powers of American over Italian children lapsed into national and ethnic stereotyping. She had slighted the imaginative powers of the poetry of Dante and Boccacio, the artistry of Micheangelo and Bernini, and music of Puccini and Verdi. Her claims about the power of the American imagination may have been reassuring to some readers but hardly a serious contribution to educational thought.

George's article resonated well with the general readership of *McClure's Magazine*. She had demonstrated that American children, like Italian children, "burst" or "exploded" into writing, reading, and arithmetic. Despite her claims of purity in transplanting the Montessori Method to Tarrytown, George was slipping unintentionally into adapting the method to meet the cultural differences between American and Italian children.

Thus far, the articles had been highly favorable pieces, extolling Montessori and her method. Although occasionally venturing into educational theory, they concentrated primarily on describing the method, especially its sensory features and didactic apparatus. McClure had learned that educators identified with the kindergarten would raise objections to the Montessori Method. Strategically, the policy questions for the editor of *McClure's Magazine* were either to: (1) avoid dealing with theoretical issues in early childhood education that were likely to bore readers; or (2) examine the issue since readers were generally familiar with kindergarten, which had become part of the American school system. Deciding that the issue could not be avoided, the editors decided to examine the comparative benefits of the Montessori Method and the kindergarten, both early childhood educational methods intended for essentially the same age group.

By the time of McClure's promotion of Montessori education, the kindergarten, a nineteenth-century import from Germany, was well established in many American public-school systems. The roots of the kindergarten-Montessori issue can be traced to their founders' philosophical perspectives. Froebel and Montessori shared similar beliefs that children possess an interior spiritual force that stimulates their self-activity to explore and learn from their environment. Both educators believed children learned most effectively in a prepared or structured classroom environment. For Froebel, this prepared environment was the kindergarten, the child's garden; for Montessori, it was the Casa dei Bambini.

Montessori, more of a realist philosophically and trained as a physician in the empirical sciences, easily rejected Froebel's mystical symbolism. She asserted that her self-correcting didactic apparatus, unlike Froebel's gifts, were empirically calibrated to the children's mastery of sensory and life tasks. There was no empirical test to verify Froebel's claims that the gifts, such as the ball or the block stimulated children to recall concepts such as the sphere or the cube that were already in their minds.[63]

Further, the Froebelian method did not lead to the child's independence since the kindergarten teacher had to intervene to reach the desired end. Montessori materials, the apparatus, itself, corrected the child who would repeat the task until it was mastered.[64]

McClure commissioned Ellen Yates Stevens, an educational expert on both the kindergarten and the Montessori Method, to write an article comparing the two educational methods. Her article, "The Montessori Method and the American Kindergarten," appeared in the magazine's November 1912 issue. An editorial introduction cited Stevens's educational credentials and stressed her subject's importance.[65]

> Miss Ellen Yale Steven, principal of the Brooklyn Heights Seminary, is known to thousands of educators in this country as one of the most thoughtful, clear-sighted and experienced American educators. Anything that she may say on the subject of primary education commands immediate attention from the members of her profession, for it bears the stamp of a wise and forceful personality and deep experience." Miss Stevens has for years stood at the head of a great school which embraces the kindergarten as a regular feature of its curriculum. Within the last eighteen months, since the beginning of the Montessori movement in this country, the kindergarten method and the Montessori Method have been issues in a great controversy which has stirred the whole educational world. The two methods have been constantly compared and contrasted, and each one has been criticized from the point of the other. The following article, coming from an educator who has for years studied and observed the kindergarten method in her own school, and who has also made a personal investigation of the Montessori schools in Rome, is one of the most interesting criticisms of the two systems that have been made.[66]

Stevens went to Rome in the fall of 1911 to make a direct field-based comparative study of Montessori schools and kindergartens in the Italian municipal school systems. Her research method combined aspects of the investigative reporting that *McClure's* readers were so familiar with and an ethnographic study of actual classrooms. Stevens used the following focusing questions to guide her research: "Is Montessori a genius? Is her book a real contribution to educational thought? Has her method something in it vital and universal? Has she broken down the wall between the kindergarten and primary classes? Is her material better than that of Froebel, and if so why? Are the children trained by it in useful physical and intellectual habits?"[67]

Stevens's seven-week investigation began with a meeting with Maria Montessori whom she described as "a woman of about forty, fine-looking, with great charm of manner, and remarkable eyes that reveal the student and psychologist." Stevens was also favorably impressed by Montessori's *Scientific Pedagogy*, which was "one of the most impressive and illuminating books I have ever read." The book, she wrote, "is a wonderful revelation of the simple, devoted, single-hearted consecration to a great cause.... Combining... scientific theory and... personal experience with original didactic material, it is unique." After reading the book and meeting with Montessori, Stevens said, "I believe fully in her genius."[68] She extolled Montessori, saying, "Where in the world can you find such a combination of genius with inheritance, training, and experience? We women should be proud that one of our sex, always considered the teaching sex, has the creative ability and scientific training which enable her to take her place as a real contributor to educational progress."[69]

Stevens next compared children in Montessori schools with those attending kindergartens and primary classes in Italian municipal schools. She observed classes in twelve schools, eight of which used all or part of the Montessori Method and four that did not use it at all. She visited the schools from one to six times, observing more than two hundred and fifty Montessori children and an estimated "two or three times that number in the ordinary primary and kindergarten classes," most of which were of the "strictly Froebelian type."[70] Stevens found the Montessori Method "more direct" and the Montessori material "more practical" than the Froebelian materials. Most importantly, Stevens found that Montessori's individualized exercises had solved the problem of matching children's readiness with appropriate learning materials. As a result of Montessori's highly significant innovation, Stevens noted that the Montessori Method had facilitated children's individual development to a much greater degree than the Froebelian system and that her method provided for "the varying rates of progress always found among children of the same age."[71]

Stevens found children in the Montessori schools "were far beyond those of their own age in the other schools in self-confidence, power of attention, interest in the work, self-control, coordination, and the ability to write, read, and work in numbers."[72]

Despite cultural differences between American and Italian children, Stevens, like George, concluded that the Montessori Method could and should be applied in the United States. But again, as with George, Stevens fell into ethnic stereotyping, writing that American children, though "less responsive to sense impressions," had more "nervous energy . . . more imagination . . . less docility . . . more initiative," and "more power of invention" than Italian children. While Italians are homogenous, in Americans are found strains of the Norse and the Celt, those northern races with their rich imagination and intuitions. Our children love the mysterious, the unreal, the myth, the fairy story; and this need should be provided for by the story, the song, and the game. I expect our children to be freer with the material—to take some of the steps more quickly and omit others altogether."[73]

Despite her laudatory praise for the Montessori Method, Stevens was not ready to abandon Froebel completely. Similar to Professor Holmes in his preface to *The Montessori Method*, Stevens proposed integrating selected elements of the Froebelian kindergarten with the Montessori Method.[74] She recommended that the American kindergarten and primary grades be reconstructed according to Montessori's philosophy and method, "using her materials, but keeping the morning circle and the story, many of the songs and games, and some of the occupations, especially the clay."[75]

The articles by Tozier, George, Montessori, and Stevens provided *McClure's* readers with the equivalent of a course on Montessori education. Tozier had introduced Montessori and the Montessori Method, emphasizing the didactic apparatus; describing the application of the Montessori Method in her school at Tarrytown, George assured them that it was well suited to American children; Montessori, writing for an American audience, explained how her philosophy of auto-education, through individualized work, led to self-discipline; and Stevens had made the case that the Montessori Method could be combined with the kindergarten.

The Montessori educational series in *McClure's* captured a wide readership who gave it a phenomenal response. Written for a popular, not an academic, readership, the Montessori articles used investigative on-site reporting by observers such as Tozier and Stevens who had visited Montessori schools. Not merely reports of an interesting educational experiment in Europe, the articles became promotional pieces telling readers of an extraordinary educational discovery that was attainable for their children.

Another reason *McClure's* readers were so attracted to Montessori education is that they were ready to accept scientific ideas from a medical doctor turned educator. In the early twentieth century, public high schools were operating throughout the country and middle-class American parents had a secondary education. These parents, many of whom read magazines like *McClure's*, were involved in their children's education. They served on school boards and were members of parent-teachers associations.

Due to the favorable response to the Montessori articles, in February 1913, *McClure's* announced a new feature section in the magazine, "The Montessori Movement in America." This "department" of the magazine would "serve as a central bureau of information regarding the progress of the movement in this country and Europe." With Stevens as its editor, a series of articles about Montessori education at home and abroad would be published regularly in the magazine.[76] Stevens said *McClure's* had "but one purpose" in giving wide publicity to the Montessori Method: "the desire to satisfy the interest of the public in the great movements and problems of the modern world."[77]

The new department provided information on the latest happenings in Montessori education. Stevens reported that Anne E. George had established a new school on the estate of Alexander Graham Bell. Enrolling nearly twenty-five children between the ages of two and a half and five, the school reproduced the environment at Montessori's schools in Rome as "perfectly as possible."

Stevens reported that thirty-nine Americans had enrolled in Montessori's month-long training course in Rome scheduled to begin January 15, 1913. The course, carefully planned by Dr. Montessori, would include "thirty lectures, thirty hours of practice work, and fifty observation lessons in the Case dei Bambini and twenty municipal schools."[78]

In *McClure's* March 1913 issue, Stevens announced Maria Montessori's plan to establish an international educational institute in Rome. The Italian educator believed that the time had come to train teachers who would disseminate her method in schools around the world. She stated that "the only way worthy to respond to the demand for the widespread diffusion of my method would be to found an institute where the method can unfold itself, be demonstrated to teachers, and to all those who desire to learn something of it first hand."[79] The new teacher, Montessori wrote, needed "to acquire a scientific method" and the new schools needed to be "laboratories for experimentation."[80] Her proposed institute would be the center of the educational revolution.

Montessori's call for an international institute caught the attention of S. S. McClure. Always alert to great new ideas, McClure saw the United States as the ideal location for Montessori's center. He especially believed that an educational institute to train Montessori teachers for American schools was an imperative need that could be fulfilled with considerable profit.

In the April 1913 issue of *McClure's* "The Montessori Movement" department featured an article, "A Mother's Experiment," about Carlos, a six-year-old boy, who was using the Montessori didactic apparatus at home, not at a Montessori school with a trained directress. Stevens said many of the letters she received as editor were from mothers who were using the Montessori apparatus and materials with their children at home. The account was apparently written by a Miss Glidden, an instructor at the Pratt Institute Kindergarten Training School, who had observed Montessori schools in Rome in the spring 1912.[81]

Carlos, the boy featured in the article, was described as "bright, active, interested in everything." His mother, who had visited Montessori's schools in Rome, purchased a complete set of the Montessori apparatus. Carlos worked with the Montessori cylinders and then the lacing, tying, and fastening frames. Next came the Montessori "Tower," which he mastered in one trial. But when he decided to make a train of the tower, his mother did not intervene. Making a train was not an approved Montessori use of the tower. His mother, later suspecting "the error of her ways . . . came to believe that Dr. Montessori had good and sufficient reasons for not wishing the didactic material to be used in this way."

After Carlos told his mother that he loved the Montessori material, she asked, "Why do you love it, Carlos?" He told her, "Because it is easy and because it is hard." His mother thought, "Why that is really just it. . . . It is easy enough to lure him on and it is hard enough to hold his interest."[82] The article ended with a strong endorsement of the Montessori Method: "The boy is not a Montessori child; his mother wishes he were. He has simply played with the material a number of times. There has been no one trained in Montessori methods to give it to him, and his mother firmly believes in training. She thinks that teaching correctly, according to Montessori methods, is a fine art, and rejoices to know that in another year the skilled American teachers who are now in Rome, studying the method, will be in this country, and will be able to give to mothers and other guardians the practical results of their study."[83]

The contradiction arises again in the "Mother's Experiment" as to the availability of purchasing Montessori's didactic apparatus to be used at home without the supervision of a Montessori directress and Montessori's injunction that only teachers trained by her in the use of the apparatus could correctly use the method. Montessori materials and didactic apparatus were being manufactured and sold in the United States, as they were in other countries, on a for-profit basis. Included in their purchase was a handbook on how to use the materials. In addition to this pedagogical dichotomy, there was an entrepreneurial commercial issue, which would eventually lead to troubled relationships between Montessori and American business people.

In "The Montessori Movement" of May 1913, Anne E. George, who had written earlier about Tarrytown as "The First Montessori School in America," returned to *McClure's* with "Rhythm Work in the Children's House at Washington." Stevens introduced the new article, stating that George's earlier article had attracted so much attention that the magazine had been deluged with orders for that issue.[84] George's topic, most likely written to appeal to kindergarten educators, was useful in stimulating children's aesthetic sensitivity as well as their sensory skills.

George, in her second year of bringing the Montessori Method to American children, had decided to incorporate music in the Bells' school in Washington. Unlike the conventional school's rigid scheduling of music to a particular time, children in the individualized Montessori class could spontaneously break into song. She told how a girl "carrying a pitcher of milk across the room, in her effort for poise, fell instinctively into the rhythmic pace" singing as she stepped, "Slowly, slowly, slowly, slow" as she completed her task without spilling the milk.

George also reported that she introduced working with clay, a favorite kindergarten activity, into her Montessori school. The children easily learned how to roll the clay and shape it into coils, and to build it into bowls, cups, and vases. George concluded "the 'imagination' is in no way hampered or coerced in the peaceful and orderly life" in a Montessori school.[85]

The June 1913 issue *McClure's* included an article within the Montessori Movement department titled "A Letter from Rome," from Janet S. Townsend, a student in Montessori's training course that had begun in January.[86] Townsend described the first meeting of the class of over eighty students—from "America, England, Canada, Germany, Australia, New Zealand, Spain, Italy, and Panama"—at the villa of the Marchess di Vitti di Marco on the Via Adda. We realized that our being there "was a great event in the history of education, as well as an epoch of note in the lives of each of us as individuals."[87] When La Dottoressa Montessori appeared, everyone "rose to their feet with one accord; . . . There was a moment of silence as she walked to her place on the platform, which was perhaps, as impressive as the applause and the cheers that presently broke forth." Townsend, in awe of the great educator, wrote: "Many of us who looked upon her for the first time felt at once the magnetism of her personality. . . . She is . . . a beautiful woman, not only in the expression of her face and the fascination of her smile, but in the delicacy of her features and the wonderful spirituality expressed in her beautiful dark eyes. . . . One recognizes at once that she is a person of distinction, and yet her manner is exquisitely simple and she has none of the unapproachableness which we so often find in so-called 'great' personalities. She is truly great, and, therefore, simple and sympathetic."[88]

Townsend told of the trainees' visit to the convent school on the Via Giusti. Observing children seated at small tables, intent and focused on their work, Townsend was fascinated by "the deftness and directness, as well as the earnestness with which the children worked . . . using their fingers with precision and deftness in tracing the outlines of various wooden insets and putting them into their frames, or in sorting into pairs the various textiles, or testing the accuracy of their sense of hearing with the sound-boxes."[89]

A high point in the course came when Montessori, herself, presented a series of practical lessons directly to the children. Completely charmed by what she saw, Townsend found Montessori's interaction with the children to be "simple and direct, absolutely free from anything approaching sentimentality, yet playful and winning."

Joining in the earlier praise by Tozier, George, and Stevens, Townsend, concluding her letter, wrote, "No one who has listened to Dr. Montessori's lectures, or who has seen her work with the children and the results obtained by her method, can fail to recognize her genius and the wonderful contribution she has made to modern education."[90]

In the August 1913 issue of *McClure's*, Stevens announced that the Montessori Department had achieved its purpose in acting as a clearing house and providing information about the Montessori Method throughout the country. The newly established Montessori Educational Association would assume the department's function in its national mission "to promote and develop in America the educational movement based on the principles and theories of Dr. Montessori."[91]

Acclaiming the Montessori Method as a revolutionary innovation in education, the articles in *McClure's Magazine* had painted a journalist's portrait of Montessori as a scientist, a woman of genius, and an "educational wonder-worker." Resonating well with their readers, they had generated a popular response. McClure, the publicist-publisher, was now ready to move to the next phase in his strategy: launching the Montessori movement in the United States that he would lead.

6

McClure and the Montessori Educational Association

The introduction and promotion of Montessori education in the United States, from 1910 through 1915 was first done by individuals such as S. S. McClure, Anne George, Dorothy Canfield Fisher, and Alexander Graham and, his wife, Mabel (Hubbard) Bell, and then by committees and organizations. The well-connected McClure, aware of the power of networking, played an important role in bringing these individuals together in the Montessori American Committee in 1912 to advance what then appeared to be a shared common cause. As the momentum for Montessori education accelerated, the larger national Montessori Educational Association, led by the Bells, growing from the nucleus of the smaller committee, was officially organized in 1913. The roles of the committee and the association can be best understood in how their members interacted with each other, how they advanced Montessori education, and how Maria Montessori reacted to them.

From the time of the Committees of Correspondence during the American Revolution onward, Americans have believed in the power of committees, associations, and organizations to set agendas, diffuse information, and accomplish goals. Alexis de Tocqueville, in his keen observations of American life, commented on the American propensity to organize and join associations. When McClure, George, and the Bells organized the Montessori Educational Association, they were following a long-lived American tradition. Because of her suspicions about what she could not control, it is doubtful if Montessori understood or even appreciated the groups that organized to promote her work. She did not like the idea of shared decision-making that diffused her control. Montessori, who consistently determined that she alone would control her method, was ill-disposed to permit others to make, or even share, in decisions about its implementation.

McClure knew the value of naming prominent, nationally recognized persons as members of organizations. They lent an association creditability, a respectful notoriety, and served to recruit others to its cause. Listing prominent persons such as Alexander Graham Bell, the noted inventor of the telephone, and Margaret Wilson, the daughter of the president of the United States, on the association's letterhead showed that important people belonged to it and drew others into the fold. Montessori accepted and appreciated the support that prominent and wealthy people, such as Queen Margherita and Baron Leopold Franchetti, had given to her in Italy. These individuals were patrons who gave her the support needed to accomplish her mission. When she first met McClure, not aware of his dire economic situation, she saw him as an American patron. She, at first, saw the association as a vehicle to attract philanthropic patrons to fund her proposed international educational center in Rome.

After running its popular series on Montessori in 1911–1912, the New York office of *McClure's Magazine* was deluged with letters from readers who wanted to know more about Montessori, how to attend her training classes, where to purchase the didactic apparatus, and the location of schools where their children would receive a Montessori education. Dorothy Canfield Fisher wrote that she, too, had received a similar overwhelming response when her book, *A Montessori Mother*, had been published. Anne George wrote that the public response to the articles in *McClure's Magazine* was so great that it overwhelmed Montessori's capacity to reply to inquiries. To assist Montessori in responding to the great interest in her method in the United States, a group of her proponents organized the Montessori American Committee in the spring of 1912.[1]

In its June 1912 issue, *McClure's Magazine* officially announced that the Montessori American Committee had been organized in response to a request from Montessori herself. It was "to direct the progress in America of Dr. Montessori's educational theories." In addition to McClure, it included such prominent individuals as Alexander Graham Bell; Byron Satterlee Hurlbut, dean of Harvard University; William H. Maxwell, superintendent of New York City schools; Robert Walker, director of the Rock Island Railway Company; Dr. A. Duncan Yocum, chair of the University of Pennsylvania's Pedagogical Department; Henry W. Holmes and Arthur O. Norton, members of Harvard University's Department of Education; Ellen Yale Stevens, principal of the Brooklyn Heights Seminary; Anne E. George, translator of *The Montessori Method*; Howard C. Warren, of Princeton University; John F. Reigart, principal of School No. 166, New York City; Edith Sharon, principal of St. Michael's School, New York City; William Morrow, secretary of the Frederick A. Stokes Company; Mrs. William Pierson (Juliet Morgan) Hamilton, the daughter of J. P. Morgan; Edward H. Bouton, of the Sage Foundation Homes Company; Mrs. Henry Copley (Rosalind Huidekoper) Green; and Mrs. Richard Cabot.

Among its first actions, the committee recommended Edith Sharon to Montessori as director of the country's first Montessori training school to be located in New York. The committee had much to learn about how Montessori worked with others, including those who sought to promote her educational method. The temperamental Italian educator was very angry when *McClure's Magazine*, without her express approval, had announced the formation of the Montessori American Committee. She believed that McClure had violated his agreement with her that there be no public announcement of the committee until she had approved of its mission and constitution.[2] On June 5, the irate Montessori dispatched a telegram to McClure clearly showing her displeasure: "INDIGNANT / ANNOUNCEMENT / CONTRARY CABLED ORDERS AND WHAT AGREED PERSONALLY MCCLURE / ANNOUNCE JULY NUMBER COMMITTEE ANNOUNCEMENT PREMATURE / THAT SEPTEMBER ARTICLE WILL GIVE MY IDEAS FULLY."[3]

The incident surrounding the announcement of the Montessori American Committee was prophetic of future tensions and disagreements between the publisher and the pedagogue. The conflicts stemmed from the sharp differences in their personalities. The announcement about the committee clearly reflected McClure's style of behavior—of acting immediately on an idea while there was enthusiasm and support for it. Montessori, however, thought and behaved very differently; she was slowly deliberate in her actions and extremely possessive of her educational method. It was her creation and belonged to her alone, not to others. McClure and the members of the committee erroneously believed that Montessori would welcome their endeavors to promote her method. Though Montessori wanted her method disseminated and implemented in the United States, she intended to be in total control of the process. What would become a point of sharp disagreement was the plan to establish a Montessori training center. If such a center was to be established, Montessori would be exclusively in charge of it—the training of directresses could not be delegated to others. The committee's recommendation of Edith Sharon as director of a Montessori training institute must have been especially vexing for Dr. Montessori.

In what would become the first of many efforts to appease Montessori, McClure was able to assure her that he was acting in good faith. In July, Montessori, too, reasserted her confidence in McClure, saying, "It will be a short time until the Institute will come into being." McClure and Montessori, in their preliminary meetings, had discussed the establishment of an educational institute for research on her method and for the training of teachers. While McClure anticipated that his promotion of Montessori education would restore his sagging finances, Montessori saw him as a famous publisher, a patron who would attract funds for her research. Looking forward to financial support from the Montessori American Committee, Montessori pointedly advised McClure that the Montessori society in England had ensured her of a "pecuniary guarantee for three years."[4]

The announcement of the committee's mission was most unusual in that such statements invariably say what a committee will do; however, this one meticulously specified what it would not do. Appeasing Montessori's uneasiness that others might try to act in her name and bowing to her insistence on controlling anything related to her method, the committee specified that it would deal "under Madame Montessori's directions with all matters relating to the educational side of the movement, such as discouraging the premature opening of schools by teachers insufficiently trained, seeing that only serious propaganda work is carried on and that only well substantiated statements about the movement are sent forth, and helping in the organization of the courses for teachers which Montessori herself will undertake."[5]

Since Montessori had not approved of a Montessori training institute in the United States, the committee decided to use *McClure's Magazine* to recruit American students for her training course in Rome. The announcement stated that "Madame Montessori intends to start, this fall, a special course for fitting teachers who wish to open training schools for teaching the Montessori method. The course is to be given by Madame Montessori personally in Rome. No training school approved by Madame Montessori will be opened in the United States this year." George, an eager recruiter for Montessori, reported that over one hundred students had enrolled in this international course, seventy of them Americans.[6]

The committee used *McClure's Magazine* as its means to communicate with the public. Until a national headquarters was established, inquiries were to be addressed to the Montessori American Committee in care of *McClure's Magazine*. Readers were advised that more information about the Montessori movement would appear in the magazine's future issues.

The committee made a special effort to note that it would not be involved in manufacturing, distributing, and selling the Montessori didactic apparatus and materials. "The apparatus is available from the House of Childhood, Inc., of which Carl A. Byoir, is president. The Committee has no financial connection with the firm which is to manufacture and sell the Montessori materials." The distribution and sale of the Montessori didactic apparatus was often controversial during the introduction of Montessori education in the United States, especially when critics decried its commercialism.

Seeking to disengage from its earlier recommendation of Edith Sharon as head of the projected Montessori training institute in New York City, the committee stated that Montessori had not authorized such a school. On April 23, 1912, Anne George, S. S. McClure, Edith Lewis, Edith Sharon, and William Morrow convened as a subcommittee at a special meeting at the request of McClure. The subcommittee reconsidered the action taken by the general committee on April 20 regarding "the advisability of retaining as members of the committee persons who have direct interest with the establishment of training schools." After

McClure expressed his opinion to the subcommittee, it approved the following recommendations to be presented to the larger, general committee:

1. That Mrs. Sharon could, for the present remain as a member of the large general committee, but that, in completing plans for regular organization, the subcommittee appointed for the purpose should not include Mrs. Sharon in the executive committee.
2. That it is advisable for the committee to avail itself of the opportunity afforded by Mrs. Sharon of having her secretary, Miss Mulheron, take care of the general correspondence for which form letters can be used; All form letters to be approved by the sub-committee working on organization, and that the answers sent by Miss Mulheron should be signed "Montessori American Committee."
3. That a brief announcement of the formation of the committee with statement of its functions, reference to the proposed establishment of training schools in Rome.[7]

Anne George, who had grown steadily uneasy about the conflict with Mrs. Sharon, wrote to McClure on May 4, 1912:

> I have just written a letter to Mrs. Sharon explaining to her that we didn't any of us understand the meeting . . . as she evidently did from the minutes. . . . These minutes . . . seem to me to bring out with startling clearness all of the dangers that I so bunglingly tried to put before you. . . . I love Mrs. Sharon dearly, and I believe that she is going to be a splendid head of the training school, but I know that she must be curbed and held in check or she will allow . . . her executive frenzy and her personal ambition to carry the method into a tangle of undesirable complications.
>
> The effect of these minutes on Mr. Morrow and Miss Lewis were so great that . . . we all agreed that it would be far from wise, in the light of Mrs. Sharon's interpretation, to make use of her secretary and of her school. We . . . have taken the attitude that since Madam Montessori has definitely cabled to us to withhold publication until the arrival of her constitution, we are hardly warranted in making our June announcement so definite as to determine the headquarters of the American committee, so are having all communication to the committee sent in care of the magazine to be forwarded, and will decide upon our permanent headquarters in time for the July announcement. . . . Please don't scold me for having taken the responsibility in the matter of not using Mrs. Sharon's address and secretary. . . . It was so evident that she never could be made to disassociate the activi-

ties connected with her training school from the more general ones of the committee.

In a postscript, George added, "I have had several long talks with Mrs. Hamilton who agrees with me entirely about Mrs. Sharon's value as the head of a training school and *just* as strongly as to the need of curbing her activities where *other* schools and other interests enter. All this confidential. Might tell Montessori of support Mrs. H. will give N.Y. training school."[8] Juliet Hamilton, the daughter of J. P. Morgan, might be, in George's opinion, a source of future funding for Montessori education in the United States.

While the committee was trying to placate Montessori by distancing themselves from Edith Sharon and her plan to establish a school in New York to train Montessori teachers, Sharon had arrived in Rome. There she met with Montessori who was very clear about her attitude regarding the teacher-training school in New York. In a letter to S. S. McClure, Sharon wrote: "We shall have to renounce our intention of a school in N.Y.—this year. . . . The Dottoressa wants money for her own school—but does not mean to pursue a center either in England or America to deflect from Rome students."

Sharon, understandably disconcerted that her position on the committee and as the once-recommended head of the Montessori training school had suddenly diminished, realizedthat her position on the committee had become untenable. She wrote to McClure from Rome: "I find Montessori very much displeased, with the committee, with Miss George & us all. . . . It's all quite impossible . . . and I am withdrawing from the whole movement. I shall decline to accept a position on the executive of any committee. I feel unable to work any longer for . . . this wonderful thing, with any dignity, or honor, or success."[9]

After calming Montessori's anger by retracting its earlier action to establish a Montessori training school in the United States, the committee, supported by *McClure's Magazine*, continued its efforts to promote Montessori education in the United States in 1912–1913. Ellen Yale Stevens, in charge of the Montessori Movement series in *McClure's*, acted as the voice of the committee. Responding to queries about the availability of Montessori directresses, Stevens answered, "The Montessori American Committee is willing to assist any who desire teachers for Montessori classes or any teachers who desire positions. Address the Committee at 443 Fourth Avenue, New York."[10]

The Montessori American Committee was also successful in recruiting seventy American women for Montessori's first international training course in Rome in 1913. Especially significant in the growing Montessori movement were the friends and associates of Alexander Graham Bell.

McClure, a friend of the Bells, often attended Alexander Graham Bell's "Wednesday Evenings," gatherings of intellectuals, scientists, and other notables at the Bell home. McClure discussed his recent enthusiasm, Montessori education, at these meetings. Bell, originally a teacher of the deaf, and his wife, Mabel, who was profoundly deaf, were intrigued with McClure's account of how Montessori had developed her method from her initial efforts in educating children with disabilities. Mrs. Bell, who had used her senses of sight and touch to overcome her auditory handicap, wanted to learn more about Montessori's emphasis on sensory training by using specially designed didactic apparatus.[11]

Prodded by the interest of their daughter, Marian (Bell) Fairchild, the Bells established a small Montessori school for their grandchildren in their home in Washington, DC. Marian and David Fairchild had two children, Barbara and Graham. The Bells' two Fairchild grandchildren were joined by the five children of their daughter, Elsie (wife of Gilbert Grosvenor): Melville, Gertrude, Lillian, Mabel, and Carol. The Bells employed Roberta Fletcher as the directress in charge of their school for their seven grandchildren, all between the ages of two and six.[12]

When the Bells went to their summer home, Beinn Bhreagh, in Canada, Miss Fletcher accompanied them. At their request, she set up a small Montessori school, which the Bells called the "Children's Laboratory," on the upper floor of the estate's warehouse. This little school was attended by the Bells' seven grandchildren and five children of friends in the area. The Bells, highly impressed with the results Miss Fletcher achieved with the Montessori Method, became dedicated converts to Montessori education.[13] The Bells' approach to Montessori education differed from McClure's. The Bells came to it through their personal reflections on the uniqueness of their own educations and from the direct instruction of their grandchildren. Because of this, they directed their efforts at establishing Montessori schools with trained directresses. McClure, who was interested in contemporary movements in science and technology, saw Montessori education as an educational innovation that would bring about social change and improvement. While these approaches were different, the Bells and McClure shared the goal of training Montessori teachers.

Their deepening interest in Montessori education led Mabel Bell and her daughter, Marian Fairchild, to seek out Anne George, the country's foremost Montessori directress, at her school on the Vanderlip estate in Tarrytown, New York, in February 1911. George recounted how the Bells put the Montessori Method into practice: "In October, 1912, at the request of Mr. and Mrs. Alexander Graham Bell, I took charge of a class of 20 children in their home in Washington. The parents of the children enrolled in this school became convinced of the value of the method for educational purposes, and determined to put forth every effort to extend the same benefit to other children."[14]

The parents of the children attending the school, like the Bells, became enthusiastic supporters of the Montessori Method. In May of 1913, they organized the Montessori Educational Association as a national organization with headquarters in the US capital and unanimously elected Mabel Bell as its president.

The association planned to publish a bulletin to disseminate information about the Montessori Method throughout the country. It would aid in establishing Montessori schools in settlement houses. Anne George was named as the association's director of Montessori work. Alexander Graham Bell believed "an educational movement of great magnitude and import has been started by Mrs. Bell."[15]

The Bells purchased a building at 1850 Kalorama Road, Washington, DC, and rented it to the association for a larger school, the Montessori Children's House, which opened on October 15, 1913, with sixty students.[16] In November, a Montessori school was established in Friendship House, a Washington social settlement. A branch of the association was also established in New England.

Sharing the same purpose, "to promote and develop in America the educational movement based on the principles and theories of Dr. Montessori," the original Montessori American Committee, largely established by McClure, was enveloped into the Bells' larger association, in which McClure was a vice president. Changes in the composition of the committee and the officers of the new association reflected its Washington location and the influence of the Bells. Of the eighteen committee members, only four held offices in the new association: McClure as second vice president; George as director of Montessori work; Morrow on the executive committee, and Alexander Graham Bell as a trustee. While the committee had five members from institutions of higher education, the association had none listed as an officer. The school administrators on the committee from New York—Superintendent William H. Maxwell and the three principals—Ellen Yale Stevens, John F. Reigart, and Edith Sharon—were not carried over as officers in the association. The school administrators holding offices in the association were all from the District of Columbia system—William M. Davidson, superintendent; Alys E. Bentley, director of music; and Edith C. Wescott, principal, Western High School. Demonstrating that the association was truly national in scope, the US Commissioner of education, Philander P. Claxton, was its first vice president, and Margaret Wilson, President Woodrow Wilson's daughter, a member of its board of trustees and executive committee.

The Bell family was well represented. Alexander Graham Bell served on the Board of trustees and his wife, Mabel, was the president. The Bells' son-in-law, Gilbert H. Grosvenor, editor of the *National Geographic Magazine*, was treasurer. The Bells' daughter, Marian Bell Fairchild, served on the executive committee. In addition to Fairchild and Grosvenor who had children enrolled in the Bells' school, three other parents were officers: Mabel B. Brooks, Mrs. Gervin Peters, and Mrs. Bailey Willis.

The association, reflecting the Bells' and the parents' interest in their Montessori school, gave paramount attention "to assist in the establishment and maintenance of schools for children and schools of observation and practice conducted according" to Montessori's principles.[17] The association's commitment to promote Montessori schools fitted nicely with the more general objective, inherited from the original committee, to promote the Montessori Method. The establishment of more Montessori schools meant that there would be a demand for more trained Montessori directresses. Montessori, McClure, the Bells, and the association all agreed with the goal of recruiting more American students for Montessori's training courses in Rome. The goal, however, carried with it some internal issues. Montessori insisted that only she could train an authentic directress. Could others, especially those trained by Montessori, train other aspirants? McClure, who believed that a training program in the United States would be a source of financial profit, wanted to share in the control of the Montessori training program.

In addition to the Bells' school on Kalorama Road, the association supported a demonstration school in the Friendship House settlement in Washington, DC. Its directress was Elizabeth Fraser whom Montessori had trained in her international course in Rome in 1913. A second demonstration school was opened in September 1914 in the Open Stair Tenement in New York. Miss Frazer, who had been directress in the school in Washington, DC, was in charge of the school in New York. Jane Kenney, who had been trained by Montessori, became directress of the school in Washington, DC. George commented on how these two demonstration schools, both located in urban settlement houses, served poor children much like those Montessori herself had taught in the first Casa dei Bambini in Rome.[18]

In April 1913, Mrs. Bell wrote to Montessori, informing her of the establishment of the Montessori Educational Association and its plans to promote her method in the United States.[19] She encountered that same anger that Montessori had shown to the earlier committee. The forming of the association violated Montessori's protocol that she had to give prior approval for such an organization. Mrs. Bell had also mentioned the association's plan to establish a Montessori training school. Montessori was adamant that only she could train directresses and that there must be no adaptations or alterations with her method. Mrs. Bell was disappointed, indeed perplexed, by Montessori's angry reaction. She decided to wait, hoping that Montessori might, with time, become more open to the association. As she waited, McClure informed Mrs. Bell that he had successfully persuaded Montessori to come to the United States to lecture in December, and the association would be listed as the official sponsor. Mrs. Bell would meet with Montessori when she spoke in Washington, DC.

The Bells and the Montessori Educational Association played a significant but an often unclear role in the introduction of the Montessori Method in the United

States. The centerpiece of the introduction of Montessori education was Maria Montessori's lecture tour in 1913, which was officially sponsored by the association. In reality, however, McClure, who held the position of second vice president in the association, negotiated the terms of the agreement and the itinerary for the tour with Montessori and then informed Mrs. Bell about its provisions. Behind McClure, who was sinking further into debt, was Lee Keedick, the lecture agent, who provided the advance money for the tour and was actually in control.

When Montessori was in Washington for a lecture on the tour, the Bells gave a gala reception for several hundred people in her honor, which had extensive press coverage. (For more on Montessori and the Bells in Washington, DC, see chapter 7, "Montessori's American Lecture Tour, December 1913.")

After the break in relations between McClure and Montessori in the spring of 1914, the association, under the leadership of Mabel Bell, continued to promote Montessori education in the United States. Its *Bulletin* was enlarged into a magazine, *Freedom for the Child*. A branch of the association was organized in New York City. However, the association, despite several efforts, had problems in communicating with Montessori, who did not reply to its queries. It was not only awkward but organizationally untenable for the association to promote the Montessori Method when the method's originator refused to cooperate.

When Montessori returned to the United States to arrange the demonstration school at the Panama-Pacific International Exposition and to lecture in California in 1915, relationships between Montessori and the association were tenuous. The issues between Montessori and the association are treated in chapter 8, "The Montessori-McClure Breakup."

Officers of the Montessori Educational Association in 1913

President, Mrs. Alexander Graham Bell; 1st Vice-President, Philander P. Claxton, U.S. Commissioner of Education; 2nd Vice-President, S. S. McClure, Founder, *McClure's Magazine*; 3rd Vice-President, Mrs. Bailey Willis; Secretary, John Dunlap, M.D.; Treasurer, Gilbert H. Grosvenor, Editor, *National Geographic Magazine*;

Board of Trustees

Alexander Graham Bell; Charles J. Bell, President, American Security and Trust Company, Washington; Miss Alys E. Bentley, Director of Music, Public Schools, Washington; John A. Brashear, Chairman, Educational Fund Commission, Pittsburgh; William Knowles Cooper, General Secretary, Y. M.C. A.; William M. Davidson, Superintendent of Schools, Washington; Mrs. John

Fisher (Dorothy Canfield); John B. Larner, Attorney-at-Law; Mrs. J. Girvin Peters; Miss Edith C. Wescott, Principal, Western High School, Washington; Miss Margaret Woodrow Wilson.

Executive Committee

Miss Edith Wescott, Chairman; Mrs. Alfred Brooks; John Dunlap; Mrs. David Fairchild; William Morrow; Mrs. Bailey Willis; Miss Margaret Woodrow Wilson. Miss Anne E. George, Director of Montessori Work

Officers of the Montessori Educational Association in 1914

President, Mrs. Alexander Graham Bell; 1st Vice-President, Philander P. Claxton, U.S. Commissioner of Education; 2nd Vice-President, S. S. McClure, Founder, *McClure's Magazine*; 3rd Vice-President, Mrs. Bailey Willis; Secretary, John Dunlap, M.D.; Treasurer, Gilbert H. Grosvenor, Editor, *National Geographic Magazine*;

Board of Trustees

Alexander Graham Bell; Charles J. Bell, President, American Security and Trust Company, Washington; Miss Alys E. Bentley, Director of Music, Public Schools, Washington; John A. Brashear, Chairman, Educational Fund Commission, Pittsburgh; William Knowles Cooper, General Secretary, Y. M.C. A.; William M. Davidson, Superintendent of Schools, Washington; Mrs. John Fisher (Dorothy Canfield); John B. Larner, Attorney-at-Law; Mrs. J. Girvin Peters; Miss Edith C. Wescott, Principal, Western High School, Washington; Miss Margaret Woodrow Wilson.

Executive Committee

Miss Edith Wescott, Chairman; Mrs. Alfred Brooks; John Dunlap; Mrs. David Fairchild; William Morrow; Mrs. Bailey Willis; Miss Margaret Woodrow Wilson. Miss Anne E. George, Director of Montessori Work

John A. Brashear, Chairman, Educational Fund Commission, Pittsburgh

Philander P. Claxton, U.S. Commissioner of Education

William Knowles Cooper, General Secretary, Y.M.C.A.

William M. Davison, Superintendent of Education, Pittsburgh,

John Dunlop, M. D.

Mrs. John R. Fisher (Dorothy Canfield), Arlington, Vermont

Gilbert H. Grosvenor, Editor, *National Geographic* Magazine (son-in-law of A. G. Bell)

John B. Larner, Attorney-at-Law,
S. S. McClure, Founder, *McClure's Magazine*
Mrs. J. Girvin Peters
Miss Edith C. Westcott, Principal, Western High School, Washington
Mrs. Bailey Willis
Miss Margaret Woodrow Wilson[20]

7

Montessori's American Lecture Tour, December 1913

Figure 4. S. S. McClure and Maria Montessori during her American lecture tour, December 1913 (Harris and Ewing, photographer, Library of Congress).

While McClure was crossing the Atlantic with Montessori, Lee Keedick, the lecture agent, was making arrangements for their arrival and for Montessori's speaking tour. Mrs. Bell and the Montessori Educational Association, too, were planning for Montessori's visit to the United States. To ensure maximum coverage, the major newspapers had been alerted to the imminent arrival in New York of the great Italian educator who had inaugurated an educational revolution. Montessori was scheduled to speak in the country's major cities about her method. While here, it was expected that she observe American schools and renew friendships with the directresses she had trained in Rome. Further, she would describe her plans for the international educational institute, training center, and model school that she hoped to establish. Her supporters, who had read about the "educational wonder-worker" in *McClure's Magazine*, were eager to see and hear her.

Montessori's party, led by McClure, disembarked from the *Cincinnati* on Wednesday morning, December 3, 1913, at the pier in South Brooklyn. Although Americans had seen photographs of her, in person Montessori made a strong impression. She was dressed in black, the color of mourning, which she had worn since her mother's death. Though showing signs of middle age, her face still carried hints of her beauty as a young girl, especially her dark, raven-colored hair. Those who saw her came away with an array of perceptions: she was regal, not maternal; reserved, not open; solemn, not vivacious. When blurred together, these perceptions made her into an imposing figure, one that demanded notice. McClure, at Montessori's side, no longer the young journalist, was slipping into his senior years. Still irrepressible, excitable, and always enthusiastic, McClure was eager to launch what he believed would be Montessori's triumphal tour of the United States, a triumph he would lead and the profits from which he hoped to share. All eyes were on them—Montessori, the great educator, and McClure, the famous editor and publisher.

Presenting the smiling Montessori to the excited throngs crowding the dock, McClure introduced her as the genius who was making the greatest educational innovation the world had ever known. Montessori was pleased to see two familiar faces in the Educational Association's official welcoming committee: Ellen Yale Stevens, who had written about her for *McClure's Magazine*, and her faithful disciple, Anne George, founder of America's first Montessori school. After the greetings, McClure and George took Montessori to her hotel, the Holland House.[1]

At the hotel, Montessori held her first of several press conferences in the United States. The reporters knew from the reception of the articles about her in *McClure's Magazine* that stories about Montessori would attract readers. The *McClure's* articles had made her familiar to many Americans. Now, they wanted insights into her life, especially how she had become the first woman to earn a medical degree in Italy. They wanted to know her opinions on women's rights and marriage. It was not generally known that she was a single mother—something that would have shocked many readers in 1913.

As photographers took pictures, reporters began their questioning. Since Montessori did not speak English, George translated the questions that Montessori answered in Italian and occasionally in French. Although an American press conference was new to her, it did not unnerve her since she was used to public speaking.

The questions in the minds of McClure, Keedick, George, and her other promoters were: how would the press portray Montessori when she stood directly before them? Would the reporters continue to emphasize the Montessori mystique as had the earlier authors in *McClure's Magazine* who described her as a "genius," "a wonder-worker," with "remarkable eyes" and "great charm"?

The answer to McClure and Keedick's question came four days after the press conference, when a very perceptive article about Montessori appeared in the *New York Times* on December 7. The unidentified *Times* reporter enticed his readers with a heading in bold capital letters, "DR. MONTESSORI TALKS OF HER MODE OF 'AUTOEDUCATION'" followed by "Her Personality Reflects Strongly the Fundamental Principle of Her System, Meditation and Serene Poise—'Meditation Means Something Growing,' She Says."[2] Montessori's supporters were assured that the positive portrayal of La Dottoressa begun by Tozier would continue.

The suite at the Holland Hotel had been noisy and crowded with reporters, photographers, and former students. A *Times* reporter who had carefully observed Montessori described her as "a heavy woman, squarely built. Her black hair is sprinkled with gray, but her face is ruddy and without a wrinkle, showing clear and bright above the black of her traveling dress. Her eyes are the expressive part of her face; they seem always to be working out formulae about you." After describing her appearance, the reporter made a surprisingly insightful analysis of Montessori's personality. He wrote, "For personality she has one of a type to which Americans are not familiar, and which one does not associate with the Latin temperament. . . . She has not the quick, flashing smile that is characteristic of her race: she smiles slowly—her face changes expression almost imperceptibly. There is no rapid alteration of mood."[3]

The reporter was puzzled by the way in which Montessori greeted her former students, the young women who had met her at her arrival and had followed her to the hotel. He found Montessori's greeting to be "curious," especially since she had known them "very intimately in her work with them" in Rome, where she had prepared them to be Montessori directresses. "There was no sudden look of recognition, no expectancy, no surprise. There was no word of greeting—only that serene smile and the Continental kiss upon the cheek."[4]

Although he had captured a fleeting insight into Montessori's behavior with her students, the reporter, of course, could not have comprehended the intricacies of La Dottoressa's expectations for her students. Montessori was almost like an abbess in a convent who was responsible for her novices' correct formation. This correctness was doctrinaire; but rather than in a religious doctrine, the formation was in Montessori's educational doctrine. She expected her students to remain loyal disciples to her and to her method. As true believers, they were not to alter the method but were to implement it exactly as she taught it to them.

When the reporter made his observation about Montessori and her students, he could not have foreseen the problems that Montessori's attitude would cause with some of her American students, who did not see their apprenticeship with her to mean that they had become lifetime disciples.

The *Times* reporter's commentary on the Italian educator's personality continued, "But she gives, above all, the impression of poise and sureness. It is perhaps that contrasted with our own nervousness, perhaps the mere fact that she is in a strange country and does not understand English—whatever the cause, she seems curiously detached. She is not aloof, she is interested in this odd and noisy place, but she is always apart, serene and untouched by it."[5]

While Montessori's detachment intrigued the reporter, McClure and those traveling with Montessori had found it more problematic. The gregarious, talkative, and irrepressible McClure still puzzled over a strategy to use to engage the often aloof Montessori. At times on the voyage from Italy to New York, McClure had found Montessori's remoteness to border on coldness. For others, Montessori's remoteness, reflecting an interior spiritual quality, was part of her attraction. Although now a celebrity in a country that loved celebrities, Montessori remained an intriguing, somewhat mysterious lady in black.

The reporter's analysis of Montessori's personality led to his commentary on her method of education. He wrote, "Those who know the fundamentals of the Montessori method will realize that it is but an expression of this serene poise. Children of three and four under the Montessori method have their 'silencio,' the period of meditation. That does not mean, Dr. Montessori will tell you, a passive, enforced, paralyzed silence. It is a voluntary, active thing. . . . Meditation means something growing. . . . This is the fundamental principle underlying the entire Montessori system, the development of growth within one's self, which is the reason for . . . the method of 'auto-education': It is this power of assimilation that gives Dr. Montessori the air of detachment and difference from her surroundings."[6]

The *Times* reporter raised the fascinating and complex issue of the relationship of Montessori's personality to her method of education: "Critics of the Montessori method of education have said that its chief defect was its absolute dependence upon (her) personality. Dr. Montessori herself, who arrived in New York last Wednesday, firmly denies this is a defect. But half an hour spent with the world-famous educator establishes the fact that the method is Montessori and Montessori is the method, and one may well have grave doubts, about how it will go with 'auto-education' when Maria Montessori's personality is removed."

The reporter's comment, insightful for a newspaper column rather than a scholarly journal, anticipated issues that would impact the initial introduction of Montessori's method in the United States, especially after her return to Italy. Montessori insisted that her method, based on her empirical observations of children, was scientific. If it was scientific, as she claimed, then it could be replicated independently of her. However, Montessori insisted that only she could properly train the directress who were to implement the method. Her insistence that her presence was necessary involved her as a person, especially her personality. Added to this paradox, McClure's promotional campaign emphasized her personality as a wonder-working genius.

The *New York Times* article included Montessori's responses to questions about the purpose of her trip to the United States, her educational method, and her attitude on women's issues, especially their work outside of the home and their struggle for greater political participation. Montessori appeared to be undaunted by the assertiveness of the reporters. She was ready to participate in the process that would make her and her method of education known throughout the United States.

Asked why she came to America, Montessori, referring to the "thousands of letters" written to her from people in the United States, replied, "My object in coming to America; . . . America more than any other country outside of my own has been interested in the method as I have worked out in the Casa dei Bambini. I have come largely to understand the spirit of this great interest with which I have been in touch, though somewhat remotely, in the teachers I have trained for their work in America. Here I seem to have many friends, many who are eager for the help that a system of child development can give."

As she went on with her answer, Montessori wanted to make sure that the people in the United States, though eager to hear about her method, really understood it; it was especially important that it was being implemented correctly in the hundred Montessori schools that had been established in the United States. Like the lecturer she had been at the University of Rome, Montessori advised, "I wish to develop and implant more deeply my educational ideas. By that I mean my underlying ideas, which are often obscured at the first by the petty and the trivial, often to their detriment. I come first to America because the work is progressing here more rapidly and I would be sure that the development is right and unhampered."[7]

When asked if she intended to extend her method to older students, Montessori responded by announcing her plan for an international educational institute. She wanted "to secure the co-operation of America in the establishing of a laboratory school, a model school for every branch of psychological research in child development." She wished "to interest American educators in my idea of this international laboratory . . . for I hope to have a branch laboratory in every country." Although Montessori was vague about her proposed international center, McClure was thinking along similar lines. While Montessori assumed her center would be in Rome, McClure saw it in the United States. If not the center itself, then certainly a branch, in which he would have a leading role.

Then in her long answer, interrupted only by Anne George's effort to keep up with her in translation, Montessori proceeded: "The school constitutes an immense field for research. It is . . . a 'pedagogical clinic.' In . . . its importance, it can be compared to no other gathering of subjects for study. We have our system of compulsory education to thank for that. There are gathered together living human beings of every social caste, of every degree of normality and abnormality. It is the field in which the culture of the human race can really and practically be undertaken, the field where seeds of perfection are sown." In her view of the school as a laboratory, Montessori was appealing to the American educators, especially the Progressives, who saw the institution as a community setting, with broad social implications.

Montessori then returned to the original question about extending the age of the students but also sought to put to rest the idea that her method was only suited for Italian children. She said, "in this laboratory school . . . I shall have not only children who are older than those of the Casa dei Bambini but children of differing nationalities, so that the adaptation to temperament can be definitely worked out. The experience of my American teachers has proved to me that nationality is no difficulty in the application of method."[8]

Montessori, who had developed a universal concept of the child, saw her method being applied internationally. She stated emphatically, "I would not imply that the Montessori school is confined to Rome and the United States, however." Pointing to the growing interest in her method worldwide, she said, "It was a peculiar gratification . . . that my book, 'The Montessori Method' is being prepared in the Japanese tongue. There are already in Japan tentative schools where the method will be adopted. Under the influence of some of the leading Protestant missionaries two schools have been established in China."

In explaining how she had developed the concept of auto-education, Montessori referred to her now well-known first school, the Casa dei Bambini in the San Lorenzo district, "the poorest quarter of Rome." She recounted her work with children from very poor families, whose parents were "often out of work, illiterate." The readers of *McClure's Magazine* knew the story; now Montessori, herself, was sharing it with the readers of the *New York Times*. She described her work with the children at the Casa as "a most eloquent experience," that gave her insights for her theory of auto-education.

It was challenging, for Montessori, speaking in Italian, to clarify her philosophy at a press conference, a setting unsuited for theoretical analysis. Trying to ground her theory in the nature of the child, she said, "The idea was to give a gradual series of psychic stimuli perfectly adapted to the needs of the child." The structured environment that she created "stimulated each pupil to his natural development. The children are free in all their manifestations and are treated with cordial affection. There was a sowing of a seed in the consciousness of the child, then a perfect freedom of opportunity for a spontaneous explosion of personality in an environment calm, warm with a sentiment of affection and peace."[9]

Wanting something more concrete for their readers, a reporter asked Montessori about results. When Anne George translated the question, Montessori, undaunted, replied, "Results? They were breath-taking. The intellectual activity of these little children was like a spring of water gushing out after a pile of rocks had been removed. We did not train nor teach; we merely allowed the child to discover itself." Contrasting her didactic apparatus with toys, Montessori continued, "We saw them despising playthings which gave them no cause to exercise their powers of reason. That is why children break their toys: because they are moved by an intellectual curiosity to know what is inside them." Montessori's talk of results most likely remained vague to the reporters. At her coming lectures, motion pictures of children working with the didactic apparatus would dramatically and clearly make her point.

As the press conference concluded, the reporters' questions turned from Montessori the educator to Montessori the women. Now a celebrity as well as a noted educator, Montessori was asked for her view on the women's movement, especially the right to vote. While sympathetic to the suffragist cause, Montessori said she was "not a militant."[10]

Early in her career, Montessori had been involved in the Italian and European women's movement.[11] She had been a member of Italy's delegation to the International Women's Congress in Berlin in September 1896, where she supported a resolution that women should receive equal pay for equal work. She had predicted that science and technology would liberate the "New Women" of the twentieth century, from the drudgery of domestic work, and free them to genuinely fulfill themselves as persons, giving them more time and energy for self-development. "Eventually, the woman of the future will have equal rights as well as equal duties."[12] As Montessori became more involved in education, she was less involved in the women's movement.

When asked if mothers should work, especially in professions, Montessori replied: "In this continual social progress of the world women are more and more taking up different lines of work. Anything that tends to broaden the mother tends to broaden the child." In 1913, working mothers were still rare, especially in the middle and upper classes. Montessori's first school was located in a working-class area where many mothers worked outside of their homes. Montessori believed that industrialization and technological change in the future would bring more women, including middleclass women, into the workforce. Schools would need to respond to this change and provide for the children of working mothers. Nevertheless, Montessori believed mothers would continue to have the greatest responsibilities for the physical and moral care of their own children.[13]

Turning to higher education, a reporter asked, "When will the children trained by your method be able to go to college? Hesitating in her reply, she paused, conjecturing the implications of the question. Then, she said, "College? That embarrasses me just a little to say. The college as it stands now is not at all compatible with such a system as we are teaching. It is totally different. When the system is established for the complete education of an individual, there will be no need for colleges as they exist now. We shall be able to do away with them entirely."[14]

When asked why some children are bad, Montessori, drawing from her work in pediatrics as a physician and from her research psychology and anthropology, answered that they were not bad but, if treated properly, were good. Citing her medical observation at the Obstetrical Clinic in Rome, Montessori said, "A knowledge of child hygiene has made it possible to silence the new-born child. There is no reason but ignorance why babies should cry and a study of rational feeding has done away with it." Montessori used the question as a lead-in to her emphasis on the instinctual need for sensation as the first means of absorbing information about the external world. "The baby, lying tranquilly in his crib, exercises his senses from about the seventh day when his attention is first attracted by a ray of light. It is then his psychological development has begun, and it is from that time he can be kept busy adjusting himself to the external world."[15]

Montessori, ready to bring the press conference to a close, raised her own closing question: "They do not ask what it is I think of America, what I think of education here. . . . But I should like to say that while I have been too absorbed to keep in intimate touch with the educational influences at work here in the United States, I have been watching the larger, general tendencies with great interest. And in its larger aspects, I think that you will find that Italian educators, myself, among them, heartily endorse the larger methods of education which the United States has been working out."

Some of the reporters either did not understand what Montessori was saying or misquoted her. The *New York Herald* misquoted her as saying, "We believe in taking the baby away from the mother as soon as he is born. The mother does not know how to care for her offspring. Parents require much training before they are to be trusted with their infants." Montessori was further misquoted as saying, "After my method has been taught there will be no college education necessary."[16]

The newspaper accounts, like the earlier articles in *McClure's Magazine*, were laudatory, extolling Montessori as "a woman easily entitled to her place among the half dozen most prominent in the world . . . a woman of wonderfully attractive personality . . . on the highest pinnacle of feminine attainment both in this country and abroad, (whose) methods of juvenile upbringing have taken a place in history next to those of Rousseau, Pestalozzi and Froebel" and "give promise of assuming worldwide predominance."[17] They praised Montessori as having done "more constructive scientific work than any other living woman, the creator of a system of education that will within a few years modify all existing educational systems and theories and as it is developed take their place thereby evolving a new and higher type of thinking and acting man."[18]

McClure and Keedick's publicity campaign did its work; an eager American public was ready to hear the "educational wonder-worker" describe her "revolutionary" method of education. McClure and Keedick were experts in getting an audience for what promised to be a momentous three weeks in the halls and auditoriums of America's major American cities.

On December 4, Montessori, accompanied by McClure and Anne George, arrived in Washington, DC, where she received a red carpet treatment similar to that given to a visiting head of state from another country. Montessori had become much more than a noted educator; she now was a celebrity.

The *Washington Post*, in its December 5 issue highlighting Montessori's itinerary and lecture, attracted readers with the bold heading, "HER SCHOOL REFORMS WON WORLD FAME." A quote from Montessori was prominently positioned at the article's head, "'Let Schools Replace Hospitals and Penitentiaries.' Her First Message to Washington Mothers—Calls Desks and Seats of Present Buildings 'Instruments of Torture.'"[19]

A bit more subdued than the New York City press, the *Post* reporter described Montessori as "a robust woman, in the early prime of middle life," with the "pronounced brunette coloring typical of the south European." Not overwhelmed by her presence, the reporter wrote that her personal appearance did not convey "an impression of her wonderful achievements" that have revolutionized methods for educating children.[20]

Next a short biography informed readers that Dr. Montessori, a graduate of the University of Rome holding a medical degree and the doctorate of philosophy, originally entered education by studying "defectives" and then turned to educating normal children. In 1906, she "began to perfect" her system, which is "attracting the attention and receiving the commendation of the leading educators of the world."[21]

The reporter focused on Montessori's emphasis on themes she would reiterate in her forthcoming lectures: children's freedom to work in the classroom without interference and the importance of establishing a foundation of sensory and physical skills for children's ongoing development. Montessori made the comment that so intrigued the reporter that he used it as the lead for his article: "The desk and seats in the average public schools are barbarous affairs. Future generations will place them in museums as examples of torturing instrumentalities in this enlightened age."

Next Montessori stressed another point she would make in her coming lectures —the difference between teachers she trained from those in conventional schools. "We do not use the term teacher, but director. The director is present to repress antisocial acts. Otherwise, the child is left free to do his work in its own way."[22]

Another statement that captured the reporter's attention was Montessori's claim she did not use punishment to control pupils' behavior. "There is no place for punishment in this system. The normal child, placed in natural surroundings, is always good. Consequently, if one finds that a child in such surroundings persists in being bad, it is patent that it is abnormal, being either physically or mentally weak. I immediately take that child to a specialist; determine what is wrong with it, and then begin to give the attention necessary to correct its failing."[23]

December 6 was a tightly scheduled day for Montessori. She visited the Montessori School at 1340 Kalorama Road, sponsored by Alexander Graham Bell and his wife, Mabel. Here, Montessori saw the work of Anne George, the first American directress she had trained. Approving George's application of her method, Montessori saw the Bells' school, situated in the United States' capital, as validating her claim that her method was universally applicable to children everywhere in the world.

The true disciple, George, was proving to be indispensable for Montessori's tour. She had translated Montessori's book, *The Montessori Method*, into English for its American publication. George, at Montessori's side during the public appearances, was her translator for the press conferences and lectures. She also was available to assist her mentor on any personal matter that arose on the tour.

After Montessori had visited the Bells' school, Margaret Wilson (1886–1944), the president's daughter, escorted Montessori on a private tour of the capitol in a White House car. Like her father, Woodrow Wilson, a former professor of political science and president of Princeton University, Margaret Wilson was deeply interested in education. Twenty-six at the time of Montessori's visit, Miss Wilson was an enthusiastic advocate of the Montessori Method and an active member of the Montessori Educational Association. Newspaper accounts of Montessori's lecture tour invariably mentioned that Montessori had the committed support of President Wilson's daughter.

A meeting with President Wilson had been planned as part of Montessori's Washington itinerary. Mabel Bell wrote to Margaret Wilson, in the month preceding the visit, expressing some concerns about Montessori's projected visit with the president. She was concerned with Montessori's rather than the president's schedule. "I have just arrived from Nova Scotia and find Miss George very much troubled about the matter of Montessori's reception by the President. It seems that she not only wants to meet the President but also Dr. Wilson the great educator and talk with him about her work. And she is coming over from Italy with the understanding that she is to have this meeting. Miss George says . . . that as Montessori is . . . to lecture in New York Monday evening it is impossible for her to wait until Monday afternoon for her audience. Besides this Mr. Bell and I are giving a reception for Dr. Montessori on Saturday and—if you would not be so kind as to receive with us."[24] Mrs. Bell and Miss George need not have worried since the meeting with Wilson was cancelled, because the president was ill with the flu.

Montessori's tour of Washington with Margaret Wilson as her guide surely was a fascinating encounter. A talented vocalist, Miss Wilson's interests ranged from music to mysticism. Her cosmopolitan outlook was open to new ideas such as those Montessori was bringing to America. In one of history's unusual coincidences, three decades after their meeting in Washington, both Montessori and Wilson would be in India. In 1938, Margaret Wilson traveled to Pondicherry, where she joined the ashram of the Hindu mystic Sri Aurobindo. Known as "Nistha," translated as "Sincerity," she lived there until her death in 1944.

In 1939, Montessori went to Adyar, in Madras, to conduct a training school sponsored by the Theosophical Society. When war was declared between Italy and the United Kingdom in 1940, the British interned Italian nationals in Great Britain and its colonies. The British authorities in India, sure that the sixty-nine year old did not pose a risk to security, released her to carry on her educational activities in India.[25] Though Montessori and Wilson were in India at the same time, there is no record that they met again. Montessori would remain in India until World War II ended in 1945.

On the evening of Saturday December 6, Montessori, at the Masonic Temple in Washington, DC, gave her first lecture to an overflow audience that filled the auditorium to capacity. Montessori did not speak from a prepared text but rather expressed the major themes of her educational method: children needed to be at liberty to learn; they expressed their inner drive to self-development through their freely chosen work; the years from birth to age six, especially from three to six, were a crucial time of sensory, muscular, and mental development; children would stay at a task, repeating it until they had mastered it; her school, a prepared and structured learning environment, with specially designed didactic apparatus, should replace conventional classrooms; her directresses, differently trained than conventional teachers, did not interfere with the children's auto-education.

Montessori would pause periodically in her presentation so that Anne George could translate her comments into English. Since she had been a student in Montessori training course and had been the translator of the English edition of the

Montessori Method, George was extremely familiar with Montessori's principles and methods.

By 1913, the use of motion pictures to illustrate lectures had become highly popular. At the urging of McClure, Montessori had brought several reels of films, illustrating children at work in the schools in Rome. Keedick, a skilled promoter, had highlighted the motion pictures in advertising Montessori's lectures. The showing of the films, following Montessori's presentation, became a standard feature in all her lectures. The depiction of children using the didactic apparatus intrigued the American audiences. The apparatus that promised rapid learning leading to the spontaneous explosions into writing and reading, had been featured in the photographs in *McClure's Magazine*. Now through the newly invented technology of the motion picture, those who had just heard their inventor speak could watch children working with the apparatus, determined to learn the skills they promised to teach.

Since the motion pictures no longer exist but were an important attraction in the Montessori lectures and a cause in the later controversy between McClure and Montessori, we have reconstructed what they might have portrayed from the still photographs in *McClure's Magazine*:[26]

- Girls at the School of San Angelo welcoming La Dottoressa Montessori
- "Little Pietro, four years old, serving soup to the other Montessori children . . . done so deftly and carefully . . . that not a drop is spilled or a dish broken."
- Two girls, Pepinella, three and a half, and Rosina, four, learning to button and lace together strips of cloth fastened to wooden embroidery frames; among the first of the Montessori exercises.
- "Training the sense of touch," showing a girl learning the difference between rough and smooth by running her fingers over coarse sandpaper and smooth cardboard
- Two blindfolded children, a boy, learning to distinguish shapes by touch as he fits geometrical insets into their proper places in a frame, and a girl, distinguishing textures by touch
- Children learning to distinguish colors by arranging colored silk on bobbins according to gradations of shade
- "Learning to write and read by touch," showing girl using her finger to trace sandpaper letters learning to know them by touch, and a boy and girl making words out of cardboard letters
- A girl making a sentence with the cut-out letters that reads, "I wish well to the lady directress, to my teacher, Signorina Mass Silvia, and to La Dottoressa Maria Montessori."

- "Little Girls in the Ghetto School of San Angelo, in Rome, Carrying the Montessori Materials from their School-room on the Third Floor to the Open Court. The Children make the journey down the steep flights of narrow steps with perfect order and security of movement."
- Queen Margherita visiting the school at San Angelo

Following her lecture, Alexander Graham Bell and his, wife, Mabel, hosted a gala reception honoring Montessori at their mansion on Connecticut Avenue. Four hundred invited guests from Washington's upper echelons stood in line to greet Italy's and now the world's most famous educator. The guests passed through a receiving line that included Dr. and Mrs. Alexander Graham Bell; Montessori, standing next to Mrs. Bell; S. S. McClure, identified in some newspaper articles as the president of the Montessori system in America; Mrs. Franklin Lane, wife of the secretary of the interior; Miss Margaret Wilson, daughter of the president of the United States; Dr. Philander Claxton, the US commissioner of education; and the Bells' two daughters, Mrs. Gilbert Grosvenor and Mrs. David Fairchild.

A "special" to the *New York Times* gave an account of the evening in which guests dined at a buffet supper throughout the evening. What is extraordinary about the Bells' reception and other events of Montessori's tour in 1913 is that La Dottoressa had become a celebrity, feted like a visiting opera singer such as Jenny Lind, or a great writer such as Charles Dickens rather than an educator with a new method of education. The *Times* list of guests at the reception was impressive: "the French Ambassador and Mme. Jusserand, the members of the Italian Embassy, German Ambassador and the Countess von Bernstorff, Norwegian Minister and Mme. Byrn, Minister from Uruguay and Mme. De Pena, Secretary of the Navy and Mrs. Davis, Count and Countess De San Estaban of the Spanish Embassy, Secretary of Agriculture and Mrs. Houston."[27]

On December 7, the Bells gave a farewell luncheon for Montessori with educators from the Washington, DC schools. After the luncheon, Mrs. Bell accompanied Montessori, McClure, and George to Washington's Union Station, where they boarded the 3 P.M. train for New York.[28]

While she was in Washington, Montessori met with Philander P. Claxton (1862–1957), the US Commissioner of Education, on December 6 at the Bureau of Education. McClure and the Bells had succeeded in enlisting the Commissioner into the Montessori movement as a vice president of the Montessori Educational Association. Claxton, who had been the superintendent of public education in North Carolina and a professor of education at the University of Tennessee, had wide interests in education that included primary schooling. As a member of the official receiving line, Claxton saw Montessori again at the Bells' reception and a third time at their farewell luncheon for her.

On December 8, the day after Montessori's departure, the *Washington Herald* ran an article with the bold headings, "MONTESSORI SYSTEM IMPRESSES CLAXTON"— "Education Commissioner Thinks Method Could Easily Supplant Kindergarten Method." The *Herald* quoted Commissioner Claxton on the Montessori system as saying "he sees no reason why it would be too expensive, proportionately, to introduce the system in public schools to supplant the present kindergarten method."

Claxton qualified his endorsement of Montessori education, however, by saying that "he had not had time deeply to investigate the merits of the system, and did not care to make a statement officially." But he then said, "I have read Dr. Montessori's book and think it very good. I rather think it will become a classic in education. The system seems to me to be worthwhile. . . . Important principles of the Montessori method are the ideas of freedom and muscular development. This tends to encourage spontaneity and the training of the senses properly. The whole system might, if approved, be introduced into our schools without much increase in proportionate cost."[29] The commissioner's comment, though expressed with qualifications, raised the possibility of the Montessori Method being incorporated into the public school system.

Claxton's presence at the Montessori events in Washington and his membership in the Montessori Educational Association was a coup for McClure and the Bells in that it added credibility to the Montessori Movement. Although the commissioner came close to endorsing the Montessori Method, he stopped short of doing it officially. While his statement was important in giving Montessori even greater national attention, the power of the US Commissioner of Education was very limited. In 1913, the commissioner of education headed a bureau within the Department of the Interior. Rather than a policy-making office for education at the national level, the Commissioner and the Bureau acted as a clearing house on educational statistics, enrollment trends, and state expenditures for schools. The Bureau's publications did give national attention to trends in education. For example, Anne George's *The Montessori Movement in America* and Elizabeth Harrison's *The Montessori Method and the Kindergarten* were Bureau of Education Publications.[30] Claxton's statements were intended to convey that the implementation of the Montessori Method could be achieved with limited expenditure. One wonders if Montessori, coming from Italy, a country with a national minister of education, understood the complexity of the American educational system where schools were under state and local control and where the US Commissioner of Education had very limited power. Claxton's comments, however, about the Montessori Method supplanting the kindergarten, surely added to the uneasiness of those dedicated to the Froebelian method.

Montessori's schedule was demanding. Returning from her gala reception in

Washington, Montessori's next scheduled event was a lecture at Carnegie Hall in New York City on December 8. McClure and Keedick's effective publicity campaign had drawn an overflow crowd to hear the great lady from Italy. That evening, Carnegie Hall was sold out. Every seat was filled and a standing-room-only crowd filled the galleries. The *New York Times* reported that over one thousand persons had been turned away. In the audience, there were educators from various schools and professors of education from universities in the area, such as New York University and Columbia University's Teachers College. If Montessori could win the endorsement of the educational professionals and professors, her method had a good chance of becoming part of the American system of education.

As the audience waited for Montessori to come to the lectern, they looked at the stage and saw large American and Italian flags and a large banner overhead, reading, "America Welcomes Dottoressa Montessori." McClure and Keedick had arranged to have prominent individuals seated on the stage, a visible indication that what Montessori was going to say would be of the utmost importance. Among the invited dignitaries were Henry Fairfield Osborn, president of the American Museum of Natural History, and Frederick A. Stokes, the president of the American Publishers Association. John Dewey, professor at Columbia University and America's foremost philosopher of education, stepped to the lectern. Dewey, a tall, thin man, a pioneer Pragmatist philosopher, and the founder of the University of Chicago Laboratory School, would preside at the event. Not a dynamic speaker, Dewey welcomed Montessori and then turned to McClure to introduce her. Not a quiet man like Dewey, McClure, who told of his visits to Montessori's school in Rome, enthusiastically presented Montessori as "the greatest woman educator in history."

Then Montessori appeared, dressed in black, accepting the applause and cheers of the assemblage. Speaking in Italian, Montessori told the story of how she developed her method at the Casa dei Bambini in Rome. She emphasized the importance of applying science to education and how her insights had come from the empirical observation of children at work and at play. At intervals, she would pause as Anne George, at her side, translated La Dottoressa's message. The *Times* quoted Montessori, "The development at which I aim includes the whole child—bodily strength, knowledge of practical necessities of life, keenness of all senses, and accurate muscular control. My pupils learn their three R's earlier than other children. A broad basis is laid for the child's future development."[31]

Montessori emphasized that children needed the freedom to act on their innermost impulses to work; through work, they developed themselves. She did not go into detail about the didactic apparatus that she had invented. The motion pictures of children using them in her school would do that for her.

Maybe it was the adulation paid to her that December night at Carnegie Hall or perhaps her growing confidence that she had moved from a small school to the larger world stage that caused her to conclude with "My larger aim is the eventual perfection of the human race."[32]

When Montessori's two-hour address ended, the audience burst into sustained applause. The lecture was a success. But one has to wonder what John Dewey thought. The professor, the pragmatist who emphasized experience and who warned against basing education on "counsels of perfection," had just heard the speaker promise to perfect the human race.

While Dewey may have been reflecting on what Montessori had said, S. S. McClure was not in a reflective mood. Unlike the philosopher, the editor-publisher who lived according to his own philosophy of enthusiasm was very enthusiastic that evening. Montessori's performance had reassured McClure that he still possessed his uncanny ability to recognize talented people and bring them forward to a large audience. Just as he had popularized the English authors Robert Louis Stevenson and Arthur Conan Doyle in his magazine, he had worked his skills for the Italian educator, Maria Montessori. Believing in acting rather than reflecting, McClure sought out Keedick. In a quick decision, they agreed that Keedick would make the necessary arrangements for a second Montessori lecture in New York City at Carnegie Hall on December 15. Meanwhile, McClure and Montessori had a schedule to keep—on to Philadelphia.

Montessori and her party next traveled to Philadelphia, where on December 9, her lecture followed the successful format used in Washington, DC, and New York. The high point of Montessori's Philadelphia visit was her emotional meeting with Helen Keller (1880–1968). Keller's remarkable story of overcoming blindness and deafness was well-known at the time of Montessori's tour.[33] Keller had lost her sight and hearing due to a childhood illness when she was eighteen months old. When she was six, her parents contacted Alexander Graham Bell who arranged a diagnosis for Helen at the Perkins Institute for the Blind. This led to the employment of Anne Sullivan, a former student at Perkins, as her governess and teacher. Sullivan patiently taught Helen the names of words by spelling them with her fingers on her student's upturned palm. Keller went on to learn braille and developed highly sensitive sensory powers. Sullivan became known as a "miracle worker" for her skill in teaching Helen. Keller, herself, became a renowned lecturer and political activist.

The meeting of Montessori, Keller, and Sullivan, now the wife of John Macy, brought together three remarkable women who had in common their use of sensory learning. Sullivan used Keller's senses in teaching her to see with her fingers; Montessori used children's senses as the first step in her method. Often, the children in Montessori's schools did their sensory activities, feeling objects and textures, with their fingers, wearing blindfolds. Alexander Graham Bell served as a link between all three. His advice to Keller's parents eventually led them to Sullivan. Montessori, with Anne George as her translator, and Keller, accompanied by Anne Sullivan Macy, met in Montessori's hotel room. Montessori's and Keller's conversation was an intricate three-way process. George translated Montessori's Italian into English for Macy, who, in turn, traced the words into the manual alphabet on Keller's hand. At the onset of the visit, Montessori embraced Keller, telling George, "Say to her that I am too much moved to express what I feel." Keller, with her hands on Montessori's shoulders, replied, "Blessed are the feet of her who comes across the sea with a message of liberty to the children of America."[34] Montessori then told Keller that she was dedicating her new book, *Dr. Montessori's Own Handbook*, to her.

When Keller referred to herself as a "product of the Montessori method," Macy agreed emphatically. Commenting on the similarity of her method with Montessori's, Macy said that when she taught Keller she was not aware of Montessori's work. But she was impressed with how the "same ideas spring up in many parts of the world at about the same time. . . . Is it the spirit of the age manifest here and there in one and another individual?"[35]

When George prompted Montessori to tell Keller about her work in the Casa dei Bambini, Montessori said, "Tell her this . . . that my children understand her; they know the triumph of the soul over difficulties. But the children of the future, the men of the future, will understand her even better than men do now, for they will be liberated and will know how the spirit can prevail over the senses."[36]

Montessori's comments about liberation generated a response from Keller, an active member of the Socialist Party, "You . . . are fighting for the freedom of children. We are fighting for the freedom of the parents, for the industrial revolution. . . . We never can have the Montessori system or any other good system of education so long as the conditions of the home, of the parents, of the workers, are so intolerable. . . . When you think of the appalling conditions . . . under which people live, it sometimes seems a miracle that the children grow up at all to intelligence and decency."[37]

Montessori, who wanted to avoid being drawn into politics in her host country, responded philosophically, "I began . . . as a sympathizer with political revolutions of all kinds. Then I came to feel that it is the liberation of this, what we have in our hearts, that is the beginning and end of revolution. . . . We must educate children so that they will know how to free themselves and others from bondage. And the first thing is to bring our children under the care of worthy teachers. You and Mrs. Macy symbolize such education, the education of the future, the development of a soul by the union of an inspiring teacher and the child whose soul has grown freely with such stimuli as it needs and without the stimuli that debase and hinder growth."[38]

Anne Sullivan Macy commented that Helen was "a revolutionist before I was. Two or three years before I cared for them, she had all these ideas. You see, I could have molded her in my own likeness. I could have made her a copy of myself. But I left her free to think." To which Montessori replied, "That is it. Liberty to think." She then asked Keller, "You will come to see our schools in Rome some time?" Keller replying that it would be a great pleasure said, "I hope . . . that the next time I see you I shall be able to speak with you in Italian—in Rome."[39] This ended one of the most unusual and poignant meetings of Montessori's trip and probably in the history of education.

The December 11, 1913, *New York Times* article "Dr. Montessori Returns" reported on Montessori's arrival in New York from Philadelphia: she was the guest of honor at a reception in the home of Mr. and Mrs. P. Stuyvesant Pillot. Among the twenty-five guests were Dr. and Mrs. Nicholas Murray Butler, Dr. John H. Finley, and S. S. McClure. The article in the *Times* then provided Montessori's busy schedule: she would lecture in the Brooklyn Academy of Music, proceed to Providence to meet with the Rhode Island Board of Education which adopted her method, and then she will go to Boston to give two lectures and return to New York to speak again at Carnegie Hall. She would conclude her trip with a lecture in Pittsburgh and two in Chicago. The article concluded with a quote that "Dr. Montessori said that she had been well pleased with the schools started in this country by her pupils. She has found, she said, that the method bearing her name is being followed faithfully with good results."[40]

On December 11, Montessori spoke at the Brooklyn Academy of Music under the auspices of the Institute of Arts and Sciences to an audience that completely filled the hall. The evening's format followed that of the other presentations. McClure, excited and enthusiastic as usual, introduced Montessori "as the greatest woman in the world" who "would revolutionize education in our time." He exclaimed that Montessori had captured the attention not only of professors and scholars but of the whole people. The pioneering journalist said, "As an editor for thirty years I have found that the only true test of real greatness and permanent worth is the approval of the masses of people."[41] McClure's words about popular approval indicated not only his style but his belief that great ideas in literature, philosophy, and politics needed to be available to the people. His inexpensive monthly magazine had made great ideas available to the masses. He was proud to be a popularizer; great ideas were not the property of the elite but were to be shared by everyone. When McClure ended his introduction, Montessori came to the stage, dressed in her usual black, to the thunderous applause of the audience.

Anne George, Montessori's translator, who wrote an interpretation of Montessori's lecture in Brooklyn, provides the most complete account of a presentation on Montessori's tour in 1913.[42] When Montessori paused in her remarks, George told the audience how very pleased Montessori was to be in Brooklyn, the city in America that sent her the greatest number of students. Moving to the theme of the child's freedom that was so popular with American audiences, George described Montessori's concept, "We must understand by liberty the right and power to grow freely . . . when we talk of the liberty that is finer and different from external liberty, that is finer than the liberty of physical nature, when we speak of the liberty of the spirit we are speaking of what is almost supernatural. We cannot discover the law of liberty which applies to this kind of life suddenly, it must take long, deep study and observation. . . . So, when we talk of the liberty of the child we must understand that this liberty includes a kind of liberty which is still a problem to us."[43]

Carefully capturing Montessori's words, George continued that liberty did not mean leaving children alone "to do what they want." That "would mean . . . abandoning the child, and, a free child is never an abandoned child." To have the "fullest and finest development of life," the truly free child needs "a very fine, a very carefully determined guidance and care."

George then repeated the story Montessori had used to illustrate how some parents had misinterpreted her idea of liberty. "A mother of one of the children who attended Dr. Montessori's school . . . thought she understood Dr. Montessori's idea of liberty and thought she applied to her child this form of liberty. She allowed him to do anything he wanted to do spontaneously, whether these spontaneous acts were helpful or not. One day, Dr. Montessori was walking with this mother and child along a street in Milan. The bells in a nearby cloister began to ring and the child stopped to listen to them. Dr. Montessori watched with interest this sign of interior activity. But, the mother, who thought it was perfectly right for the child to do whatever he did spontaneously while at home, thought that when in the street the thing to do was to walk, so she said, "Come along! Come, hurry along!"[44] The mother had interfered with the child's freedom to engage his senses in hearing and appreciating the tolling of the bell.

The story led to Montessori's principle of the child's freedom to learn through the senses, especially touch. "It is much easier for him to understand . . . things through the sense of touch than through the other senses. He needs to perfect this method of recognition in order to help him to understand and recognize them by the more complex senses." Despite the clear evidence that children need to touch objects to develop their powers of sensation, adults persist in admonishing the child, "Don't touch! Learn to let things alone! Learn not to touch things!"

George emphasized Montessori's principle that children needed the freedom to act on their impulses which, in turn, led to their self-development. Dr. Montessori's method, which "leaves them free to work . . . gives the greatest importance to the environment that is necessary for . . . the full mental and physical development of the child. . . . Her materials are constructed to supply the child with the simple sense training exercises . . . which he must have."[45]

Reiterating Montessori's comments, George told of her mentor's discovery of a new base for education—"the phenomenon of activity awakened by the presentation of a rational stimulus." In contrast to the old way of instruction in which something is imposed externally on the child from the outside, Montessori presents a stimulus that sets in motion "an activity" that leads to more actions that develop the individual. She refers to how these chains of activity lead to "explosions" of reading and writing, a favorite expression in the Montessori educational lexicon. "'For example," said George, "the act of writing takes place after the children have had and have mastered exercises which prepare them for writing and give them the ability to write spontaneously."[46]

Since George was the first American who had been trained by Montessori, George was especially sensitive to Montessori's comments about the characteristics of Montessori teachers. Thoroughly understanding Montessori's precise prescriptions for her teachers, George carefully translated her words:

> To give this kind of orderly instruction and freedom to the child it is necessary that the teacher shall have a new attitude, that she shall be different from the teacher who has conceived as her mission to force into the child's mind right concepts. She must learn to watch for activity once it has been stimulated. This teacher must come to have an attitude of humility. She must become at the same time an observer of the freely developing child and a wise director of the spiritual growth of the children about her. She must perfect herself to the point where she will not intervene: she must learn to abolish her own personality, her own ego. She must at the same time learn from her observations to distinguish which are the acts she must encourage and leave free, and which are those rare acts which lead to debasement, and therefore, which she must check. . . . She must be like a mother who guards her child when he is in danger of falling, but she leaves the child free to play when he is in a beautiful garden, leaves him free in the enjoyment in which he is safe. She must learn to intervene, to check the harmful things, but to vanish when the child shows that activities which are helpful have been awakened and allow the child to have the illusion that he has accomplished it all himself.[47]

As she ended, Montessori moved as she had done in her address in New York from the child's little world to the larger world of humanity. George translated Montessori's closing remarks that the school, which she was establishing, would prepare "people who will be stronger morally and spiritually, who can better fight the evils existing in the world about them, who will be better able to combat the difficulties which may come to them. We . . . need in the future . . . a race not only stronger physically, but stronger mentally and spiritually. . . . The important fact is that man carries in this body a mind and a soul that can attain to the progress of civilization."[48]

After Montessori and George had made their presentations, the now famous films of children in Montessori's schools in Rome were shown. They presented children working with the didactic apparatus and learning practical life skills. The format that had developed—McClure, the famous progressive publisher and editor; Montessori, the gifted educational innovator; and George, the dedicated disciple, was a success. Each highly promoted lecture set the stage for the one to follow.

The tour was tightly scheduled and strenuous. December 13 found Montessori, McClure, and George in Boston where the schedule was even more demanding in that Montessori lectured in the morning and evening. Her talks in Boston were attended by members of the Harvard faculty. After the Boston lectures, Montessori went to Rhode Island, where she met the governor and members of the state board of education. She also met with Thomas Edison who gave her a private tour of his laboratory at West Orange, New Jersey.[49]

On December 15, Montessori was back in New York City to give her second lecture at Carnegie Hall. A week earlier on December 8, many people had been turned away from Montessori's first presentation, so McClure and Keedick had immediately arranged for a second lecture. Tickets at 50 cents, one dollar, and $1.50 had sold out.[50]

The program began at 8:15 P.M. with McClure, identified as the Montessori Educational Association's vice president, making his usual laudatory introduction. Montessori spoke without notes, at times following her usual themes but also voicing on-the-spot insights as they occurred to her. Anne E. George again acted as translator. The December 16, 1913, issue of the *New York Times* covered the highlights of the lecture under the heading, "GIVE CHILD LIBERTY SAYS DR. MONTESSORI." This was followed by three subheads: "Young Must Have Complete Freedom For Natural Development, Asserts Educator"; "EXPLAINS HER METHODS" and "Stimuli Offered to Awaken and Nourish the Inner Self—Her Last Lecture."[51]

Montessori enlarged on her familiar theme of the "child's freedom to learn." The *Times* quoted her, "The child must grow in liberty if he is to grow well and there is no other way in which his natural development can take place. The primal impulse of the child is to become a man, and he must have liberty to find those conditions and that help which will enable him to become in the fullest possibilities, the man he was destined to be."[52]

The *Times* reporter, alluding to the hundreds of mothers and fathers in the audience, commented that Montessori "criticized the practice of many parents of not allowing their children to touch things on a table or desk, not realizing that the child at this age gains many of his perceptions from the sense of touch, whereas adults have outgrown this stage of development." The reporter paraphrased Dr. Montessori who said "that the stimuli she gave the children corresponded to their needs and were just sufficient to awaken, develop, and nourish their inner self.... The joyous child was the one which grew strong and sturdy in body."[53]

The article returned to directly quoting Montessori, "Contrary to the statements of psychologists, that between the ages of 3 and 6 a child's attention is very hard to hold, I was first struck with their constancy in the first week of my school at San Lorenzo. There was a child playing with large and small cylinders designed to be fitted one into the other. I tried many times to distract his interest in the cylinders, even going as far as to have the other children sing and play, but I counted forty-two times after the singing began that the child continued to manipulate the cylinders. Surely, this shows with what intensity a child rivets its attention on something in which it is interested."[54]

The *Times* continued: "Dr. Montessori said that this constancy was the essence of children's spontaneous development and that they should be allowed to do over and over again the work which interested them. As the child's activities increased, Dr. Montessori found, those of the teacher diminished. It often happened, she said, that visitors to the school commented on the fact that the teachers had nothing to do but to give the child what he wanted, and then, 'take it easy.'" Hearing this comment, the teacher smiling replied, "No, I don't even have to do that. The children come in and get their own work themselves."[55]

The *Times* article reported that Montessori told the audience that a new science of education needs to replace the obsolete traditional ideas about education. The old-fashioned school's emphasis on group instruction, rote learning, and memorization was an impediment to true education. The first six years of a child's life, she said, was a crucial period for auto-education in sensory, physical, and intellectual self-development. The didactic apparatus that she had invented captured children's attention to the point that they would persevere in using it until they had mastered a skill.

According to the *New York Tribune*'s account, Montessori advised mothers against giving children toys to idle away their time or of turning them away when they are busy. She said, "The child should be allowed to work with the mother. Imitation is the first instinct of the awakening mind."[56]

Montessori continued, "The child wants to do something sensible. Useless play without a meaning does not appeal to him; neither do so many of the tasks set for children in the ordinary schools. That is why children are rebellious and naughty."

"People often say to me, 'What about the naughty child? Your method may do very well for the young angel, for the child who is naturally gentle, who is capable of happy mental development. What about the rebellious child, the capricious, headstrong child, who cannot be managed by gentleness?' I answer always, 'There are no bad children. What seems like caprice is really only rebellion against the denial of their parents of their desire for a natural environment. I have come to this conclusion only after several years of the most careful observation. . . . If children are allowed free development and given occupation to correspond with their unfolding minds their natural goodness will shine forth. This I have called the conquest of goodness. It is fact not theory.'"[57]

As with her previous lectures, Montessori received a standing ovation. On December 17, Montessori continued the heavily scheduled tour, speaking in Pittsburgh where the format of the earlier lectures was repeated. Newspapers in Pennsylvania covered Montessori's American tour. Reporting the "Montessori fever" sweeping the country, the Honesdale *Citizen* stated the Montessori Method "makes a child direct its own education." The child is so "anxious to learn" that "it need never be driven, the streams of its ever active intelligence require only channels to lead it from the things it already touches, sees and hears, to an association with things, names and ideas that make up the stock of knowledge of mankind." Montessori was quoted, asserting that her method was so fundamental that "it applies to children of any nationality."[58]

Montessori's remaining lectures were two scheduled in Chicago on December 19 and 20. McClure had arranged for a suite in the elegant Blackstone Hotel, where, as in the other cities, Montessori met with local dignitaries, educators, and reporters. She spoke to capacity crowds at the Illinois Theater. The educator, Ella Flagg Young, introduced her at her first lecture and Jane Addams at her second presentation.

The *Chicago Daily Tribune* reported a meeting Montessori had with Chicago educators on December 18 at the Blackstone Hotel. Noted as meeting with Montessori were Miss Susan McGorrisk, of the Chicago Montessori School, on Chicago's South Side; Miss Mary Knudsen; Mrs. Alice H. Putnam; and Miss Elizabeth Harrison, president of the National Kindergarten College. Harrison, a nationally recognized kindergarten leader, was an especially important guest. Her views on the relationship of the Montessori Method and Froebel's kindergarten could have a telling effect on the possible amalgamation of the two approaches to early childhood education.

With the headline, "New Ideas on the Training of Children—Dr. Maria Montessori Tells of Her Methods," the *Tribune* article began with Montessori's definition of education as "so presenting ideas that they shall awaken and set into action the forces of self-building."[59] Then the article reported that Montessori "exploded many theories advanced by psychologists, condemned the unconditional teaching of sex hygiene, and said children are neither stupid nor capricious by natural tendencies, but are made so by poor instruction and lack of freedom."[60]

As she had done throughout the tour, Montessori reemphasized the importance of sensory training in her method: "A child—and I speak from experiments with children between the ages of 3 and 5 only—is taught to discriminate forms and colors; he learns to distinguish the smallest things in his environment. When he compares he is continually forming judgments and deciding. He begins to associate ideas when he observes the differences in the color and form of the various things in his environment."[61]

Next, Montessori connected sensory training to repetition, also a reoccurring theme in her lectures. She told the educators at the Blackstone, "The principal [*sic*] of my method is to let a child experiment with a thing himself and repeat exercises such as putting cylinders in cylinders and repeat processes of building and construction until he has learned the correct and easy way to do his exercises. By the frequent repetition of an exercise the child acquires constancy and ability to give attention, which is the basis of character building."[62]

Montessori's discussion of character formation led to questions about children's natural goodness and the importance of developing their individuality that had followed her throughout her speaking tour. Elizabeth Harrison undoubtedly was alert to Montessori's comments on these matters. The *Tribune* reporter, like the reporters in other cities on the tour, seized upon Montessori's contention that "Children never are bad through natural tendencies. They may be capricious, but it is invariably the result of lack of freedom—because they have not been given the proper opportunity of asserting their individuality."[63] Up to this point, Harrison, a disciple of Froebel, could easily concur with Montessori's rejection of any tendency to evil in a child's nature.

Defending her emphasis on children's individuality, Montessori stated, "I have been criticized on this score because persons believe too much development of the individual is harmful to the society in which the individual lives. In answer I would say children who have been developed individually are more ready to understand their debt to the society in which they live than those who are not, and more readily lend their individuality to the good of the whole."[64] Some kindergarten and progressive educators had criticized Montessori's method as inadequately providing experiences for the child's socialization—the ability to interact with other children in commonly shared activities. Harrison, most likely, would have found Montessori's comments an insufficient means to bringing children into social interaction.

Montessori's comments in Chicago were interesting in that she entered into a discussion of psychology, particularly the recently evolving field of child psychology. She asserted, "I believe experiments in child psychology will show that the tendency of modern psychology is wrong and psychologists will have to adjust their theories to conform with actual experiments. The new school of which I am head in Rome I prefer to call a laboratory for experiments in child psychology. The psychologists are wrong when they say children at the age of 3 or 4 years have to be forced to give attention. It has been my experience that they show a desire to give attention to certain things. Children were asked by me to listen to kindergarten stories and when they got tired they could run away without first asking permission. I learned in that way that the mental development of the child of 3 is not such that he could give attention to long stories, but children 5 and 6 years listened through the stories without compulsion."[65]

Montessori commented on the controversial sex hygiene program. She stated, "I am afraid the teaching of sex hygiene should be more restricted than it is at present in your schools. The teaching of sex hygiene of itself might arouse curiosity about things a child should not know. If accompanied with spiritual teaching and taught a child correctly developed, whose individuality has been asserted in his moral, physical, and mental acts, sex hygiene might prove of advantage. Otherwise I believe it would be worse than worthless and even harmful. The curiosity of the child should be aroused, but upon only those subjects which he should be allowed of himself to have full knowledge. . . . Information about the body will never prevent evils unless accompanied by a corresponding mental development of the child upon coordinating subjects."

Montessori continued, "Psychic hygiene should be taught wherever sex hygiene is taught. Nervous children have been sent to my school and they have become calm when they were allowed to act according to the needs of the body and the laws of life. Children afflicted with insomnia have acquired sleep and those with loss of appetite have eaten heartily. It was not as a result of rest but the acquisition of things which satisfy the needs of life that the children became calm."[66]

In addition to its report of Montessori's meeting with Chicago educators, the *Tribune* also carried an unusual article, "Jurists' View of Montessori," featuring opinions of the judges of the Chicago Municipal Court. The judges were asked to give their opinions on the possible effect Montessori education might have on criminals. Judge Fisher stated that "under present economic conditions I can't see what good any educational system will do. If the blight of poverty were removed from such a vast number of people educational methods would make a difference."

Judge Hopkins, more optimistic, commented, "The only way to keep children off the street is to interest them in something that will be good. Children must be taught in an interesting way that which is good for them, as they will turn to

Figure 5. Above: "Training the sense of touch. Learning the difference between rough and smooth by running fingers alternately over sandpaper and smooth cardboard; distinguishing different shapes by fitting geometric insets into place; distinguishing textures." Below: "Learning to read and write by touch. The child at the left is tracing sandpaper letters and learning to know them by touch. The boy and girl are making words out of cardboard letters." (Both from Maria Montessori, *The Montessori Method: Scientific Pedagogy, as Applied to Child Education in "The Children's Houses."* Translated by Anne E. George, Fifth Edition. New York: Frederick A. Stokes Company. 1912. p. 282.)

Figure 6. Above: "Children touching letters. The child on the left has acquired lightness and delicacy of touch by very thorough preparatory exercise. The one on the right has not had so much training." Below: "Making words with cardboard script." (Both from Maria Montessori, *The Montessori Method: Scientific Pedagogy, as Applied to Child Education in "The Children's Houses."* Translated by Anne E. George, Fifth Edition. New York: Frederick A. Stokes Company. 1912. p. 283.)

interesting things that aren't so good." Judge Sabath, even more positive, stated, "The Montessori method, as I understand it, trains the mental powers of the child. Of all things that is most needed to prevent crime."[67]

Very pleased with the success of the Montessori lecture tour, McClure wrote to Mabel Bell, the Montessori Educational Association's president, from Chicago on May 20, 1913:

> We have got safely through & once more I am able to breathe freely.
> Miss George has been more than an angel. I have come to regard her as the most remarkable woman I've ever known in many respects.
> The Dottoressa has been successful every where & excepting her neurasthenia & resulting fatigues, she has been a very good traveling associate.
> Chicago has done us proud & loudly applauded Miss George.
> I cannot adequately thank you & the Association for your most important & vital assistance. I can only say that I am eager to reciprocate in any way where I am able to serve you.[68]

With her taxing lecture tour completed, McClure had arranged for a weekend of rest and relaxation for Montessori at the Battle Creek, Michigan, sanitarium of Dr. J. H. Kellogg. McClure and his wife, Hattie, who frequented the sanitarium, were sure it would restore Montessori's energy. Dr. Kellogg's Sanitarium was, indeed, a fascinating health spa. An advertisement for the sanitarium stated: "Brain fog—mental confusion—indecision—lack of vim and chronic weariness are evidence of something wrong with the body. To determine the causes of ill health by a complete scientific "inventory" of each patient's entire organism is an essential feature of the Battle Creek Sanitarium System. . . . Then follows a course of health training adapted to each patient's special needs—diet scientifically regulated, graduated body-building exercises, outdoor methods, the scientific application of electric light, hydrotherapy, electricity, mechanical and electrical exercises, radium, the X-ray, massage and all other up-to-date remedial means."[69] Unfortunately, Dr. Montessori's professional opinion, as a medical doctor, of her stay at the sanitarium is not available.

Apparently, with her energy renewed, Montessori returned to New York. There she was honored at a farewell reception at the Women's Cosmopolitan Club on the evening of December 23, the night before her departure for Europe.

On the morning of Christmas Eve, McClure and members of the Montessori Educational Association were at the pier to bid farewell to La Dottoressa. They were all pleased with what had proved to be a highly triumphant tour. Before boarding the *Lusitania*, she made her farewell statement address, praising her three-week experience in the United States. America, she said, was "one of the hopes of the civilized world" and "would leave its children a great heritage."[70]

Montessori boarded the *Lusitania* with a feeling of elation; her tour was a great success. She was now known on both sides of the Atlantic. McClure, standing on the pier waving farewell, too, was elated. He congratulated himself on his decision to promote Montessori education. In the three weeks of Montessori's tour, it seemed certain that the United States would be the country where the Montessori Method would be rapidly and enthusiastically implemented. It looked to him like a sure thing.

8

The Montessori-McClure Breakup

A mutually beneficial professional relationship between S. S. McClure and Maria Montessori was based on the American editor's discovery of the remarkable Italian educator in 1910 followed by his subsequent publicity about her work in *McClure's Magazine* in 1911 and 1912. By April 1914, however, the business partnership between these two compelling individuals had ended badly, due primarily to Montessori's belief that McClure, along with other Americans, profited from her educational ideas at her expense.

In December 1913, Maria Montessori, in response to an invitation by S. S. McClure, had undertaken a triumphant lecture tour of the United States, which generated widespread publicity for her method. McClure and Montessori initially had a warm, trusting relationship. In her correspondence with McClure, Montessori praised her American friend and business colleague, "You have always remained very strong and chivalrous as a person beyond reproach and without fear as the gentlemen and friend who remains in my trust for life."[1]

In her introduction to her 1912 book, *The Montessori Method: Scientific Pedagogy as Applied to Child Education in The Children's Houses*, Montessori gratefully acknowledged McClure: "I know that my method has been widely spoken of in America, thanks to Mr. S. S. McClure, who has presented it through the pages of his well-known magazine. . . . To *McClure's Magazine*, a mere acknowledgement of what I owe them is a barren response; but it is my hope that the method itself, in its effect upon the children of America, may prove an adequate expression of my gratitude."[2]

Harvard Professor Henry W. Holmes, in his introduction to Montessori's book, stated: "An audience already thoroughly interested awaits this translation of a remarkable book. For years no educational document has been so eagerly expected by so large a public. . . . That this widespread interest exists is due to the enthusiastic and ingenious articles in *McClure's Magazine* for May and December, 1911, and January, 1912."[3]

There were six major strands in the complex web that entangled McClure and Montessori that led to their eventual break in relations:

1. The educational apparatus produced by the House of Childhood Company and its owners, Carl Byoir and, later, James M. Pierce;
2. Montessori's lecture tour in the United States in December 1913 and the lecture agent, Lee Keedick;
3. S. S. McClure's lectures on Maria Montessori and her educational method;
4. The ownership and use of the films of Montessori's classes in Italy
5. Montessori's teacher-training courses in the United States, and
6. The Montessori Educational Association.

S. S. McClure was involved in every one of these issues. Montessori suspected that McClure, along with other Americans with whom she did business, used her educational ideas for their own profit. This included Carl Byoir and James M. Pierce, successive owners of the House of Childhood, and Lee Keedick, the lecture agent, all who had financial motives for their connection with Montessori as did S. S. McClure. Although many educational issues were involved in McClure's efforts to popularize Montessori education in the United States, the actual cause of their breakup was financial—the issue of who would profit from the Montessori Method. At the beginning of the relationship in 1911, McClure, carried along by his usual enthusiasm, was swept away by Montessori's educational ideas and wanted to revamp American education according to her principles.

The House of Childhood, the company that manufactured and sold Montessori's didactic apparatus in the United States, was a pivotal financial issue with unfortunate consequences for the business relationship between Montessori and McClure. Montessori had authorized similar companies to manufacture her didactic apparatus in Italy, England, Germany, and China, but the United States posed special problems for her.[4]

The original American franchise holder of the House of Childhood was Carl Byoir, a young man from Iowa who first learned about Montessori education in the pages of *McClure's Magazine*. Sensing a profitable financial opportunity because of American parents' enthusiastic response to Montessori's method, he acquired the franchise for the House of Childhood from Montessori in 1911.

Byoir was born June 24, 1888, in Des Moines, Iowa, the son of Jewish immigrants Benjamin Byoir and Minna Gunyan, from Kinishin, Poland.[5] Hardworking, ambitious, and in need of funds, Byoir became a reporter for the *Iowa*

State Register in Des Moines while a high school junior. After graduation from high school, he was hired as the city editor of the *Waterloo* (Iowa) *Times-Tribune*, where he worked for more than a year. In 1906, he entered the University of Iowa and graduated with a Bachelor of Arts in 1910.

Paralleling McClure's earlier experiences in student journalism at Knox College, Byoir financed his University of Iowa education by working as a stringer for several Iowa newspapers, winning college debating and writing contests that had cash prizes, and becoming the general manager of an annual publication, *The Hawkeye*. Byoir's success with *The Hawkeye* prompted him to write a *Manager's Manual* for future college annual managers. He then developed a plan to offer college annual managers at other universities a package deal that included his *Manager's Manual* plus a contract with a printer to print and bind their annuals. He enlisted a local printer, James M. Pierce, the publisher of a farmers' magazine, the *Iowa Homestead*, in Des Moines to handle the printing. Pierce, who was well equipped, had a stand-by press to back up his regular printing press and an engraving department.[6] Both Pierce and Byoir profited from their alliance. By summer 1909, Byoir had negotiated printing contracts with thirty-seven college annual managers, earning $9,500 in commissions.[7]

After graduating from the University of Iowa, Byoir attended Columbia Law School in New York City. Returning by train to New York in the fall of 1911, Byoir read Josephine Tozier's "An Educational Wonder-Worker: The Methods of Maria Montessori" in *McClure's Magazine*. (For more on Tozier's article, see chapter 5, "*McClure's Magazine* Publicizes Montessori"). Byoir took special notice of Tozier's prediction that Montessori education "will spread far beyond Rome and Italy."[8] Tozier's article, highlighting Montessori's ground-breaking educational practices with young Italian children that led to their early amazing ability to read and write, captured the enterprising Byoir's imagination. He took a special interest in the photographs of the educational apparatus Montessori used in her Case dei Bambini. In place of the Italian children using Montessori's didactic apparatus—the blocks, wooden squares with geometrical insets, sandpaper letters, and lacing and buttoning devices—Byoir saw American children whose parents would be likely buyers of these items. Tozier quoted Montessori's forecast of the disappearance of traditional teachers, "For the mistress will be substituted *didactic apparatus* which itself controls errors and places the child on the path of auto-education."[9]

Byoir's entrepreneurial instincts were sparked when he learned that an Italian, Baron Franchetti, the husband of an American Montessori devotee, Alice Hallgarten,"had arranged for the international patent of the didactic apparatus that Maria Montessori has invented."[10] Byoir speculated that he could make a substantial profit by marketing Montessori's educational apparatus to American parents and teachers. He decided to acquire the American franchise for the apparatus, which, as far as he knew, was not held by anyone else.

On his return to New York, Byoir contacted *McClure's Magazine*. Edith Lewis, who became Willa Cather's longtime companion, was then an editor at *McClure's*. She directed Byoir to Roberts Walker of the Wall Street law firm of White & Case. Walker had just months earlier represented S. S. McClure in his unfortunate loss of ownership of his magazine.

When Byoir approached Walker regarding the Montessori franchise, the lawyer cautioned him it would be a risky investment. Walker, attempting to dissuade the young man, warned him he would lose his money. Undeterred, Byoir boldly told Walker to protect the interests of his client, Madame Montessori. He was prepared for any losses that might occur.[11]

Since Byoir was undaunted, Walker drew up the House of Childhood contract between Carl Byoir and Maria Montessori. Walker wrote to Edith Lewis: "I have today delivered to Mr. Byoir the applications for patents and the assignments to the House of Childhood, Inc., accompanying same that you received from Italy with Mr. Bruno's letter of April 3rd. Mr. Byoir has already furnished Madam Montessori with a copy of the contract with her."[12] Alfredo Bruno, Maria Montessori's Italian lawyer, would reappear later in the Montessori-McClure saga.

Investing $6,000 in his project, Byoir set up The House of Childhood, a corporation to manufacture and market Montessori's didactic apparatus in the United States. While Montessori, who had invented the apparatus, held 20 percent of the corporation's stock, Byoir owned the majority, 80 percent.[13] Thus, Byoir gained the exclusive American sales rights to the Montessori apparatus.

Byoir's next step was to manufacture the educational apparatus that would be reproduced from an original set of materials from Italy. When the materials were late in arriving, an impatient Byoir sailed to Rome to meet with Montessori. In his thesis on Byoir, Robert Bennett wrote, "She provided him with a complete set of the physical equipment required by the Montessori system and a thorough understanding of his new product. In Italy, Byoir studied every aspect of the system under Dr. Montessori's personal tutelage."[14] Two aspects of the Byoir-Montessori relationship were unusual. One, the usually suspicious Montessori was agreeable and open to the young American businessman; two, the beginnings of Montessori education in the United States, unlike most other educational movements, were marked by profit-making commercial motives as well as pedagogical ones.

After graduating from Columbia University's School of Law in June 1912, Byoir focused his energies on his House of Childhood. The articles in *McClure's Magazine* that led to Byoir's investment had also attracted many readers, especially potential customers for the apparatus. Byoir, trained in the use of the didactic materials by Maria Montessori herself, stimulated the demand by lecturing to educational groups and women's clubs. He also wrote a manual instructing teachers and parents on the proper use of the didactic apparatus. There was, however, a major inconsistency in the use of the didactic apparatus that Byoir and, apparently, Montessori disregarded. Montessori insisted that only trained directresses, which she herself had prepared, could be Montessori teachers. However, the sale of the apparatus implied that even untrained parents could use them.

By the fall of 1912, Byoir's efforts were paying dividends. His House of Childhood corporation had a New York headquarters. His storehouse was stocked with the sets of the apparatus that he was manufacturing, and there was a backlog of orders from eager buyers who wanted their children to teach themselves to read and write. The Montessori didactic apparatus, which cost only $11.75 to make, sold for $50 a set.[15]

Byoir's House of Childhood resulted from a contractual agreement between Byoir and Montessori in which McClure had no involvement. As previously mentioned, the only connection was that Edith Lewis, a *McClure's Magazine* employee, had recommended Roberts Walker, an attorney who also represented S. S. McClure, to Byoir. Neither was Byoir associated with the Montessori American Committee. In fact, when *McClure's Magazine* announced the formation of the Montessori American Committee in May 1912, a caveat was added that the committee was not associated with the House of Childhood. The contract agreement stated the committee "[will] work under the direct instructions of Madame Montessori, and will supervise all matters pertaining to the Montessori movement, with the exception of the manufacture and sale of the Montessori apparatus. The manufacture and sale of this apparatus is under the control of the House of Childhood, Inc., Carl A. Byoir, president. The Committee has no financial connection with the firm which is to manufacture and sell the Montessori materials."[16] In an interesting aside, McClure, a father and grandfather, who had ordered a set of apparatus, received a letter from Byoir about a delay in filling his order, "I am informed at the factory that they cannot make delivery of your set of the Montessori Didactic Apparatus until Thursday of this week." Byoir's letter to McClure with a letterhead designating the House of Childhood as the "SOLE LICENSEES, THE MONTESSORI CHILDHOOD EDUCATIONAL SYSTEM" warned, "The Montessori Didactic Apparatus has been patented, and other patent applications are pending: infringers and imitators will be vigorously prosecuted."[17]

While Byoir's House of Childhood was the exclusive American distributor of the Montessori didactic apparatus, Byoir was well known to and cooperated with McClure and other proponents of Montessori education in the United States. Josephine Tozier's article, "The Montessori Apparatus," in the January 19, 1912 issue of *McClure's Magazine*, which provided a detailed illustrated description of the didactic apparatus, was an incredible marketing tool for the House of Childhood's educational products. Tozier also advertised Byoir directly, "The didactic apparatus will be put on the market about the first of January by the House of Childhood, 603 Flatiron Building, New York City, under the management of Carl R. Byoir."[18]

Frederick A. Stokes Company, publisher of the English translation of Montessori's *Il Metodo della Pedagogia Scientifica applicato all' educazione infantile nelle Case dei Bambini*, recognized Byoir's American franchise. "Grateful acknowledgement is made to . . . The House of Childhood, Inc., New York, for use of the illustrations of the didactic apparatus. Dr. Montessori's patent rights in the apparatus are controlled, for the United States and Canada, by The House of Childhood, Inc."[19]

In July, 1913, a special section of *McClure's Magazine*, "The Montessori Movement," published a bibliography of books on Montessori education. The compiler of the bibliography, Ellen Yale Stevens, included the entry, T. L. Smith and C. R. Byoir, *Montessori System: Introduction to the Houses of Childhood*, 1912. Byoir's coauthor, Theodate Louise Smith, who had earned a PhD from Yale, was a lecturer at and librarian of Clark University's Children's Institute. Smith was a research assistant to and coauthored articles with the highly recognized authority on child psychology and education, G. Stanley Hall. (Although the authors have not been able to locate the Byoir-Smith publication, it is most likely the "companion manual on instruction" referred to by Bennett that accompanied the educational sets of equipment sold by the House of Childhood.) Similar to the *Manager's Manual* which Byoir had written for college annual managers, this publication was given academic respectability by its coauthor, Theodate Smith, a prominent American educator and author on the Montessori Method.

As early as 1911, Smith had commented on Montessori's didactic apparatus and the House of Childhood in her article entitled "Dr. Maria Montessori and Her Houses of Childhood" in the *Pedagogical Seminary*. She alerted her readers that an English translation of Montessori's *Metodo della Pedagogia Scientifica* would be published by the Stokes Publishing Company in early 1912. She added that Montessori instructional items were being prepared at the House of Childhood, 603 Flatiron Building, New York City.[20]

In 1912, Harper & Brothers published Smith's book, *The Montessori System in Theory and Practice: An Introduction to the Pedagogic Methods of Dr. Maria Montessori*. Smith's final chapter, "An American Teacher's Experience," related how she and her fellow teachers initially used directions and photographs from Montessori's *Scientific Pedagogy* to improvise their own apparatus. Referring to purchasing a partial set of didactic apparatus and specially designed furniture from the House of Childhood, Smith wrote, "we have added the tables made by the 'House of Childhood,' as they are lighter than our former ones."[21]

In 1913, Byoir sold his 80 percent interest in the House of Childhood to James Melville Pierce (1848–1920), president of the Homestead Company of Des Moines and publisher of the *Iowa Homestead*. Pierce was the Iowa printer who had partnered with Byoir in the college annuals deal. Byoir had been successful "as chief salesman and managing director of 'The House of Childhood,'. . . . He ended his one-year Montessori sales effort with $63,000 profit, after he sold his valuable franchise to Pierce."[22] In 1913, James M. Pierce was listed as the president of the House of Childhood located at 200 Fifth Avenue, New York, in Florence Elizabeth Ward's *The Montessori Method and the American School*.[23]

Byoir, who lived until 1957, displayed no further interest in Montessori education after selling the House of Childhood. He was a public relations pioneer who worked for the Hearst organization and served on the Creel Committee on Public Information in World War I. President Wilson named Byoir to the American delegation at the Versailles Treaty Conference that ended the war. Byoir's assignment was to publicize American peace goals. Byoir later founded his own public relations firm, Carl Byoir and Associates, and the Cuban dictator, President Gerardo Machado, was a client. Byoir inaugurated President Franklin Delano Roosevelt's Birthday Balls, fundraisers for the Warm Springs Foundation that took place from 1934 to 1937, which raised millions of dollars for research on infantile paralysis.

Because of the extensive publicity in *McClure's Magazine* about the Montessori Method, allegations were made that the magazine's owners profited from the sale of Montessori's books and educational apparatus. A Montessori enthusiast raised these concerns with the editor of *McClure's Magazine*, "I take the liberty of asking you whether anything you could say or do to refute the false idea that has been such a drawback of this wonderful system of education,—that it is only a money making scheme because patents have been taken out and the price of the materials used having been so high that only the rich can possibly obtain them."[24] *McClure's Magazine* responded, denying the charge: "This is a plain statement of the relation of *McClure's Magazine* to the Montessori method of teaching children. . . . A young man from Des Moines, IA, came forward with the proposition to organize a company for the manufacture in the United States of the apparatus used in the Montessori schools. An arrangement was made with Mr. Byoir whereby a part of the profit in the apparatus would go to Madam Montessori. . . . No one in any way connected with the Magazine has any financial interest of any sort in the sale of the apparatus."[25]

While Byoir and then Pierce were marketing her didactic apparatus in the United States, Montessori, the creator of the materials, disenchanted with the

American way of doing business, was growing more and more suspicious. In particular, she was distressed by the trifling revenue she received from the successive owners of the American House of Childhood company, Carl Byoir and James Pierce, who had earned large profits from the sale of the educational apparatus she devised. Her legitimate complaint was that after the House of Childhood had operated for three years in the United States, she learned that the "dividends that are due to me [are] $500.00."[26] Given that Byoir, who owned 80 percent of the company, made a profit of $63,000 in the company's first year, Montessori's 20 percent profit for that year alone should have been almost $16,000. Three years later, she should have received double or triple that amount, certainly not just $500.

Feeling cheated and misused by her American business partners, Montessori complained to McClure about "the crazy expenditures of Mr. Byoir. . . . Everyone can spend without limits or earn from my work—while I alone remain with nothing."[27] Her dissatisfaction extended to McClure, her key American contact, though he had no legal connection to the House of Childhood.

In December 1913, while Montessori was lecturing in the United States, a meeting was arranged to address her problems with the House of Childhood. Silas L. Egly, the company's secretary-treasurer, informed McClure that James Pierce would attend both Montessori's Chicago lecture on December 19 and the post-lecture business meeting, presumably between Pierce, Montessori, and McClure, "I sincerely hope that all matters pertaining to The House of Childhood can be adjusted at your conference."[28]

On the day before sailing for Rome on December 24, 1913, Montessori negotiated with both James Pierce and S. S. McClure in regard to the House of Childhood. Montessori sought better terms from Pierce. At this time, McClure's plans to have Montessori conduct teacher-training courses in the United States in the summer of 1914 depended on maintaining her continued good will toward him. McClure was willing to purchase the House of Childhood from Pierce so that he could arrange terms that would placate Montessori and make her agreeable to his next business proposal. He wrote to his wife, Harriet, "When I get this contract I am after, I can go on with ease of mind and peace."[29]

At this point, the course of events regarding the House of Childhood is unclear. From the correspondence after Montessori returned to Rome in late December 1913, it appears that, in January, Pierce still owned the House of Childhood; he, Montessori, and their lawyers were still working out new terms. Confusingly, Harriet McClure claimed that McClure and Montessori had reached an agreement regarding the House of Childhood before Montessori sailed on December 24.

After her return to Rome, Montessori mentioned her meeting with James Pierce and confirmed her continued trust in McClure: "I have not written to Mr. Pierce so as not to complicate the conditions: I hope that you will make it clear to him that it is you in whom I have confidence—and if you so recommend—I would also like to have a word with him."[30] Montessori's American attorney, Hans Von Briesen, of the New York firm of Briesen and Knauth, which specialized in patent law, was to negotiate a deal with Pierce. However, Montessori added in a letter to S. S. McClure that if Pierce "prefers to address me directly, he may send me his proposals—and I will take these into consideration myself."[31] Montessori advised McClure that Pierce could write to her Italian attorney, Alfredo Bruno. Whatever deal was being worked out, both Pierce and S. S. McClure were involved. Still regarding McClure as a trusted business partner, she cabled him, "SENT COPIES CONTRACT PLEASE CONTINUE WRITING DAILY WE MUST CONQUER ALL MY FAITH RESTS WITH YOU."[32] It is unclear to what contract Montessori is referring. Is it the House of Childhood contract drawn up in New York prior to her sailing for Rome?

Reiterating her distrust of Carl Byoir, Montessori decided to give James Pierce another chance. "It is up to him to demonstrate to me that there are people who are loyal to me—that he will understand the value of my work—that he will see me as a person on an equal footing—and that he will also understand how much Byoir has betrayed my trust in the House of Children. But Pierce is not Byoir—and I am perfectly willing to start believing again in a reformed House of Children."[33]

Harriet McClure referred to Montessori's ambivalence about whether to continue working with Pierce or accepting McClure's offer to take over the House of Childhood. Harriet's timeline of events is different in that she states that Montessori and McClure reached an agreement regarding the acquisition of the House of Childhood before Montessori returned to Rome. According to Harriet McClure: "The last evening of Dr. M.'s presence in N.Y., in my presence, she appealed to S. S. to arrange this business (H. of C.). . . . The same evening she announced her decision, in my hearing, to accept the terms obtained for her by Von Briesen with Pierce. But Sam begged her to adhere to the arrangement sketched by them together, which I was engaged in copying for her signature. . . . So, trusting Sam's disinterested devotion to her in her work . . . she entered into and signed the agreement."[34] If Harriet McClure's recollection was accurate, there would have been no reason for either Montessori or her associate, Maria Maraini, to be upset with James Pierce's operation of the House of Childhood in January 1914.

Despite the confusing timeline, the agreement reached by Pierce and Von Briesen did not satisfy Montessori; she accused Pierce of revoking his previous promises. Her associate in Rome, Maria Maraini, gave McClure a detailed account of Montessori's grievances, "Dottoressa is unfavorably impressed by Mr.

Pierce on this account: When Mr. Pierce was in Rome he made the following promise to Dottoressa before witnesses—what he also has confirmed by writing, namely: That having been on the point . . . to cover the entire amount of his investment by selling 400 sets of the material—he would pay out to Dottoressa between 3,000 and 4,000 dollars as her share in the dividends. . . . Dottoressa's impression through her conversations with Von Briesen has been that Mr. Pierce wants to draw back completely from these assertions . . . which . . . represent only the fair share to Dottoressa on the basis of her contract."[35] Mariani then quoted from Pierce's letter of June 1913 to Montessori, "'I am glad to say that by the time this letter reaches you the factory will have made up, finished and boxed ready for shipment, something over 400 sets of the didactic apparatus. If we could sell in the next two or three months, these 400 sets at 50 dollars it would bring in 20,000 dollars.' (of these one-fifth 4,000 dollars to Dottoressa)."[36]

Mariani then continued to present Montessori's case against Pierce to McClure, telling him that Pierce failed to honor his commitments to Montessori who was advised by Hans Von Briesen, her New York attorney, that she had no legal recourse. She related Montessori's frustration in dealing with American businessmen, "Dottoressa's impression through her conversations with Von Briesen has been that Mr. Pierce wants to draw back completely from these assertions he had made in writing and personally and which after all represent only the fair share to Dottoressa on the basis of her contract."

Mariani, indicating that McClure was involved in the business arrangements between Pierce and Montessori, asked him to use his influence to set matters right for Montessori, "I know that you are very anxious for Dottoressa to show her good will toward Mr. Pierce. . . . You know also that this contract was not at all advantageous for Dottoressa. . . . Dottoressa was very surprised when Mr. Von Briesen seemed to imply that there were no means of making Mr. Pierce keep his engagements—You should . . . try . . . persuading him to keep his engagements."[37] Mariani's letter was written January 10, only three days after Montessori's telegram to McClure stating that: "ALL MY FAITH RESTS WITH YOU."[38]

McClure, who needed to maintain good relations with Montessori, sought to find a way to resolve the impasse regarding the House of Childhood. He believed that his role in his plan to hold Montessori training courses in the United States would yield profits, rescuing him from his dire financial plight. McClure arranged to have his brother Robert Bruce McClure purchase the House of Childhood from James Pierce in early 1914. The House of Childhood company would become a component of McClure's proposed Montessori Company, which would sponsor American teacher-training courses taught by Montessori and her associates. S. S. McClure's success in this endeavor depended on a trusting relationship with Montessori, which she makes abundantly clear to him. "Most of the fruit of the movement, is tied to me (my person)—and to win my perfect trust, would also facilitate your business."[39]

S. S. McClure's intentions to please Montessori were confirmed by Robert B. McClure, who wrote to his brother, "In drawing up the papers you had been careful to provide in every way for the protection of her interests, that in furtherance of these plans I had, at your suggestion, purchased. Mr. Pierce's interest in the H. of C."[40] S. S. McClure, who referred to himself as "the real responsible head of her interests in America," brought his brother into the transaction instead of buying the business himself because of contractual limitations imposed by Lee Keedick for whom he was lecturing on the Montessori Method.[41] Still, S. S. McClure considered his brother a figurehead and bristled when Robert thought otherwise. He advised his wife, Harriet, "When we would consult together about the H. of C. he would always say 'I' shall do this or that. . . . Robert got his chance because the contract with Keedick ties me up. But *I* am the real head."[42] Silas Egly, Secretary/Treasurer of the House of Childhood, understood which brother was the real head of the House of Childhood. He sent sales reports to S. S. McClure, not to Robert.

The House of Childhood, under Byoir, initially sold only complete sets of the Montessori didactic apparatus, but in 1914, under the McClures' ownership, partial sets, referred to by Egly as "different sections and miscellaneous parts," could be purchased.[43] To a mother of a small child, McClure wrote: "Since Dottoressa Montessori was in America, she has given permission to sell a part of the apparatus, so if you wish to you could get for $20 a part of the set which would be quite all that your little boy would want for a year or two."[44]

By late March 1914, Montessori was no happier with the McClures' operation of the House of Childhood than she had been with the previous owners, Byoir and Pierce. She claimed that instead of receiving better terms than Pierce offered, the McClures had not even met those terms. In addition, still another American, Robert B. McClure, was now profiting from her work. Attacking S. S. McClure in a scathing letter, Montessori wrote, "Don't tell me, I beg you, that you took the House of Childhood for me: because, if it were true, you would have tried to preserve at least those modest conditions that Mr. Pierce had made for me. . . . The only difference is that Mr. Pierce made me promises that Mr. McClure found impossible. . . . Mr. McClure your brother . . . are more persons than before to earn from the House of Childhood—and that I will never have anything: and this with the written approval of your lawyers."[45]

S. S. McClure, tied up in lecturing obligations with Keedick, dispatched his brother Robert to Rome in April 1914 to negotiate his proposed Montessori Company contract with Montessori. Robert McClure received a hostile reception. Much of Montessori's anger was focused on her small payments from the American House of Childhood. As Maraini warned S. S. McClure, "This point is very important to Dottoressa just now."[46] Apparently, S. S. McClure had made a serious error by underestimating just how important the House of Childhood revenue was to Montessori.

Montessori finally agreed to negotiate with Robert McClure on the condition that she would have more favorable arrangements with the House of Childhood: "For what concerns the House of Childhood, I ask, instead of the 40% on the net dividends, the 30% as royalty. . . . This royalty should be calculated from the day in which Pierce gave the business."[47] Alfredo Bruno, Montessori's lawyer, confirmed Montessori's stipulation in regard to the House of Childhood. "The current House of Childhood contract with Pierce, which you recommended and wanted, must be rewritten and reformulated on another basis. Dr. Montessori's terms would consist of a claim on every educational apparatus system sold, as used for books, of 30% of the catalogue price." Bruno also reversed the sale of partial sets of equipment and specified that "only whole and complete systems—may be sold."[48]

Bruno contrasted Montessori's financial difficulties with the American House of Childhood to her positive experience with the European educational apparatus companies. He advised S. S. McClure, "The contract, originally drawn up with Byoir and now in effect with Pierce who succeeded Byoir, did not lead to any profit for Dr. Montessori. . . . This fact is very strange since the factories which manufacture Montessori's educational materials in other cities made profits from their first months of operation though the Montessori method movement in those countries does not even compare with the American movement."[49]

Once S. S. McClure's efforts to please Montessori by acquiring the House of Childhood had failed, he felt the ethical and, indeed practical, course under the circumstances was to void the House of Childhood contract and allow Montessori to make new agreements with whomever she chose. Harriet informed her brother-in-law, Robert McClure, "What Sam now wishes is to be able to say to Dr. M. and her counsel, that since she has re-considered the proposition sketched together with him and since she is unable to carry out its provisions, and does not wish him to carry out his part of them, he will simply withdraw."[50] However, Robert McClure's ownership of the House of Childhood remained as an obstacle to terminating the earlier agreement between S. S. McClure and Montessori. S. S. McClure, who wanted to restore his relations with Montessori, so that he could pursue his main objective of getting her to cooperate in his projected Montessori Company, was in an awkward position.

Harriet believed that Robert McClure's meetings with Montessori in Rome had only worsened matters. Beseeching Robert to divest himself of the company, she wrote, "It thus becomes a breach of trust and a dishonorable act for Sam to withdraw the H. of C. from her disposal where it was that night."[51] Harriet cited the fact that Montessori did not have a lawyer present when, in New York, she signed a contract with McClure that Harriet had handwritten. "Since this was done without advice of her counsel and without the presence of any friend of hers to advise or protect her, this agreement is in no sense binding on her. She has a perfect legal right to change and re-consider it." Harriet also explained that Montessori did not anticipate Robert B. McClure's acquisition of the House of Childhood. That arrangement occurred because "Sam was so concerned for your health and welfare at that moment, he made the offer to you to place you in that work. . . . The whole affair was hers, and hers only. It was not ever Sam's, except as her trusted agent and partner. It certainly was not . . . yours to dispose of. . . . It was not because he needed you or your money that he gave you this opportunity to serve Dr. M.'s interests . . . but purely out of his brotherly love for you. . . . He does not ask you to be at any loss in this matter. . . . He needs you to declare your willingness to sell the business you bought *in trust for her purposes*, to any buyer who will reimburse you, and pay you for your services in time and ability applied, and who will at the same time meet her views as to terms to be made with her, such as paying her 20% of list price as royalty, as she is receiving in London and Milan."[52]

Robert B. McClure's role in the S. S. McClure and Maria Montessori relationship came to a sudden end with his death in May 1914. In response to a condolence letter from Anne E. George, S. S. McClure wrote in mid-June: "I am hoping my brother's death will not delay or complicate the matters in regard to the House of Childhood."[53] That month, S. S. McClure, through his lawyer, Brodek, offered to sell the House of Childhood to Montessori's lawyer, Von Briesen. Harriet reported to her husband: "I saw Mr. Brodek this morning. About the H. of C. he has heard nothing since he offered it for $25,000.00 to Mr. Von Briesen, who was to see if he could find the money to buy and then report."[54]

In early 1916, the House of Childhood was purchased by Adelia McAlpin Pyle, a wealthy young woman from New York whom Montessori had trained as a directress. Pyle had served as Montessori's translator when she returned to the United States in 1915 to lecture and conduct a demonstration school in San Francisco. Pyle purchased the House of Childhood as an agency of the newly formed National Montessori Promotion Fund. Montessori was the honorary president of the fund, directed by Helen Parkhurst, another directress Montessori had trained.[55]

Another contentious financial issue between S. S. McClure and Maria Montessori were the payments from her American lecture tour in December 1913. McClure had used his magazine, especially the Tozier articles, to promote Montessori education in the United States. Though sincere in his high regard for Montessori's accomplishments, McClure also saw this connection as an advantageous business opportunity. After losing control of his debt-ridden magazine and desperate for new sources of income, he had taken to the lecture circuit, speaking on Montessori education. After obtaining an advance on his earnings from Lee Keedick, his lecture agent, the virtually destitute S. S. McClure traveled to Rome in November, 1913, to meet with Montessori. In a letter to his wife, McClure wrote, "My tip[*sic*] cost $500 to Mr. Kedrick[*sic*]. I had urged it."[56]

McClure's original purpose in making the trip to Italy was to obtain Montessori's permission to use her films of Italian school children during his lectures on the Montessori Method. True to McClure's ebullient nature, his original purpose quickly expanded. As McClure told Montessori about the enthusiasm for her method in the United States, Montessori, in turn, was elated by the adulation she was receiving from the great American publisher and editor. Montessori was not aware at the time that McClure had lost control of his magazine and was in difficult financial straits.

As was typical of McClure, one idea—the rights to Montessori's films—led to another more ambitious one—a Montessori lecture tour in the United States. It was one of McClure's more brilliant ideas. Elated with his success in dealing with Montessori, McClure wrote to his wife, "There is a possibility that she & one of her teachers may come to America for the month of December, with the idea of giving a few great conferences in New York, Washington, Chicago & Boston at very large prices."[57]

As his discussions with Montessori progressed, McClure realized that tour expenses, including Montessori's transportation between Italy and the United States, rental of the lecture halls, hotels, and railroad tickets, would have to be paid before any revenue was generated. Without financial resources of his own, McClure again turned to Keedick, his lecture agent, to underwrite Montessori's tour. Keeping his wife, Harriet, informed of the developments, McClure wrote, "I've cabled to Keedick asking if he could guarantee expenses for the two & $1000. . . . & if Keedick can manage the American end of it there is a strong possibility that we will get Mme. Montessori to spend December in America & give some talks."[58]

McClure was successful with both Montessori and Keedick. The typically suspicious Montessori had been won over by the publisher's enthusiasm for her ideas. Aware of the increasing interest in Montessori in the United States, Keedick saw a successful and profitable lecture tour on the horizon. On November 11, McClure, in a celebratory mood, wrote to Hattie telling her that he had successfully set up the Montessori lecture tour. Keedick, a professional lecture agent, would underwrite Montessori's lecture tour and make all the necessary preparations. He shared his good news: "At last I've arranged matters. . . . Mme Montessori is to spend December in America under Keedick's management."[59] However, a few days later,

McClure confided to his wife his concern that his negotiations with Montessori might still fail, "It seems that people in Rome have not been slow to spread the news of my downfall."[60] Montessori had heard that McClure had lost control of *McClure's Magazine*, information he had chosen to withhold from her. This was bad timing for McClure. Instead of working with the affluent, powerful editor of a prominent American magazine, Montessori learned that she was dealing with a man who had recently lost his business. She was justifiably suspicious and had second thoughts about the American tour. McClure, keeping his wife informed about his delicate and difficult negotiations, wrote, "The dottoressa was pulled hither and thither."[61]

Miraculously, McClure triumphed. Despite serious back-and-forth twists in their negotiations, McClure had convinced the cautious and suspicious Montessori to come to the United States and share with an eager public her message of educational change. On November 14, 1913, Maria Montessori and S. S. McClure signed a contract covering, in the second clause, her American speaking tour, "Memoranda of Agreements entered into between the Dottoressa Maria Montessori of 5 via Principessa Clotilde, Roma, and S. S. McClure of 1126 East 24th Street, New York City, on the 14th of November, 1913" (Clause II): " It is agreed that Dottoressa Montessori, during her coming visit to America, will lecture from 6 to 12 times under the management of S. S. McClure and that in compensation she is to receive 60% of the net profits of these lectures, and further to be guaranteed that these profits shall equal or exceed 600 dollars, which sum is to be placed at her disposal immediately."[62]

Although the contract identified McClure as Montessori's American manager, the individual holding the real financial power was Lee Keedick, the lecture agent, who had advanced the five hundred dollars that McClure needed to pay for his trip to Italy. Also, Mabel Bell, the president of the Montessori Educational Association, which would formally sponsor Montessori's lecture tour, was informed after the deal had been finalized. McClure, of course, was following his own method of doing business—act now and pay later.

In a celebratory letter, Sam told Hattie, "The Dottoressa always remembers how good my advice was and . . . she retained her faith in me in spite of powerful adverse influences. If I had failed in this contract, it would have been a serious disaster."[63] He was right; there had been no room for failure in his plan. Three days later, on November 18, an ebullient McClure announced, "This has been a difficult & most important piece of work & complete success has come to me."[64]

McClure, who was already lecturing on the Montessori Method for Keedick's agency, at first believed that he and Montessori were embarking on a joint speaking tour in which he would be the main speaker. He wrote to Hattie about his planned format for the lectures. Montessori "comes and lectures in co-operation with me and the films, for three weeks. . . . This is how I imagine it. Carnegie Hall I speak forty minutes, telling of our visit to Rome May 1911, and . . . give the essence of her principles. Then I show the moving pictures, with brief explanations. . . . Then I introduce the Dottoressa, and she speaks half an hour. Then I, or Miss George . . . give the gist of her talk."[65] (For the actual format in which Montessori was the principal speaker, see chapter 7, "Montessori's American Lecture Tour, December 1913").

McClure was confident that he would substantially profit from Montessori's tour. Acting as her agent, business partner, supporter, and companion, he accompanied her to New York from Italy. "The Dottoressa Montessori sails November 21 from Naples on the *Cincinnati* arriving there December 3rd. I've decided to come on the same ship. . . . I am pretty sure Keedick & I will make a great deal of money on her talks during December. . . . I am hoping we may be justified in taking Carnegie Hall."[66] After her strenuous speaking tour, McClure took Montessori to the Kellogg Clinic in Battle Creek, Michigan, for a few days of rest. While there, Sam told Harriet that he would have to accompany Montessori on her return voyage. Although he had found her difficult to deal with, he was anxious to maintain her good will for upcoming business deals. He wrote "Miss George says if I do not return with her, I will plant the seeds of distrust for the whole future. . . . I must not jeopardize the future. . . . We have had a difficult time. . . . But we got through without any explosion or serious trouble."[67] In fact, McClure did not accompany Montessori to Rome. A young man from the Wm. Heinemann Publishing Company, C. Bang, was designated to accompany her. A pleased Montessori thanked Bang after her return to Italy, "My journey toward Rome was excellent. . . . I have told of your great courtesy to me, and I may now write the thanks of my friends with my own. They are so grateful to you for having given me so much help & relief, at the end of my journey, when I was overcome with fatigue. I shall always retain a most grateful recollection of all you did for me."[68] She then commended Bang's services to McClure, "Mr. Bang has accompanied me all the way to Paris—with a good-heartedness and patience that could not be inferior to the inimitable perfection of Mr. McClure."[69] Bang, however, gave his own account to McClure of his crossing with Montessori. "Dr. Montessori felt very fit when I met her, but she was rather sick of the sea trip and she had not spoken to a soul for five days. . . . When we finally reached Paris, Dr. Montessori became very ill indeed with Neuralgia, and very nearly collapsed. However, after having spent half the night in taking baths and massage, etc., she felt much better the next day and was able to travel to Rome where . . . she had an excellent reception."[70]

Back in Rome after her triumphant American lecture tour, a grateful Montessori was glowing with admiration for S. S. McClure, "ARRIVED HAPPILY EVERY-

Table 1. Maria Montessori's December 1913 Lecture Tour Report of Net Receipts (Montessori's, Keedick's and McClure's Shares of Net Receipts in Dollars)

Net Receipts of Montessori Tour	8,265.93
Dr. Montessori's share (60% of net receipts)	4,959.56
Lee Keedick's share (40% of net receipts)	3,306.37
Less McClure's expenses abroad and $25 for cables	525.00
Lee Keedick's share after above deductions	2,781.37
S. S. McClure's share (half of Mr. Keedick's share)	1,390.69

Based on a report from Josephine B. Kuauer of the Lee Keedick office to S. S. McClure, January 28, 1914, McClure Mss., Manuscript Collections, Lilly Library, Indiana University, Bloomington, Indiana.

BODY HERE LOVES AND ADMIRES YOU."[71] McClure had every reason to think all was well in his business and personal relationship with the difficult Montessori when he received a second telegram from her, "ALL MY FAITH RESTS WITH YOU."[72]

Montessori's warm feelings toward McClure quickly cooled. After receiving a less-than-expected payment from her American lecture tour, Montessori's trust in both S. S. McClure and Lee Keedick significantly diminished. Since the lecture tour contract was with McClure, she held him responsible. A statement from Lee Keedick's office sent January 28, 1914, to S. S. McClure included an accounting of the Montessori lecture tour (table 1).

In this statement, Montessori's sixty percent share of the net proceeds of her tour was listed as $4,959. Keedick, who advanced the funds for the tour, split the remaining 40 percent with McClure after deducting additional expenses incurred by McClure. Keedick and McClure actually shared 33.5 percent of the net receipts: $1,390.69 each. It is unclear what amount of profit McClure expected from the Montessori tour, nor whether he was satisfied with what he received.

Approximately five weeks later, after March 3, 1914, an undated two-page document detailed the proceeds and expenses from Montessori's lecture tour.

The net receipts in March are fifty dollars less than Keedick's January 28 report. Dr. Montessori's share, according to the contract with McClure, was 60 percent of the net profit, listed on the January statement as $4,959.56 or, at least $4,929.20, based on the March net profit figure of $8,215.33.

On December 23, before starting her return voyage, Keedick paid Montessori $3,250 and S. S. McClure paid her $200, totaling $3,450. She received an additional $184.46 on March 3, totaling $3,634.46, 44 percent of either set of figures and 16 percent less than her contractual share.

Montessori's tour expenses, including her passage to and from the United States

Table 2. Maria Montessori's December 1913 American Lecture Tour Receipts and Expenses

Gross Receipts	
Lecture Location	Earnings (in dollars)
Washington, DC, December 6	1,184.50
New York City, December 8	3,780.75
Philadelphia, December 9	1,945.22
Brooklyn, December 11	1,719.40
Boston, December 13, Morning	2,184.00
Boston, December 13, Evening	1,321.00
New York City, December 15	1,127.00
Pittsburgh, Pa., December 17	1,357.00
Chicago, Ill., December 19 and 20	3,315.50
Gross Receipts	17,934.37

Expenses	
Lecture Location	Expenses (in dollars)
Washington	479.14
New York City	995.43
Philadelphia	754.75
Brooklyn	659.34
Boston	751.21
New York City	921.63
Pittsburgh	396.10
Chicago	1,185.59
Miscellaneous	3,575.95
Total Expenses	9,719.14

Based on a report from an undated document issued after March 3, 1914, McClure Mss., Manuscript Collections, Lilly Library, Indiana University, Bloomington, Indiana

and hotels in New York, Pittsburgh, Philadelphia, and Chicago, were deducted from her 60 percent share of the profits rather than from the gross receipts. Montessori was also charged for expenses incurred by Anne George, who translated the lectures, including $137.19 for personal articles purchased for Dr. Montessori. S. S. McClure's expenses of $331.68, including $192.75 for passage to America, $45.07 for fare from Paris to Rome, $39.55 for press clippings for Dr. Montessori, and

Montessori's expenses in the United States of $54.31, were also deducted from Montessori's share of the profits.

The Hotel Schenley in Pittsburg cost $32.19, which also included railroad tickets. One bill at the Holland House Hotel in New York, which included railroad tickets, was $125.11, while another bill on December 28 was $17.28. The Plaza Hotel in New York City charged $50.30. The Blackstone Hotel in Chicago cost $69.60 while the Bellevue Stratford Hotel in Philadelphia was $7.65. Montessori's passage and personal articles amounted to $863.45 and her expenses while in the United States amounted to $431.23. Those two sums, which totaled $1,294.68, comprised the amount at issue, the difference between 44 percent and the 60 percent stipulated in her contract. Keedick, the lecture agent, was responsible for the accounting procedures, not McClure, who was practically penniless, and, by nature, generous to a fault.

Montessori's resentment toward Lee Keedick was problematic for McClure who depended on Montessori's good will for further joint ventures. When Robert B. McClure, S. S. McClure's brother, was dispatched to Rome in the spring of 1914 to negotiate S. S. McClure's proposal for a Montessori Company in the United States, he learned the depth of Montessori's anger. Robert warned his brother, "Something has happened to completely change Montessori's attitude towards you. . . . Keedick's method of charging her expenses seemed to them matters of grave dereliction."[73]

Feeling cheated of what her demanding lecture had earned, an irate Montessori wrote to S. S. McClure on April 14, six days after his brother had warned him that something was amiss, "Mr. Keedick . . . promised me the night in New York, the eve of the departure, after I signed the receipt of the account, to send me a residual of about 6000 Italian lire. . . . . Instead of that sum, Mr. Keedick, then sent me one check of 950 (nine hundred and fifty). The excuse is that my expenses were high. . . . I was in the hands of managers that had promised to sustain my expenses. So this proceeding greatly shakes my confidence."[74]

Determined to receive what she believed was the money due to her from her lecture tour, Montessori referred the matter to Alfredo Bruno, her Italian lawyer. Bruno lodged a protest with McClure about Montessori's small share of the profits, "I have reviewed the lecture report and I saw to my great surprise that you have deducted Dr. Montessori's travel expenses to America and her travel expenses while in America from her share of the profits while the expenses of all the other people who worked on the lecture program appear in the general expenses. . . . The expenditures for Dr. Montessori's travel to and her visit in America must be considered the most basic general expenses. They should have been deducted from the gross profits of the lecture tour, not from the net due to the doctor. Please . . .

send the corrected payment to her. (Her share is 60 percent of the profits after the expenses of the tour have been deducted.)"[75]

Montessori's suspicious attitude toward further business deals with McClure was evident in a terse telegram she sent to him in April: "DO NOT DO ANYTHING WITHOUT REGULAR CONTRACTS FORBID PUBLICATION LAST YEARS LECTURES."[76]

Still another cause of the Montessori-McClure breakup revolved around McClure's lectures on the Montessori Method in which he showed films of Italian children in the Case dei Bambini. In December 1911, McClure, though still nominally editor, was finally forced to surrender control of his magazine to a group of financiers headed by his son-in-law, Cameron Mackenzie. His difficult financial straits forced McClure to turn to lecturing on a variety of topics to earn income.[77] In response to an invitation to speak at the Knox College commencement in 1912, McClure confided that: "I have had very serious business experiences and just avoided bankruptcy a few months ago with great difficulty."[78] In turn, his lecturing brought McClure increasingly under the control of Lee Keedick, the lecture agent who arranged his speaking schedule.

McClure, whose magazine had popularized the Montessori Method in 1911–1912, thought he could capitalize on his Montessori connection by lecturing about Montessori education. As he indicated to his daughter Eleanor, "This new discovery of Mme. Montessori is the greatest of our era & we can make a good income from teaching & lecturing."[79]

In the early twentieth century, lecturers had incorporated the newly invented motion picture in their presentations. McClure felt that his lectures would be greatly enhanced by showing the films of Montessori's school children. In his meetings with Montessori in Rome in November 1913, in addition to arranging Montessori's American lecture tour in December 1913, McClure hoped to gain her permission to use the films of Montessori's schools during his lectures. McClure, who kept his wife informed of his most recent ideas, wrote to her, "Yesterday I saw the moving pictures of the schools. They were quite interesting & will greatly help a lecture. . . . It is sublime and wonderful material. . . . I am after the world rights on moving pictures of her schools & work, *exclusive* for a term of years, & the lecture rights in the English speaking world."[80]

After Montessori agreed to lecture in the United States, McClure envisioned her tour as a beneficial marketing strategy for his own lecture series. He told Hattie, Montessori "may come to America . . . & also assist in launching the moving picture lecture which I am to give."[81]

In a running commentary to his wife about his trials and then eventual success in negotiating with Montessori, McClure wrote on November 11, "I got the moving picture rights for North America."[82] The next day, an elated McClure, optimistic about the potential financial profits from his Montessori lectures, informed Harriet, "I am thinking out my lecture & I feel that I can do a good thing. The films are very interesting. . . . There will be great profit in lecturing with the films. . . . This business is going to make my lecturing very much more profitable."[83]

On November 14, 1913, McClure and Montessori signed an agreement in regard to the films of the Montessori schools.

> "Memoranda of Agreements entered into between the Dottoressa Maria Montessori of 5 via Principessa Clotilde, Roma, and S. S. McClure of 1126 East 24th Street, New York City, on the 14th of November, 1913.
>
> I
>
> In return for the exclusive rights in the Moving Picture Films of the Montessori schools in Rome for North America, S. S. McClure agrees:
>
> 1st. to pay the cost of the negative;
>
> 2nd. To pay 10 % of the net profits on such lectures as he delivers, after 10% of the net profits of the lectures equals the cost of the films. And to pay 5% of the net profits of lectures by others he may employ after 5% of the net profits of the lectures equals the cost of the films.
>
> 3rd. to pay 25% of the profits from marketing the films elsewhere in North America.
>
> (It being mutually understood that this agreement to pay 25% is provisional and subject to re-adjustment in New York City between Maria Montessori and S. S. McClure, if further investigation should show that 25% is too little.)
>
> II
>
> New films on the schools are to be offered and accepted on the same terms."[84]

McClure was thrilled with the contract. Elated he told his typically supportive but patient wife, "Sole rights in her films in America! Think of that. Then she comes and lectures in co-operation with me and the films . . . and in the future we control . . . the films for her school for all time, and perhaps for the whole world." McClure envisioned his lectures on Montessori as a long-term undertaking. "I can add a new lecture or two each year. But only on fundamental subjects" such as "'Educational Reform according to Montessori method.'"[85]

McClure's belief that he had exclusive rights to Montessori's films "for all time" was challenged by Montessori herself. After she had returned to Rome following her American tour, Montessori began to question her commitments to the American publisher, including control of her films. On March 5, 1914, Montessori sent an urgent telegram to McClure asking for a negative of the films, "SEND NEGATIVE OUR FILM USELESS."[86]

The issue over the motion pictures grew increasing problematic to Montessori. As with the House of Childhood issue, Maria Maraini, Montessori's close associate, took up the matter of the films. In a long letter to McClure, Maraini expressed Montessori's irritation,

> Dottoressa is leaving for a lecture in Holland and is not at all pleased at not being able to take a film with her –in fact there is none here at present as the one that existed when you were here was only a proof—and being very imperfect has been destroyed by the people of the Times who knew that Dsse. had taken two with her and was in possession of the negative. Why has this negative remained in America? Now Dottoressa is unable to get a film for her own use—and in the same time whilst she has referred the people who asked for films to you (and she had good reasons to do so) you refer these people back to her—putting her in an embarrassing position. First—because as I told you she really is not in the possibility of giving the films;—second because you should at least have let these people understand that there must be conditions attached to the getting of these films. . . . Whilst now they are writing, telegraphing, insisting in a way which is very upsetting to Dottoressa—and very naturally so.[87]

Unrelenting, Montessori, following up on the issue of the films, wrote again in March to McClure, "Please again I ask you kindly to send me the negative of the films (which is my property) not having not even one of the copies myself nor the possibility of having one of them."[88]

Feeling the pressure about the motion pictures and still trying to salvage his deteriorating relationship with Montessori, McClure appealed to Lee Keedick, who had arranged and underwritten Montessori's lecture tour in 1913. In 1914, McClure was under contract to Keedick's lecture agency. A hard-headed businessman, Keedick was not about to rescue McClure from the film imbroglio, at least not at any cost to him. Keedick wrote to McClure, "Concerning your letters regarding the negative, I certainly got the impression from your correspondence that we owned the negative. This was the reason I paid the customs duty of one hundred dollars on the negative. If we send the negative to Italy we will have to pay duty on all the films we have imported, and, furthermore, it will be necessary to have the films copyrighted, which will cost a couple of hundred dollars more. Under the circumstances why wouldn't it be better to have a set of the films made here, Dr. Montessori to pay for the actual cost of the films. We can have the films made here as cheaply as in Italy so you see she would not be losing anything. I dislike to go to the expense of paying one hundred dollars customs duty on the negative and two or three hundred dollars to copyright these films when Dr. Montessori will probably not want more than one set of films herself. Please let me hear from you at once."[89]

In April 1914, Montessori's attorney, Alfred Bruno, continuing to press the issue of the films, addressed McClure, "I must lodge two complaints. Remember that in accordance with the contract, which I was not involved in drafting, the cost of producing the negative film from the positive was paid in advance to the *Times* but the fact is these payments were withdrawn from Doctor Montessori's net profits. This literary and artistic property, which obviously has a value infinitely superior to the basic expenses incurred for the development of the photographs, belongs to the Doctor, who is the only one who has the right to produce and make positive films. The negative was arbitrarily processed in America procuring much damage to Dr. Montessori now. I also know that a positive has been sold to the Heinemann publishing company in London contrary to the provisions of the contract. This topic requires new agreements also, because those provisions hastily concluded in Rome without sufficient examination have proven in practice to be unsatisfactory. Does it seem fair to charge Montessori for the cost of the films when such an expenditure is of a general nature, indeed the most basic of the general expenses."[90]

While the controversy over the films was raging, Robert B. McClure, whom S. S. McClure had sent to Rome as his representative to negotiate with Montessori, found himself in the middle of the conflict. S. S. McClure, under contract to Keedick's lecture agency, sent his brother Robert in an effort to keep Keedick out of his plan to create a Montessori Company in the United States. The time was not propitious to propose yet another McClure initiative to Montessori. The muddle over the House of Childhood and the issue over the motion pictures put Robert in an extremely delicate and difficult situation. Robert advised his brother that Montessori regarded his failure to return the negative a serious matter. "They made me feel as if they thought there was almost an attempt at fraud."[91]

Montessori, who no longer trusted S. S. McClure, was not receptive to his brother Robert as an emissary. She brought up McClure's lectures on the Montessori Method, protesting that she had not received her five percent share of the income from them. When Robert told her that his brother's lectures were serving to advance Montessori education in the United States, she rebutted his claim. Robert wrote to his brother that Montessori said this was McClure's "own project—inferentially for your own benefit . . . Then yesterday Montessori complained that she had received no statement showing her 5% share of the proceeds of your lectures with the moving pictures. It was easy for me to explain why this had not been attended to as yet, also that many of the lectures had not paid expenses but the fact remains that this was seized upon as a ground for complaint."[92]

In fact S. S. McClure's lectures were hardly lucrative. He spoke to small groups in churches and schools and a typical fee was $100.00. From that amount, his hotel and railroad expenses were deducted. The net amount was then split 50–50 with Lee Keedick, his agent. On a New England trip to Lewiston, Maine, and Burlington Vermont on January 21, for example, $39.09 in expenses was deducted from the $200 lecture fees. McClure was paid $80.46. He had earned $43.68 from a January 26 lecture in Lancaster Pennsylvania.[93] Montessori's 5 percent share from these lectures would have been $6.21. If Montessori was unhappy with the small financial returns paid by Keedick, so was McClure, who complained to his wife, Harriet, "If I can only get free of this Keedick contract I shall be able to live at home again."[94]

While the House of Childhood and the motion pictures each had a negative impact on the relationship between S. S. McClure and Maria Montessori, the final scene of the drama, alternating between comedy and tragedy, between the publisher and the pedagogue, was McClure's ambitious proposal to create a Montessori Company. In early 1914, S. S. McClure, always a man of multiple ideas, developed yet another proposition to benefit from his relationship with Maria Montessori. The Montessori Company was a business that would offer teacher-training courses taught by Montessori and her associates in the United States. Profits would be based on student tuition less the travel and living expenses of the Italian teachers and the fees charged by the participating educational institutions. According to S. S. McClure's plan, 60 percent of the Montessori Company stock would be held jointly, though not equally, by Robert L. McClure, S. S. McClure's son, and Robert B. McClure, his brother, while 40 percent would be held by Maria Montessori. As he planned his next move, Sam advised Harriet, "I want the company when organized to have the stock altered as follows

40% for Montessori
40% to R. L. McClure
20 % to R. B. McClure."[95]

In McClure's plan, Maria Montessori would be a minority stock holder in a company whose only assets were a teacher named Maria Montessori and her unique educational method. S. S. McClure would organize the classroom venues as well as the travel and living arrangements for the Italians—basically the duties of a lecture agent like Lee Keedick, but without Keedick sharing in the proceeds.

S. S. McClure's letters to Hattie suggest that he originated the teacher-training idea. However, in Montessori's March 25, 1914, letter to McClure, she indicates that Lee Keedick had proposed a course in Chicago to her before she returned to Rome after her lecture tour of December 1913. This discussion took place in S. S. McClure's home in his presence.

In a letter to S. S. McClure, Montessori complained that Keedick's lawyer believed that she and Keedick had finalized an agreement regarding the course but Montessori denied that; she indicated that she expected to conduct further negotiations on the contractual terms. She told McClure, "Mr. Keedick's lawyer wrote to me as if I had agreed to the terms Mr. Keedick spoke about in Mrs. McClure's house, with regard to the large course in Chicago. . . . I did not accept the proposals of Mr. Keedick—so much so that they not only were left suspended—but in your many, many letters you indicated that conditions in regard to classes would be negotiated before finalizing the memorandum."[96] Obviously, Maria Montessori supposed that Keedick and S. S. McClure were jointly organizing the American teacher-training program as they had her American lecture tour. Harriet McClure confirmed Montessori's assumption, stating: "It was her understanding that all these arrangements were to include Keedick, and were to rest on his capital and business organization, which he was more than willing to set at her service."[97]

However, for personal and financial reasons, McClure decided to exclude Keedick from the Montessori Company. Since the beginning of his career as editor of *The Wheelman*, McClure resisted working under another's supervision; he did not enjoy lecturing under Keedick's control. Financially, Keedick and McClure had worked together during Montessori's American lecture tour in 1913 and had evenly split 40 percent of the net profit. Keedick and McClure also evenly split the net profit from McClure's own lecture series.

S. S. McClure had decided that he, his son Robert L., and his brother Robert B. would act as the agents for the Montessori Company so as not to have to split the net profit with Keedick. He confided to Harriet, "I have definitely decided not to take in Mr. Keedick. We may be able to secure his service by a percentage of the profits & I think that 10% would be quite enough."[98]

McClure's plan to exclude Keedick from his proposed Montessori Company led to some complex maneuvering. It had to be kept secret from Keedick until Montessori signed the contract. Since S. S. McClure was lecturing for Keedick, canceling his lectures to go to Rome would alert Keedick that something was afoot. Also, S. S. McClure did not list himself as a stock holder of the Montessori Company because of provisions in his lecture contract with Keedick. S. S. McClure decided to send his brother Robert, in his place, to negotiate the contract with Montessori. Sam explained to Harriet, "Robert must understand that I have said to him plainly that I am not in this new Company & cannot be in without Mr. Keedick's permission."[99] His next letter advised Harriet, "Robert got his chance because the contract with Keedick ties me up." He told Harriet that his income from the Montessori Company would be a McClure family matter based on private arrangements with his son and brother.[100]

While McClure had relied on Keedick to underwrite Montessori's speaking tour in 1913, S. S. McClure was without funds to launch his Montessori Company project. In addition to his wife, Harriet, S. S. McClure, despite his deep indebtedness, was supporting a number of relatives such as his son Robert L. and his family, his wife's aunt Sophie Hurd, his mother, Elizabeth Simpson, his oldest daughter, Eleanor, his young adopted son, Enrico, and his brother John and his family. S. S. McClure could not even afford to send his son or brother to Rome to negotiate the Montessori Company contract with Montessori. He told his wife that he needed to "borrow enough in Chicago to send his brother, Robert to Europe."[101]

Always imaginative when it came to finances, S. S. McClure devised a plan for financing the Montessori Company. To implement his plan, he had to rely on his brother Robert. Financially independent, Robert B. McClure, who had profited from the sale of the McClure Syndicate, had managed *McClure's Magazine*'s London office. Sam wrote to Harriet about his plan to start the Montessori Company: "It has . . . come to me that if my brother Robert could loan the new company up to $5000, that the new company could pay him, 1st 6% & that then the 60% owned by the McClure's might be drawn upon for an additional return that is, say 5% of the profits the McClures' get. . . . If there were 500 pupils, there would be a profit of say $100,000, supposing dividends were declared distributing $80,000 of which Robert would get $2,400, which would make a profit to him of nearly 50%. This might be better than getting money outside."[102] In S. S. McClure's imagined and most optimistic financial projections, the McClures would be well compensated. Montessori would receive $32,000—40% of $80,000—while the McClures would get $48,000 or $45,600 after Robert B.'s interest was paid. S. S. McClure's restive imagination took him to financial heights. His old associate John Phillips had brought McClure financial flights down to the ground in the past. But now, there was no Phillips to check him. For his plan to work, Montessori had to be convinced to join the company that bore her name.

McClure, who believed that he had figured out how to finance the Montessori Company, had turned his attention to the location for the projected Montessori teacher-training course. Montessori, of course, had not yet committed herself to the project. McClure, who had placed his son Robert L. in charge of finding venues for the projected Montessori teacher-training course, wrote to him, "Chicago is much more an integral part of U.S. More people are easily got here. The country would be more easily influenced. The suburbs of Chicago have many mothers who would become pupils. These Middle West States are full of ambitious teachers & all the Southern states send great numbers to summer courses in Chicago. Californians would come in greater numbers. . . . I believe you will decide in favor of Chicago."[103]

In March 1914, S. S. lectured in Chicago and wrote to Harriet of his effort to enlist influential Chicagoans, "I had hoped to see Jane Addams for advice as to schools in Chicago but she is away. I shall try to see Ella Flagg Young."[104] As the Superintendent of Schools in Chicago, Young could be useful to McClure. McClure again wrote to Harriet, "The general impression, I find is favorable to Chicago for a summer school. Many serious teachers consider the railroad fares & the living expenses. Also this region is fresher & more enthusiastic in regard to the Montessori principle. . . . I'll be in Chicago several days next week & will make preliminary inquiries. I shall see Mrs. Emmons Blaine—sister of Cyrus McCormick. I am sure she will be very helpful. She is an enthusiast & very rich. Chicago seems to me to be the logical place."[105] Blaine was a notable supporter of progressive education in Chicago.

S. S. McClure, who was a vice president of the Montessori Educational Association, decided it would be propitious to include the Bells in his plans. The national association, based in Washington, DC, could assist in recruiting students. He informed Robert L., "As to Washington, we want them solid. I suggest that they be allowed a commission on every teacher they get—like 10% and 10% for each subscription to magazine in addition to outlay for stamps & circulars up to say $2,000 a year, for the use of their name & run the business like the *National Geographic* Magazine. That is every subscriber becomes a member of the Montessori Association."[106]

While McClure's fertile mind was devising ways of imaginatively funding the startup of the Montessori Company and determining a location for the projected teacher-training course, he was orchestrating the strategy to bring Maria Montessori into the fold like a cloak and dagger spy maneuver. He was the man behind the scenes, hidden from public scrutiny, who was pulling the strings. Just as he had kept Keedick out of the scenario, McClure also needed to have his role in the Montessori Company hidden from the members of the Montessori Educational Association. He told Harriet, "Nothing can be said to the Washington people until the contract is expired in Rome. I myself could say nothing."[107] As an officer of the Montessori Educational Association, S. S.'s financial interest in the Montessori Company would be a conflict of interest. He advised his son Robert L. "It would be a sufficient reason for me not to own stock in the Montessori Co. to avoid criticism & the impungment [*sic*] of my motives which would greatly lesson [*sic*] my influence in the movement."[108]

Moving forward with his plans, McClure hoped to have the Montessori teacher-training courses up and running in the summer of 1914. He emphasized the need for large enrollments which would generate funds, "*Numbers* is what we want. I do not think there will be difficulty in getting practice schools anywhere. . . . as soon as teachers begin to enroll, working capital will come in."[109]

S. S. McClure had not yet concluded the most important detail of all, Maria Montessori's agreement to join his Montessori Company. In mid-March 1914, S. S. McClure's major problem was getting Montessori on board. He told Harriet, "Nothing can be done, excepting in a preliminary way in regard to feeling the outlook for little schools, raising money, etc., until the contract is signed in Rome."[110]

As McClure eagerly waited to hear from his brother Robert B. that Montessori had signed the contract establishing the Montessori Company, he wrote to Hattie, "It is really important that the course opens in July. . . . Robert must make clear to her . . . a big showing is possible only during vacation."[111] McClure, sure that Montessori would agree, began to think about specific arrangements: "The details as to how many people should be brought over by Dr. Montessori etc. can be determined before she sails. Also the details of her method of living. I suggest a Battle Creek regime & nurse & an English speaking staff around her. Whatever she wants she must have." As usual, the near bankrupt McClure was willing to spend lavishly. He announced that Montessori's expenses were to be deducted from the gross receipts—unlike Keedick's accounting practices of Montessori's lecture tour that had angered her so much. He told Harriet, "All her expenses & staff expenses from Rome, back to Rome come out of the gross receipts & all the expenses of Robbie, the same. Also she can arrange to sail very cheaply from Naples. She should be allowed $125.00 for her own fare to N.Y. & 100 for each of the assistants."[112]

Initially, Montessori was amenable to training teachers in America. In mid-February she expressed concern that a commitment in Italy might interfere with those plans. She wrote to McClure, "The Minister of Public Education—here in Rome—would like to engage me for an experiment of three months in primary schools. I think that this would put the movement in America at risk, because I am sure that my presence in the United States would be necessary for our ideas." Further, Montessori believed that she alone could prepare teachers to use her educational method. She wrote, "If I do not prepare the . . . teachers, . . . everything must come to an end. All that the others can do at this point is make preparations, for instance prepare the material, prepare a newsletter et cetera."[113] The Montessori Educational Association members were the "others" that were referred to by Montessori.

Montessori viewed her educational method as a work in progress and hoped to supervise additional educational experiments in America. She asked McClure's assistance in arranging schools for this purpose, "Before engaging me, I ask you: would it be possible for me to find a primary school in America that would be devoted and prepared to carry out experiments with the three first stages?. . . .

Maybe Mr. Montego might help me for two or three years in America. . . . Three classes of roughly twenty pupils each would be sufficient for me."[114] Montessori's reference to two or three years in America indicated a long-term commitment.

Montessori saw a bright future for the American Montessori movement including a role for the Montessori Educational Association that "could make preparations for the future of the movement in America—with training sessions, schools, conferences and influence on the authorities—they could turn this into a huge project."[115] Ironically, a year later in 1915, Montessori claimed that she was unaware of the association's mission and did not know many of its members. At this point, however, Montessori appeared ready to join McClure's project.

Yet unlike McClure, Montessori was much more practical and realistic. As early as January, she had asked about enrollments in the proposed teacher-training courses. McClure learned of her inquiries in a January 13 telegram from Zoe Bateman, an associate of Mrs. Bell, in the Montessori Educational Association, "MONTESSORI ASKS NUMBER ENROLLED SO FAR FIVE PAID ABOUT EIGHT MORE APPLY BUT NO CHECKS REPORT MAY DISCOURAGE HER MORE CERTAIN TO ENROLL . . . HAVE CIRCULARIZED TWO THOUSAND SENDING OTHERS DAILY WHAT DO YOU ADVISE CAN YOU NOT OBTAIN MORE PUBLICITY."[116]

Together with his lawyer, Charles A. Brodek, McClure formally established the Montessori Company. He then vacillated between sending his son Robert L. or his brother Robert B. to Italy, to negotiate the Montessori Company agreement. Initially, S. S. McClure had planned to send his son Robert L. to Rome. He told Harriet, "Robert's two important things are to get a definite date from Dr. Montessori for these schools (& as early as possible) & to get her to sign a contract with the new company. Uncle Robert & the lawyer can advise him greatly."[117] In the end, however, he reluctantly chose his brother Robert B. as his emissary to Montessori.

At S. S. McClure's direction, his attorney, Charles Brodek, prepared the legal documents Robert needed for his mission to Rome. Brodek confirmed to S. S. McClure, "I enclose herewith a power of attorney from you and also one from the corporation to R. B. McClure, which may have to be presented by him at Rome and under which he will execute the agreement with Dr. Montessori. . . . All the other papers will be ready for Mr. R. B. McClure to take with him on Tuesday."[118] After he had received the Montessori Company stock certificates prepared by S. S. McClure, Brodek confirmed, "I have forwarded Dr. Montessori's certificate to Mr. R. B. McClure at Rome and have sent your son his certificate. The two certificates made out in the name of R. B. McClure, I am holding subject to his orders."[119]

Robert B. McClure sailed for Rome on March 24, 1914. Meanwhile, S. S. McClure was having second thoughts about Robert's negotiating skills and his ability to keep Keedick's name out of the arrangements. He apprised Harriet, "My great anxiety now is lest he bring up my contract with Keedick. He must bring up nothing new, or we will likely lose her. He is somewhat headstrong and to a degree egotistical. . . . Nothing can be done . . . until the contract is signed in Rome." S. S. McClure was also worried that as of March 18, he had "not heard from Dr. Montessori for several weeks."[120] Knowing first hand that Montessori was suspicious and difficult to work with, this was an ominous portent for the future.

With his hopes for his financial future resting on the deal with Montessori, S. S. McClure decided to clarify his role in the confused and somewhat tangled mysterious situation into which he had sent his brother. He wrote to his son Robert L. a principal shareholder in the projected Montessori Company,"I can serve her just as well as if I had no contract. . . . Further with you at work, & with what I can do & advise I will . . . in any event, be able to render adequate service." He then directed Robert L. to send an explanatory cable to Rome, "So we might send such a cable as this: 'Solely to avoid criticism and loss of influence it is best ~~for me to be able to say~~ that I own no financial interest in Montessori society. ~~This will not interfere in slightest with my work.~~ But shall lecture only on Montessori & ~~shall~~ work exclusively for propaganda. If necessary limit contract to North America. Another contract can be made later for other countries. Cable instantly contract closed ~~so work may begin~~.'" (The deletions are McClure's.)[121]

From the beginning, Robert's mission was doomed. A telegram from Montessori on March 26 ordered him not to sail for Europe, but Robert had already left for Rome. Montessori also indicated that S. S. McClure should not act until he had heard from her. Worst of all was her announcement regarding new courses. "SUSPEND SAILING WAIT LETTER IMPOSSIBLE NEW ENTRIES COURSE."[122]

Montessori's letter of March 25 to S. S. McClure, referred to in her telegram, was in a harsh, critical tone. She accused the American business people she had dealt with of defrauding her while profiting from her work, "I do not know anything about business, I know, however, that, in spite of contracts and lawyers . . . that, ultimately, everyone can earn . . . on my work—while I alone remain with nothing." Ominously, she added that "I think that the same will happen in the future."[123]

Montessori's March 25 letter signaled a serious turning point in the Montessori-McClure relationship. Her dissatisfaction with her proceeds from the 1913 lecture tour and the House of Childhood raised her suspicions about McClure's proposed Montessori Company. She told S. S. McClure that "these proceedings greatly shake my trust." Directly addressing the Montessori Company proposal, Montessori was outraged by the financial terms S. S. McClure had proposed. "It does not seem fair that I get 40% of the net on work done exclusively by me. . . . It would be well for you, an intelligent person who studies everything, to not dare to offer what you are proposing—namely *40% on the net in the Course*." Pointing out the differences between lecturing and teaching a course, she told S. S. McClure "while the fatigue of the lecturer at a conference is equal whether 100 or 1,000 people are in the audience, in a Course, fatigue increases with the number of pupils. . . . One need only think of the final exams that I must give all the students. They are in themselves a long and huge toil and every student is entitled to personal care for their preparation." Chastising him on the unfairness of offering her only 40 percent of the profits from the projected large enrollments while the McClures, as managers, took 60 percent, Montessori told S. S. McClure that once the classes had been arranged, "the larger number of students does not represent any additional difficulty for the managers."[124]

Montessori was offended by S. S. McClure sending his brother to Rome instead of coming himself. She wrote to him, "I was quite happy when you wrote me that you would be coming to speak to me in person before making a contract: because it would have been a great pleasure for me to see you again; and because I recognize you as a person of superior mind/heart and of broad ideas, which can include my situation and necessity of my work. But then I became disappointed when you wrote me that your son would have come instead: not because I do not regard him highly enough, but because it was not with him that I began the initial project that had grounded my trust in you personally."[125] While Montessori believed that S. S. McClure would be represented by his son Robert L., he decided to send his brother Robert B. as his emissary instead. It was an unfortunate choice, because months earlier, Robert B. had suffered a recurrence of severe mental problems. In late October 1913, Hattie wrote to her husband, "What a pity that brother Robert is broken down again! . . . . Robert himself must have serious care. He can no longer direct and care for himself. Two or three weeks in a Sanitarium at his present stage will not accomplish any durable improvement. He will have to be made over."[126]

Robert B. McClure met with hostility in Rome. He informed his brother S. S. McClure, "My . . . reception in Rome has been unlike anything that either of us expected. . . . The distrustful attitude of her entourage in Rome has made her thoroughly dissatisfied with her arrangement with you." Robert defended his brother's good intentions to Montessori. Referring to the Montessori Company as the Montessori Society of America, Robert referred to an agreement that Montessori and S. S. McClure had reached while she was on her lecture tour in 1913. "I . . . stated that in organizing the Montessori Society of America you had strict regard to the plan she and you developed during the American tour and had briefly expressed in the . . . memorandum signed by both just before she sailed for Rome and that in drawing up the papers you had been careful to provide in every way for the protection of her interests."[127] (Robert McClure used the terms "Montessori Society" interchangeably with "Montessori Company." His use of Montessori Society also needs to be distinguished from the Montessori Educational Association.)

Robert B. McClure, who had expected a receptive Montessori, found her to be recalcitrant and highly suspicious of the proposals he had carried to her from his brother. Bluntly telling Robert that S. S. McClure had absolutely no authority to establish the Montessori Company, Montessori said "that she did not authorize the organization of a company until all the documents had been submitted to her for approval, that in doing so you had exceeded your authority. . . . She did not want a company in any circumstances; her experience with the H. of C. was so unsatisfactory that she did not care to do business in that way."[128]

After dispelling any notion that she had a prior agreement with S. S. McClure, Montessori then opened the door, just a bit, to negotiations about training Montessori directresses in the United States. However, she had some nonnegotiable preconditions that had to be met. First and foremost, there would be no Montessori Company, and she, not McClure or anyone else, would be in charge of organizing and establishing her training classes. Then, and only then, she informed Robert, "If all these conditions were met she would talk about a training school, but it must be understood that it was *she* who was organizing the class, that it was *her* enterprise, that if we had anything to do with it it was to be as her agent, everything must be submitted to and approved by her."[129] Clearly, Montessori saw herself as the necessary principal party in the proposed American enterprise; if the McClures were to have a role, it was a secondary and subordinate one. The proposed Montessori Company in which the McClures were the majority stock holders was dead. Montessori would arrange teacher-training classes herself. She briskly informed Robert, "that other people had offered to pay her to come to America to teach, that schools had been offered to her and that in short she did not need anyone to help her in getting up a class."[130]

Seizing the initiative in the negotiations from Robert, Montessori told him that the only role left for the McClures was publicizing her classes and recruiting students. Determined not to be cheated again as with the proceeds from House of Childhood and her lecture tour, Montessori raised the specific issue of the McClures's compensation in the proposed enterprise. Robert told his brother, "She then asked me what share of the receipts we would expect for promoting the class—i.e., getting pupils and organizing small schools . . . and her question as to what percentage we wanted in case she placed the work in our hands. . . . For doing everything pertaining to our end I asked 20% of the net. This was instantly and vehemently rejected by everyone in the room."[131]

Robert B. McClure was clearly at a disadvantage as his negotiations continued. Montessori proposed that "We (are) to advance funds necessary for advertising and other incidental expenses. This money to be repaid in any case *but* if only 300 pupils are secured (the number might be changed in subsequent discussion) we get nothing for our work. Between 300 and 500 . . . increasing up to 1000 when the maximum of 20% would be reached. Another plan was hinted at—we pay for all advertising and for rental of buildings if they cannot all be had free of course and retain 20% of gross receipts to recoup our outlay and for services. On the basis of 600 pupils we might, with careful management, clear about $15,000 or more."[132] Robert's much smaller estimate of $15,000 of income from 600 students is in stark contrast to S. S. McClure's projections of $100,000 from 500 students of which the McClures would receive 60 percent, $60,000.[133]

Robert B. McClure knew that the possibilities for successfully negotiating with Montessori were steadily diminishing. He wrote to his brother S. S. McClure, "I have not given up the fight by any means but the obstacles are many and hard to overcome." He remarked on Montessori's lack of gratitude to S. S. McClure, "Never once any recognition of the great service you have rendered in making her work known in America years before it could have penetrated the mind of the public but for your insight and effort on her behalf."[134]

Robert B. McClure and Montessori never reached an agreement regarding the Montessori Company. A letter from Montessori's lawyer, Alfredo Bruno, written days after Robert reported his struggles to his brother, confirmed the failure. Bruno informed S. S. McClure, "Dr. Montessori has examined the contract plan prepared by you and relative to a series of business connections that we should establish with the Montessori Company of America recently established, but she cannot in any way feel obliged in such a broad and open-ended way. Her health condition does not allow her to commit or promise her personal work for the future, with such a great distance of time, and the limitations of freedom that would result, would certainly be damaging to the productivity of her work." Making it clear that there would definitely be no teacher-training courses in the summer of 1914 in the United States and telling S. S. McClure that his relationship with Montessori had ended, Bruno wrote, "Dr. Montessori's heavy workload does not permit her, without seriously impacting her health, to make commitments for next summer. I regret that she cannot consider your brother's proposal to teach a course in America this year. . . . In fact, she does not want to make any business commitments regarding teaching of courses so that she maintains complete freedom regarding them."[135] Bruno then demanded that the Montessori Company change its name: "This Company will have to be renamed and the name "Montessori" must be left out of the new title. Dr. Montessori does not allow the use of her name without her consent. So please give another title to the Company without *using the name Montessori*."[136]

When Robert B. McClure's negotiations had reached an impasse with Montessori, S. S. McClure told his brother to withdraw from the discussions and return home. Still hopeful, the self-confident S. S. McClure decided to go to Rome himself in May to resume negotiations. On April 18, while he was lecturing in Decatur, Illinois, he asked his wife to send a telegram to Robert which read: 'Strongly advise suspend negotiations return will go Rome *May* Sam.'"[137]

Despite her husband's unfailing optimism, Harriet McClure was enough of a realist to see that the Montessori Company proposition had collapsed. Though she was, as always, sympathetic and supportive of her husband, Harriet pointed out that by May, it would be too late to schedule summer classes. "You could never, by going to Rome, patch things up in time to carry out the scheme of the summer school in this country. Besides, she has agreed with the Italian government to carry on her work in Rome instead of over here."[138]

In Harriet's opinion, her husband's hard work on Montessori's behalf had been met with ingratitude and broken promises; further, his relationship with Montessori was beyond repair. She wrote to Sam, "You have carried out all the arrangements desired by Dr. Montessori, and have devoted your entire winter and spring to her interests, uncompensated, and now she has gone back on everything she had expressed a desire for. How can you revive relations with her? There is no peace for you in connection with her . . . one who has performed great services but has no further direct responsibility."[139]

Earlier in 1913, S. S. McClure had successfully negotiated agreements with Montessori regarding her American lecture tour and the rights to her films and had such a trusting relationship with her that she had given him her powers of attorney. Montessori's lawyer, Alfredo Bruno, asked McClure to return Montessori's powers of attorney, "Since there are now fewer reasons for which Dr. Montessori's lawyer originally gave you two powers of attorney relating to the protection of Montessori's patents and business, in Dr. Montessori's name and on her behalf, I petition you to return the relevant documents. Dr. Montessori intends to protect her business affairs herself and will only assign powers of attorney for individual subjects and particular businesses when necessary."[140]

Finally, even the usually ebullient S. S. McClure, who had pinned his hopes for repairing his tattered finances on striking a deal with Montessori, knew he had lost. Angry with his treatment by Montessori, McClure confessed to Hattie, "I do not expect any better news from Rome. . . . Nor do I feel that I can renew business relations, with her. She is too utterly ignorant and piggish. If Robert can pull anything off I will let him. I feel that I want peace."[141]

S. S. McClure did not go to Rome in May. Bruno, Montessori's lawyer, verified the futility of further negotiations with Montessori unless all of her conditions were met. In a postscript to Bruno's letter to S. S. McClure, but in a different handwriting than the rest of the letter, was written: "We understand that you are planning to visit Rome shortly. We would be happy to greet you but I am obligated to tell you that it is well known that at this time Dr. Montessori is unwilling to modify any of the issues that I have outlined in this letter."[142]

The Montessori Company never materialized and S. S. McClure realized that he and Montessori would never work together again. Robert B. McClure's failed negotiations with Montessori greatly strained his relationship with his brother. Robert L. McClure, S. S. McClure's son, felt that his father was overly critical of his uncle. Harriet reported that "Son Robert is deeply distressed at your idea that your brother is not fairly disposed toward you in this business, and thinks you are mistaken."[143]

S. S. McClure blamed his brother for the failure to implement the Montessori Company deal. This was probably unfair as by the time Robert arrived in Rome, Montessori was justifiably angry about her income from the lecture tour as well as the House of Childhood and her lack of access to her films. It was evident that Montessori no longer trusted S. S. McClure. Montessori had been approached by other individuals and groups in the United States, asking her to lecture and offer training courses. She no longer needed, nor depended, on McClure to make arrangements for her in the United States. Indeed, in 1915, she would be appearing in California. In late May, Norman Hopgood, the editor of *Harper's Weekly*, advised S. S. McClure, "I think it much better to drop the Montessori matter altogether."[144]

The McClure brothers' ruptured relationship was particularly unfortunate as in late May 1914, only weeks after his failed mission in Rome, Robert McClure committed suicide in his New York home. Peter Lyon, a McClure descendent and biographer, states that S. S. McClure's "youngest and favorite brother, Robert, shot and killed himself, late in May 1914, in his house at Yonkers, New York. Robert McClure was a sick man, an alcoholic, and the suicide was the result of that illness; but S. S., in his grief, could recall only that his last words to Robert had been spoken in anger because of a disagreement provoked by the Montessori tour."[145] Robert had a history of mental illness and had suffered several mental breakdowns.

Mabel Bell, president of the Montessori Educational Association, sent her condolences to McClure and commented on his shattered relationship with Montessori, "We have all been terribly distressed to hear of your brother's death. We know how you must feel it—particularly after all the hard times you both have been going through. . . . We were your friends and realized thoroughly your chivalry toward Dr. Montessori. No one could have done more for her or have been more loyal to her. The trouble I feel sure lay in the great difficulty of perfect comprehension between two people who knew each other's language so imperfectly. Miss George showed me a letter of hers in which she spoke of you most appreciatively."[146]

S. S. McClure, who said he wanted peace, sailed for Ireland, his childhood homeland. Harriet wrapped up loose ends in the McClure-Montessori saga. "I ought to tell you that I sent the book and photo to Dr. M. some days ago."[147]

9

Montessori Education in the United States Post-McClure

As S. S. McClure and Maria Montessori's relationship reached its unhappy conclusion in the spring of 1914, both the publisher and the pedagogue were angry about the events leading to its unsatisfactory termination. They each had their personal interpretations of these events from their own perspectives. McClure, who once held boundless hopes for a successful and profitable relationship with the famous Dottoressa, now viewed the "educational wonder-worker" as much too difficult and unappreciative of his efforts. Montessori, in turn, who once regarded McClure as a great American publisher and loyal supporter, now assessed him as an opportunist who had manipulated her for his financial gain. McClure, whose name was once virtually synonymous with progressive investigative journalism in the United States, was beginning his gradual descent into obscurity, a minor figure at American history's margins. Maria Montessori's fame, in contrast, was steadily rising as she moved from being a noteworthy Italian educator to the center of the international education stage. Ironically, as she was gaining worldwide recognition, interest in the Montessori Method, which had reached a peak during her 1913 tour, was beginning to decline in the United States.

At the very time that Montessori education was being introduced to an American audience, Progressive education was starting to dominate teacher education programs in colleges and universities. As public enthusiasm for her method waned, professional educators, especially Progressive professors of education who adhered to John Dewey's pragmatic Experimentalism, grew more openly critical of Montessori and her method. Their private doubts about her and her method now became open condemnations. Walter Halsey, a professor at the University of Omaha, decried Montessori's method as a "fad promoted and advertised by a shrewd commercial spirit" that had been foisted on an ill-informed "novelty loving American public."[1] Halsey was condemning the entrepreneurial efforts to manufacture and sell Montessori didactic apparatus.

LECTURE BY S. S. McCLURE, FOUNDER OF McCLURE'S MAGAZINE

SUBJECT:

"The Montessori Method of Education"

Lecture illustrated with excellent motion pictures made in Dr. Montessori's own school in Rome.

S. S. McCLURE is one of the Vice-Presidents of the Montessori Educational Association of America and is responsible for the introduction of the Montessori Method in this Country. He accompanied Dr. Montessori on her triumphant lecture tour of America in December, speaking from the same platform. He has made an exhaustive study of the Method in Dr. Montessori's School in Rome and has been chosen by her to deliver lectures on the Method in this Country.

In the history of education, epochs are marked by the names of the men who evolved and gave to the world the various methods of instruction. It is in accordance with the trend of twentieth century propensities that the most pronounced departure in educational methods in many years should have a woman as its founder.

The achievements of Dr. Montessori are of the greatest importance, not only to teachers and parents, but to everyone interested in human progress. First appearing as a method of child education, her work is seen to be based on the deepest foundations and to point to the improvement of the human race individually, biologically, and socially. The Twentieth Century needs sorely what she has to offer. And her contribution is real because she gives us, with the enthusiasm of genius, only theories that have been scientifically tested and methods proved to be successful.

NEW YORK TIMES.—Dr. Maria Montessori lectured on her method of education last night to an audience that filled Carnegie Hall. More than 1000 persons were turned away. Dr. Montessori spoke under the auspices of the Montessori Educational Association. Dr. John Dewey, President of the National Kindergarten Association, presided. The lecture last night, it was supposed, would be Dr. Montessori's only public appearance in this city, but so much interest has been manifested that she will deliver a second lecture in Carnegie Hall on Monday, December 15.

NEW YORK SUN.—Carnegie Hall held one of the largest audiences in its history last night. It was an audience of mothers and fathers who were eagar to hear Dr. Montessori explain how she was able to make children advance rapidly in learning, make them polite, self reliant and charming by giving them complete liberty and without rewards or punishment. Dr. Montessori delivered her lecture in Italian, but Miss Anne George, one of her pupils in the Montessori method, translated. The audience listened with perfect attention and there were bursts of applause frequently. A series of moving pictures brought the Houses of Childhood before the eyes of last night's audience, and the little folk were displayed in the different stages of their advancement.—December 8th, 1913.

The Montessori lectures illustrated with motion pictures are all under direction of Lee Keedick, 150 Nassau Street New York City.

Figure 7. Postcard advertising S. S. McClure's lecture series on the Montessori Method. 1914 (Special Collections and Archives, Knox College Library, Galesburg, Illinois).

A more scholarly critique came from William Heard Kilpatrick, a leading Progressive professor at Columbia University's Teachers College, who had visited Montessori's schools in Rome. Kilpatrick's book-length deconstruction of the Montessori Method, *The Montessori System Examined*, in 1914, challenged *McClure's Magazine*'s laudatory claims of Montessori as an "educational wonder-worker." Specifically, Kilpatrick summarily dismissed Montessori's assertion that her method was based on scientific findings. Kilpatrick found her method was deeply flawed by her limited knowledge of contemporary educational psychology.[2] For the pragmatist professor, the Montessori Method was definitely not innovative, modern, nor experimentally scientific. It was, he wrote, a mid-nineteenth century piece "fifty years behind" modern educational thought.[3]

Now that McClure's ambitions to head the Montessori movement in the United States had perished, the professors' attacks on Montessori did not concern him. McClure had his own struggle. He would not willingly go to the periphery of American life. The publication of *My Autobiography by S. S. McClure* in 1914 gave him a chance, another moment, to be on the public stage.[4] McClure's "autobiography," actually written by Willa Cather, had been serialized in *McClure's Magazine* from October 1913 through May 1914. While Kilpatrick's attack on Montessori was being read by a few educators, McClure's autobiography, published as a book by the Frederick Stokes Company in the United States and John Murray Publishers in the United Kingdom, was reaching a much larger audience. The fact that McClure's autobiography was really a biography written by Cather was never hidden; McClure himself acknowledged Cather as the real author. Cather, who had worked on *McClure's Magazine*'s editorial staff from 1906 through 1912, truly liked McClure and willingly wrote his life story.[5] One can imagine McClure pacing back and forth recalling the events of his life—a poor immigrant Irish lad in Indiana, attending Knox College, marrying a professor's daughter, founding his magazine—and Cather taking the notes she would weave into his life story.

Artfully crafted by the gifted Cather, McClure's autobiography was well-received and favorably reviewed. Llewellyn Jones titled his review of McClure's autobiography in the *Chicago Evening Post* "The Life Story of a Genius." Jones praised the book as "simple, human, intensely interesting and more provocative of fruitful thought than any biography our readers are likely to have seen for a long time." The reviewer credited McClure as the editor who knocked down the props for the "prevalent illusion" that "there is a high brow literature" for the elite and another inferior version "that makes no demand on the intellect" for the "great mass of people."[6]

McClure's autobiography devoted only three pages, accompanied by a photograph, to Montessori. This is most likely due to the fact that McClure's promotion of Montessori from 1911 through 1914 was concurrent with his work on his autobiography. When McClure's autobiography was published, his relationship with Montessori was still ongoing.

Overruling his staff's opposition to publishing the initial Montessori articles, McClure, in his autobiography, recounted, "Not infrequently the magazine's biggest successes were articles whose interest, was generally doubted, even in my own office, until they had succeeded."[7] The Montessori articles had generated such an enthusiastic response that McClure believed that "people everywhere had been waiting for her message." He related that Alexander Graham Bell confided to him that he regarded "the introduction of the Montessori system in the United States as the most important work that *McClure's Magazine* had ever done."[8]

When his relationship with Montessori had disintegrated, McClure, mired in debt, faced a desperate financial future. A clause in his agreement with the new trustees who now controlled *McClure's Magazine* stipulated that McClure could no longer engage in publishing. He was forced by economic circumstances to turn increasingly to the lecture platform under the exclusive management of Lee Keedick. But, after Montessori broke with him, he could no longer lecture on the Montessori Method, nor use the motion pictures of children in the Montessori schools in Rome that had made his lectures so popular. (For the issue of the Montessori films, see chapter 8, "The Montessori-McClure Breakup").

Billed as the "Founder of McClure's Magazine" and featured as a "publicist, author, and traveler," among McClure's topics were "Editing as an Art; or the Making of a Magazine; The White Slave Traffic; The Commission Form of Government;" and "The Five Greatest Problems in Our Civilization." Keedick's promotional brochure promised that McClure's "time is worth ten times more than any lecture association can afford to pay for it. . . . But other considerations than financial ones have induced Mr. McClure to undertake the work. He feels that he has a message worth while for the men of America. He is in a position to tell them things they need to know, and tell them with the inspiration of a man whose life is in the work. Surely the true ends of the lecture platform could not be better served than by a man like Mr. McClure. In the great struggle for political righteousness Mr. McClure has been a powerful leader."[9] McClure's lecture tours required him to travel by train across the country, usually speaking to local organizations in small towns. McClure, a man who never gave up, was constantly searching for new possibilities to recoup his declining income. For a while, he planned to enter the field of educational motion pictures. But this venture, like other of his enthusiasms, faded quickly and unsuccessfully.

While McClure's fortunes were at near bottom by 1915, the momentum that marked Montessori's lectures in 1913 was beginning to dissipate. Still a well-known, indeed a world-renowned educator, Montessori would return to the United States to lecture in California and to establish a demonstration school at the Panama-

Pacific International Exposition in San Francisco. However, Montessori's arbitrary manner in dealing with her American supporters, such as those in the Bells' Montessori Educational Association, had begun to tarnish the halo polished in 1911–1912 by *McClure's Magazine*'s highly laudatory articles.

The year after her break with McClure, Montessori returned, in 1915, for her second visit to the United States. She came to California to lecture, offer teacher-training courses, and conduct a demonstration school. Montessori's engagements were scheduled to coincide with the Panama-Pacific International Exposition being held to commemorate the opening of the Panama Canal. Although World War I was raging in Europe, the International Exposition proceeded as planned in the then neutral United States. A nine-month series of gala events, the Exposition attracted more than eighteen million visitors to its midways. Despite Italy's entry into the war on the side of the Allies, Montessori made what German submarines had caused to be the perilous trans-Atlantic crossing to America.

McClure, who had arranged Montessori's 1913 lecture tour, had no part in Montessori's 1915 visit. The identity of Montessori's sponsors in San Francisco is not clear. Although Montessori was formally sponsored by the National Education Association, Robert G. Buckenmeyer suggests her support may have come from leading Italian-Americans such as Ernesto Nathan and A. P. Gianini.[10] Nathan, a former mayor of Rome and a friend of Montessori, was Italy's Commissioner to the Exposition. Sol Cohen also suggests that the Montessori Alumnae Association in Los Angeles, organized by Katherine Moore whom Montessori had trained in 1913, also cooperated in arranging Montessori's visit.[11] Montessori's funding for her 1915 visit was much-more limited than during the 1913 lecture tour arranged by McClure and Keedick. Although articles about Montessori's lectures and demonstration school appeared in West Coast newspapers, Montessori's national press coverage was less than that of her earlier tour.

Montessori arrived in New York City on April 18, 1915, accompanied by Mario, her now acknowledged seventeen-year-old son, and her educational disciple, Anna Fedeli.[12] En route to California, Montessori was joined in Chicago by Adelia McAlpin Pyle and Helen Parkhurst, two students she had trained in Rome in her second international training course in 1914.[13] Pyle would act as Montessori's translator and Parkhust as her assistant during her stay in California. Anne George, the country's pioneer Montessori directress, was not part of her entourage. George had accompanied McClure on the 1913 tour, serving as Montessori's translator and all-around aide. Mrs. Bell only learned indirectly that Montessori would be in the United States. The Dotteressa had not responded to her letters inquiring about the trip and a possible role for the association.

Montessori and her entourage went first to Los Angeles, where, from May 1 to July 28, she conducted her third international training course. She next went to San Francisco where her fourth course was scheduled for August 1–November 30.[14] Montessori settled in a house in San Francisco, living with Mario, Anna Fedeli, and the two Americans, Adelia Pyle and Helen Parkhurst. These American women would play a role in the ongoing history of the Montessori movement in the United States. Parkhurst, who became Montessori's trusted confidant, for a time was delegated as Montessori's official representative in the United States. Pyle faithfully maintained a typescript of Montessori's San Francisco lectures.[15] The daughter of a wealthy New York family, Pyle purchased the House of Childhood after Robert McClure's death and Montessori's break of relations with S. S. McClure. (For the issue of the House of Childhood, see chapter 8, "The Montessori-McClure Breakup.")

Montessori's lectures and demonstration classes were scheduled to coincide with the meetings of the National Education Association and the International Kindergarten Union, which met in the San Francisco area during the International Exposition. Montessori addressed both groups and also gave a training course for teachers in San Francisco from August through November.

One of the noteworthy aspects of Montessori's second visit was the glass-walled model demonstration school that she set up in the exposition's Palace of Education and Social Economy. In operation from August through November, the school attracted scores of visitors who observed the children through glass walls. The class enrolled twenty-one children, between the ages of three and six, who had been selected from more than two thousand applicants. The twenty-eight-year-old Parkhurst worked as the on-site directress under Montessori's supervision.[16] While Montessori had relied on motion pictures of her school in Rome to illustrate her method during her lectures in 1913, she now used children who actually performed the life skills and worked with the didactic apparatus. A highly popular attraction, Montessori's glass-walled classroom was in operation for four hours in the mornings. Accounts indicate the children, with their attention focused on their work with the apparatus and other materials, were not distracted by their spectators.[17]

Although national attention on Montessori and her method had lessened, Montessori still attracted audiences to hear her discuss her new book, *Dr. Montessori's Own Handbook*. Montessori included a "Note by the Author," with her signature, prominently placed before the *Handbook's* preface. It read: "As a result of the widespread interest that has been taken in my method of child education, certain books have been issued, which may appear to the general reader to be authoritative expositions of the Montessori system. I wish to state definitely that the present work, the English translation of which has been authorized and approved by me, is the only authentic manual of the Montessori method, and that the only other authentic or authorized works of mine in the English language are

'The Montessori Method,' and 'Pedagogical Anthropology.'"[18] Montessori was making it perfectly clear to her American readers that she and she alone was the authentic voice of the Montessori Method. As McClure had learned, Montessori was suspicious of imitators, especially those she believed were using her name for their own profit. Her note was intended to discredit the publications of Americans who had usurped her method such as Dorothy Canfield Fisher's *The Montessori Manual for Teachers and Parents*, Florence Ward's *The Montessori Method and the American School*, and Theodate L. Smith's *The Montessori System in Theory and Practice*.[19]

During Montessori's 1915 visit, the issue of who would be in charge of Montessori education in the United States when she returned to Europe remained unresolved. The Montessori Educational Association, which had been organized in 1913 by McClure, Mabel and Alexander Graham Bell, and Anne George, was still functioning. McClure, a key mover in the association's founding, was no longer active but continued as the association's second vice president and as a member of the Board of Trustees. The Montessori Educational Association, with nearly seven hundred members including a number of prominent individuals, had functioned throughout 1914 and remained a presence on the country's educational scene in 1915.

The ending of the uneasy relationship between Montessori and the Montessori Educational Association closes the curtain on the first phase of Montessori education in the United States. Between the time that Montessori sailed for Italy on December 24, 1913, after her first American lecture tour and her return to Europe on December 8, 1915, and after her presentations in California, the situation was still ambiguous. Mrs. Bell and her associates were aware that the Montessori-McClure relationship had ended, but they sought to continue their efforts for Montessori education.

During the sixteen months between Montessori's first and second visits to the United States, Mabel Bell and the other officers of the association had to chart their own course with no guidance from the woman whose cause they had espoused. In 1914, the association encountered problems that would reappear as persistent issues when Montessori returned to the United States in 1915. The Montessori Educational Association, like Montessori, had the problem that local Montessori societies were springing up around the country that neither Montessori nor the association had approved. In an attempt to regulate these independent, autonomous organizations, the association's board of trustees recommended on April 7, 1914, that "Affiliated societies may be organized elsewhere than in the District of Columbia, in which case every member of such society shall be a member of the Association." These affiliated societies were to follow rules in their governance approved by the association's Board of Trustees and were to be designated as "Montessori Educational Association," followed by their local name.[20]

In October 1914, the Montessori Educational Association's Executive Committee considered two matters that caused conflict earlier between McClure and Montessori: Montessori training courses in the United States and the House of Childhood. Anne George reported that "in accordance with Dr. Montessori's wish to conduct a training-course in this country she had induced the New York University to make a most liberal offer for that purpose; but that Dr. Montessori had preferred a counter-proposition by Mrs. Roger Boyle that she should give a course of lectures at the American University." The matter became further complicated when Mrs. Boyle, who was invited to attend the meeting, read a letter expressing in general terms the American University's desire to arrange a lecture course by Dr. Montessori. Boyle also said that she had received a cable from Dr. Montessori, giving her approval, and asking her to complete arrangements. At this point, Anne George read a letter from Montessori "placing the matter in her hands" but "urging" an "immediate decision." Mrs. Boyle responded that Chancellor Franklin Hamilton of the American University was "out of town and had refused to discuss the matter before his return." The Executive Committee instructed George to write to the chancellor and urge him to make a definite offer.[21]

The Executive Committee next took up William Morrow's concern, brought to it by Anne George, that the association keeps "entirely independent of the Montessori's Children's House." The Children's House was a reference to the House of Childhood Company. The committee instructed its secretary to write to Mr. Morrow that "such distinction existed and should be maintained absolutely."[22] (For the persistent issue of the House of Childhood, see chapter 8, "The Montessori-McClure Breakup.")

On November 2, 1914, Anne George received a letter, presumably from Chancellor Hamilton, that the American University had not yet opened and that classes would not begin for at least another year. George was told, "You can without hesitation advise Madame Montessori that there is no possibility of the institution being able to pay her for any lectures this winter. While perhaps the University might be glad to have her give some lectures, there is not the remotest possibility that they will be able to make her any payment for them."[23]

The unresolved matter of the association's sponsorship of a training course or lectures by Montessori continued. It was further complicated when it was learned that Montessori might be coming to California. William Knowles Cooper, the General Secretary of the YMCA and a member of the Montessori Educational Association's Board of Trustees, wrote to Gilbert Grosvenor, the association's treasurer, on November 10, 1914, informing him that two friends of the Montessori movement, Mrs. Boyle of Georgetown and Mrs. Hitz of Chevy Chase, had contacted him regarding Montessori's proposed visit to the United States. Cooper wrote, "As I understand it, Dr. Montessori is prepared, indeed I think anxious, to come to this country during this winter. She has so assured Mrs. Boyle. Moreover, I understand, she has entered into correspondence with supporters of her movement in California and perhaps other states."

Cooper advised Grosvenor that Mrs. Boyle "is of the opinion that the Montessori Educational Association ought to take notice of this desire on the part of Dr. Montessori and give direction to the proposed visit." However, Mrs. Boyle has the impression from Mrs. Bell that the association would not assume responsibility for Montessori's visit. Cooper concluded his letter with the recommendation that the Board of Trustees meet in the near future to determine a definite course of action.

Next in the sequence of events was the calling of a special meeting of the Montessori Educational Association on November 28, 1914, chaired by John Larner, the vice president, rather than Mrs. Bell. Both Anne George and Mrs. Boyle reported on their correspondence with Montessori. After discussion, Margaret Wilson moved the following resolution that passed unanimously: "That this meeting suggest to the Board of Trustees of the Montessori Educational Association the advisability of appointing a representative committee to correspond with Doctor Montessori with reference to a visit from her to this country, to canvass the situation and ascertain where her services could be most helpfully employed."[24] A meeting of the board of trustees was set for December 10.

Prior to the December meeting of the Board of Trustees, Gilbert Grosvenor, the Bells' son-in-law, on December 4 at his wife Elsie's request, wrote to Mabel Bell about his apprehension should Montessori return to the United States. His very candid letter provides thoughtful insights not only about Montessori's relationships to Mrs. Bell and the association but also to Montessori's earlier break with McClure. In his letter, addressing Mrs. Bell, his mother-in-law, as "Dear Little Mother," Grosvenor wrote:

> Personally, I think Montessori can advance her own cause better staying in Italy than by coming to America. <u>This, however, is a matter for her to decide</u>, and I understand she has decided to come to America. Therefore we should not oppose her, <u>but do what we can to help her</u>.
>
> It is going to be very difficult to have any business dealings with a woman of her peculiar disposition. She is undoubtedly a genius and has all the irresponsibility's of a genius, but at the same time she seems to me of a very suspicious nature. I should hate very much to have any business dealings

> with her, and I should be sorry if you had any with her. We do not talk Italian and all conversations with her must be made through an interpreter.
>
> She seems to me to lack the faculty of knowing who her friends are. We all know Mr. McClure's weaknesses, but I think his promotion of Madame Montessori and her ideas was entirely altruistic. She owes her entire success to him, and yet, because she thought he ought to have sent her $100 more than he actually did send, she writes him a most insulting letter and discontinues all dealings with him. This action on her part, in my judgment, is inexcusable. McClure obtained for her a profit of $3,600 for a lecture tour in the worst month of the year, namely-December. This profit was net, and to it should be added all her expenses from Italy and in America, including the expenses of a maid, etc.
>
> Furthermore, I don't like the way Madame Montessori has conducted herself with Miss George. She asked Miss George to arrange a course of lectures for her, and then goes right over Miss George's head and makes a tentative agreement with somebody whom she had never heard of before. I refer to Mrs. Boyle. The result has been that everything had been tied up, and considerable hard feeling has developed in Washington which was very evident at the meeting last week.
>
> My hope is that if Montessori comes to America you will retire as President of the Association. You gave the Association the benefit of your name and experiences and financial help at a time when it sorely needed it. But the situation will be very different when Montessori reaches America. She will then be the whole movement in America, and I am afraid there may be unpleasantness. Anyway you would be worried to death over her uncertainties and idiosyncrasies and her utter lack of responsibility.
>
> I think it will be much better for some business man like Mr. Conklin or Mr. Morrow—some man in New York to become President of the Association. You could give it the benefit of your counsel as a member of the Board. Of course, you would not state that your retirement was caused by Montessori's coming to America. The movement is so far along now that what is needed is a good business administration of the Montessori patents, etc. The educational mission of the Association will be superseded or taken over by Madame Montessori herself.[25]

(For a detailed account of the financial issues between McClure and Montessori to which Grosvenor referred, see chapter 8, "The Montessori-McClure Breakup.")

On December 10, Mrs. Bell presided over a meeting of the Montessori Educational Association's board of trustees that adopted Margaret Wilson's motion authorizing a special committee: "To communicate with Dr. Montessori to insure the execution of her wishes and plans; To communicate with the friends of Dr. Montessori and to cooperate with them in making plans for her work in this country; To present plans when formulated to the Board of Trustees and also present to the Board of Trustees plan for raising money for the work of Dr. Montessori while in America."[26]

Despite the association's efforts to reach an accord with Montessori on her second visit to the United States, matters drifted with a great deal of uncertainty. Grosvenor's reading of future events regarding Montessori's relationship to Mrs. Bell and the Montessori Educational Association were keenly prophetic. When Montessori returned to the United States in 1915, the Montessori Movement centered entirely on her. Her relationship to the association remained confused, conflicted, and aloof. She either did not understand or did not like the American approach to shared decision-making as practiced by the well-meaning Bells and others in their association.

Although Mrs. Bell had witnessed how Montessori's relationship with McClure and George had soured, she kept her commitment to the Montessori Method and sought to improve the organization's relationship with Montessori.[27] Firmly believing in the Montessori Method's educational efficacy, Mabel Bell was desperately searching for a way to cooperate with its originator. She and her husband, Alexander Graham Bell, had established Montessori schools at their estate in Nova Scotia and in Washington, DC.

Despite Grosvenor's warnings, Mabel Bell still believed that she could salvage the Montessori Educational Association's relationship with Montessori. Thus, she sent a representative, Bailey Willis (1857–1949), whose wife, Margaret, was a member of the association, to meet with Montessori in San Francisco.[28] Willis, a distinguished geological engineer, was a recognized expert on seismology, especially earthquakes. From 1884 to 1915, he headed the Areal Division of the US Geological Survey; from 1915 to 1922, he was a professor and chairman of Stanford University's geology department. On August 21, 1915, Mabel Bell wrote to Willis about his forthcoming meeting with Montessori: "Since its beginning I have heard of increased friction with the Dottoressa & her disavowal of us. All this requires consideration and I await with interest the result of your interview with her, but so far I have heard nothing that alters any opinion of her as expressed here. She has done much for little children. Much therefore must be forgiven her. You of course will know how to uphold our dignity."[29]

Although Willis's specific purpose in meeting with Montessori in San Francisco was to assess her attitude to the Montessori Educational Association, his correspondence with Mrs. Bell provides not only a clear account of Montessori's attitude toward the Montessori Educational Association but also a highly insightful analysis of Montessori's personality and her behavior.[30] It can also be read as a prescient retrospective on why Montessori's relationship with McClure ended as it did.

Willis met with Montessori in late August 1915 at a house that Montessori had rented in San Francisco. As agreed to in advance, Montessori and Willis communicated with each other in French. Willis, with the scientific objectivity that characterized his research in geology, listed the major issues he intended to discuss with Montessori:

> (1) the factors in the educational problem in America, namely, the people to be educated, the pedagogs [sic] to be convinced, the Montessori teachers to be directed; (2) the need of co-operation and the value of societies in accomplishing that end; (3) the exploitation of Dr. Montessori's name by unauthorized persons for personal advantage; (4) the teaching of mixed Montessori and kindergarten or other methods; (5) the "Washington" Association, its purpose, organization, Montessori (?) work, and possible dissolution; (6) Dr. Montessori's ideas or plans for organizing a center and local societies; (7) Dr. Montessori's relation to the proposed center and societies and to the Montessori Educational Association.[31]

These issues had arisen but had gone unresolved during the three years (1911–1914) when McClure had been promoting Montessori and her method. McClure, who enthusiastically jumped from one idea to another, was not temperamentally suited to dealing with them systematically. The Montessori American Committee and the Montessori Educational Association had been established to promote generally Montessori education in the United States, but their specific functions were never well-defined. McClure, who knew the value of enlisting the support of wealthy and well-known individuals, believed the Montessori Educational Association would give his promotion of Montessori academic respectability. Montessori, herself, did not want to share control of her method with others, especially an association. Suspicious and controlling, Montessori believed she had been exploited by individuals like McClure, Byoir, and Dorothy Canfield Fisher. Neither would Montessori let others share in the training of Montessori directresses.

Willis's strategy was to raise these difficult issues indirectly rather than head on, "One does not talk to a brilliant Italian woman, full of dignity adorned with feminine graces, in terms of a table of contents, so the above is rather my analysis of what we did talk about than any record of the sequence. . . . Dr. Montessori's attitude was one of well-feigned ignorance of the Association's purposes, and of a desire to be informed. She was sincerely anxious about the misuse of her name, the purity of her method. She repeatedly said she did not want the Association to dissolve. She expressed a high regard for Mrs. Bell, and incidentally remarked that she did not know the other people associated with her. "[32] However, Montessori had met several of the members of the Association when she spoke in Washington and had been a guest at the Bells' home. For example, she had a meeting with Philander Claxton, the US Commissioner of Education, and had been escorted on a tour of Washington, DC, by Margaret Wilson. Both Claxton and Wilson were on the Association's Board of Trustees. She, of course, knew Alexander Graham Bell, and Gilbert Grosvenor, the Bells' son-in-law.

Willis proved adept at analyzing the woman who sat across from him. He wrote that: "At no point did she take the lead. She has a way, that might be disconcerting to some people, of remaining silent, contemplating what has just been said, with an absolutely non-committal expression, for so long that you wonder whether she has understood."[33] In retrospect, one can imagine how the irrepressible and voluble McClure must have dealt with Montessori's silences. If he had taken time to consider them, he most likely interpreted Montessori's reticence as signifying agreement with his plans.

Willis continued his analysis of Montessori: "I studied her closely and tried to understand her position. She has both principle and method which she considers hers. She anticipates both opposition to and more or less misuse of her method. She feels herself a stranger, facing unknown influences, distrustful of would-be friends. She is jealous, somewhat fanatical, independent, and intensely feminine. She demands a loyalty to her ideas, which is perhaps not consciously a demand for loyalty to her person; but she is very exacting and critical, although she herself suffers when she feels that anyone whom she cares for, like Miss George, has failed her. She will be neither practical, nor reasonable, nor constant in her relations. Yet relations with her there must be, amicable or otherwise, and preferably amicable. And my object is to establish them."[34]

Returning to his stated purpose, Willis brought up the issue that was so sensitive to Montessori: the exploitation of her name "by unauthorized persons for personal advantage." Stating that he was representing "the American Montessori Educational Association," Willis said he "took a chance and said that I knew neither Mrs. Bell nor any other officer would be willing to use the name unless the Association truly represented her principles, and she, as I had anticipated" stated that she did not wish the Association to change its name.[35]

However, Montessori complained that the Montessori Educational Association had been established without her knowledge, consultation, and approval. She claimed she did not know its officers, its by-laws, and its organization. Responding to the challenge, Willis wrote: "Knowing beforehand that she had said that it would be most unfortunate if the Association bearing her name should dissolve,

I told her boldly that some of the officers were inclined to advocate that action unless an understanding could be reached with her."[36]

Montessori, obviously prepared for the issue of her affiliation with the Montessori Educational Association, handed Willis a memorandum, "General Regulations for the Formation of an Authorized Montessori Society." Telling Willis that the memorandum was provisional, she asked him to consider the relationship of the Montessori Educational Association to her plan and to suggest possible changes. Thinking that the "General Regulations" might provide the association with some guidelines, Willis said he would forward the document to Mrs. Bell for her consideration.

As he continued his discussion with Montessori, Willis said, "I made her say she had no organization, no editor, no plan, and pushed her to the statement that 'I am of a special temperament. I can do some things but not all. I cannot organize.'" Sensitive to Montessori's insecurity that unauthorized individuals would distort her ideas, Willis suggested that the association's journal might contain a statement that "Dr. Montessori is not responsible for the views on education expressed in the articles accepted by the Editor . . . unless signed by her." Then Willis asked Montessori for an article on the educational situation in America, on the training courses, and the advanced materials. Although he thought that Montessori was pleased with his suggestions, she did not commit herself.[37]

Willis raised the increasingly delicate issue of Anne George's relationship with Montessori. George, the first American trained by Montessori as a directress, had played important roles in the introduction of Montessori education to the United States. She had established the first Montessori school in the country and was in charge of the Bells' school in Washington; she had translated the English-language edition of *The Montessori Method*; she was the author of articles on the Montessori Method that appeared in *McClure's Magazine* and *Good Housekeeping*; she stood by Montessori's side as her translator for the 1913 lectures. George, who tried to remain a Montessori purist, was also a personal friend of S. S. and Hattie McClure, the directress of the Montessori school sponsored by the Bells in Washington and the Montessori Educational Association's Director of Research. Now, there were signs that Montessori had grown suspicious about George's loyalty.

Pointedly, Willis asked Montessori if she had confidence in Miss George. Montessori, he said, answered the question slowly and with some feeling, replying "Oui, j'ai beaucoup de confiance en Miss George." Willis said he told Montessori "that the Association had consistently regarded Miss George as her authorized exponent, and that if either Miss George or the Association had failed to represent her correctly, it had been involuntary and because we had not known what her wishes might be."[38]

After an hour and a half, the meeting between Montessori and Willis ended. In his notes, Willis wrote, "For myself, I enjoyed it. The fine presence, the feminine subtlety, the defensive merriment, the deep sense of purpose, the contemplative thought, the quick response to a flash of mutual suggestion, marked her as an infinitely variable personality, with whom discussion was as dangerous as it was fascinating. Possibly the door has been opened a little to something of an understanding."[39] However, when Willis and Mrs. Bell had the opportunity to study Montessori's "General Regulations," they would see that the door was closing rather than opening on the possibility of future cooperation with the Dottoressa. Montessori's "General Regulations for the Formation of an Authorized Montessori Society" indicates Montessori's need to control; further, it specifies as much what a Montessori association cannot do as to what it can do.

The section, "Condition of Authorization," stated: "In order to form an authorized Montessori Association it is necessary that one or more of the proposed members be graduates, that they hold a certificate of work completed under Dr. Montessori herself from the year 1913 and on—i.e. from the time of the first International Course held in Rome—and bearing her signature or official seal after said date."[40] This was especially pointed at Anne George who was the association's director of Montessori work. In a bold move, Montessori attempted to remove George and the early group of Montessori teachers trained before 1913 from organizing or having any role in Montessori societies in the United States. In addition, Montessori wanted to ensure that she alone directed all programs that trained American Montessori teachers. In 1915, there were a growing number of Montessori teachers in the United States. Many had been trained by Montessori and others were self-styled imitators of her method.

The "Bylaws" stated, "Each Chapter shall defend the Montessori Method from false interpretation and in so far as possible, guarantee the integrity of its application. It shall also help to spread the method by every possible means."[41] The section on "Necessary Members" stated, "The society should at once seek to have among its members lawyers, that they may study the legal questions relative: 1. To the legal defense of the Method, of the name Montessori and of the rights of the graduates in order that no school or society may assume the name of Montessori without authorization."[42]

The section, "Montessori Schools" specified that "Such schools shall be held only by a Montessori graduate and they must be exponents of the pure Montessori Method without any admixture of other methods, without additions or modifications."[43] The section on the "Bulletin," specified that "No society shall be authorized to publish a bulletin. The bulletin must come from the Center." Montessori specified that the '"Center" meant the "office of Dr. Maria Montessori herself and is the place where the method continues to be developed under her direction and work."[44]

Montessori's "Regulations" made her intentions perfectly clear about the direction of Montessori education in the United States. Her memorandum reflected her experiences with McClure who had organized a "Montessori Committee," without her approval. While McClure, always eager to act, had thrived on ambiguity, Montessori, with a controlling personality, wanted specificity in her relationships, not open-endedness. She wanted it understood that as the Montessori Method's originator and patent-holder, the method was legally hers alone. No local society would be allowed to use the name "Montessori" in its title without her expressed authorization. Unlike her past relationship with McClure, any future promotion of her method in the United States was to be based on a "just and righteous propaganda" that included "public lectures, benefits, popular meetings," and "visiting days" in authorized Montessori schools so that her method could be observed and accurately reported in articles in newspapers and magazines.

As McClure had learned, Mabel and Alexander Graham Bell were now learning that Montessori was a woman with a strong, determined, and controlling personality. She had created the educational method that bore her name, and she alone would control Montessori education as a movement. Determined to maintain the Montessori Method in its unadulterated state, La Dottoressa had to protect it from those who would exploit it, like McClure, and from those who might misinterpret it like Dorothy Canfield Fisher. She also made it clear that she did not intend to incorporate other methods such as the kindergarten into her method.

On September 25, 1915, Mabel Bell, shocked by Montessori's "Regulations," wrote to Willis, "I must confess to you on the spur of the moment that nothing I have seen or heard so far had so completely discouraged and revolted me as this paper. . . . It is throughout so illiberal, so at variance with my conception of all the Montessori idea stands for that I simply do not know how to go on any further." How can any seeker after Truth say that a method must be held 'without additions or modifications'? . . . Montessori herself is reported . . . as having said, 'If it is not experimental, it is not my method.' Also in the early days she did not want it called the Montessori Method; she wanted it called the scientific method. . . . Neither she nor any one mind, however wonderful, has the monopoly of scientific ways of doing things. Therefore she could not then have claimed any exclusive property in her principles. All she has the right to claim is the patent right to her apparatus"[45]

Mrs. Bell then turned to the crucial issue of the Montessori Educational Association's relationship to Montessori. "I suppose she has the right to refuse the use of her name; and if so I do not see how we can continue to use it without submitting to all her conditions and that I certainly for one will not do."

Mrs. Bell was especially saddened by Montessori's treatment of Anne George. She had long worked with George, the directress at the Bells' school in Washington and the Association's designated Director of Montessori Work. Calling George Montessori's "best and greatest graduate," she found Montessori's treatment of George to be especially painful. Montessori's "utter ingratitude and lack of justice" for Miss George's "faithful" work was shown by the "careful way in which Miss George is barred out from any participation in the proposed new organization! I don't know how to pardon that."

Showing her dismay, Mrs. Bell told Willis, "That Dr. Montessori should want to be the directress of Montessori work as long as she remains in the country is perfectly legitimate and Miss George would be the first to admit it and I the second, but that she should so deliberately affront and disavow an association from whom she has in the past received so much help and under whose auspices she herself elected to visit America is more than I feel prepared to condone now. . . . To think of Miss George's slaving for her during those weeks of traveling, acting as ladies maid, secretary and general protector and nurse, of our own real loss in the efficiency of our school, and know that it all counts for nothing as she proposes to employ lawyers and business men to defend her against us."[46]

Despite Montessori's efforts to curtail the activities of the Montessori Educational Association, Mabel Bell was still not ready to depart from the Montessori scene,

> I am going on with the schools I and my friends have established and will continue to do all I can to persuade other parents to bring up their children in the principles for which Dr. Montessori's name has become synonymous, and to use the didactic material invented by her, for I think it is so far the best that I know of. But I wish it did not have to bear her name. Nevertheless I think I should fight to retain it, because it had become identified with these principles and whether she admits it or not, we are carrying on her method and we are carrying it on in all its purity, even when we do add to it or modify it so long as we adhere to the ideal of Freedom for the Child. To yield it now would be to cast discredit on all our previous work, upon all Miss George's loyalty and devotion. Further consideration and advice may alter my ideas as to what is our best course, but at present my feeling is to continue our claim to be the Montessori Educational Association and our schools true Montessori Case dei Bambini, whatever the Dottoressa says.[47]

Another significant but not overtly stated issue in Montessori's relationship with the association was her need to attract funding for her educational activities. When she began cooperating with McClure, Montessori had anticipated that the publisher's personal connections would bring financial support from American philanthropists for the international educational institute she wanted to establish in Rome. Early in her negotiations with McClure, Montessori had pointedly hinted that the American association might emulate the Montessori society in the United Kingdom, which had pledged financial support of her plan to establish her institute in Rome.

By 1915, Montessori was pondering how to attract funding in the United States. Just before her departure from New York to conduct a training course and school in Barcelona on December 8, Montessori dealt with the funding issue. She authorized the establishment of the National Montessori Promotion Fund, with herself as president, and her new trusted American associate, Helen Parkhurst (1887–1973), as her designated representative. With her own American Promotion Fund in place, financial support, Montessori hoped, would come directly to her rather than indirectly through other channels over which she had no control.

At this point, twenty-eight-year-old Parkhurst, not Mrs. Bell or the experienced Anne George, became Montessori's designated deputy in the United States. Parkhurst replaced the faithful Anne George as Montessori's foremost American disciple and spokesperson. Despite her youth, Parkhurst was not a novice in education. When she met Montessori in 1914, Parkhurst had been a teacher of children in the primary grades and had been an educator of primary school teachers. Born in 1887 in Durand, a small Wisconsin town, she had earned her bachelor of science degree from the State College, at River Falls, in 1907. She also matriculated from Columbia University's Teachers College in 1909. Parkhurst taught in rural schools in Wisconsin from 1907 to 1909 and in the primary grades at the Edison School in Tacoma, Washington, from 1909 to 1911, where she began her experiments with the "laboratory method." She had entered teacher education as the Supervisor of Primary Teacher Training, from 1911–1913 at the State Teachers College at Ellensburg, Washington, and then as Director of Primary Training at the State Teachers College at Stevens Point, Wisconsin, from 1913–1915. In 1914, she was granted a leave of absence from Stevens Point to study anthropology at the University of Rome. While in Rome, she attended Montessori's international training course. She was granted a second leave to serve as Montessori's assistant at the Panama-Pacific International Exposition in 1915.[48] Taking notice of the intellectually alert and engaging "ebullient young woman with a quick smile," Montessori affectionately called Parkhurst "Margherita."[49]

Like many other directresses, such as Anne George, whom Montessori had trained, Parkhurst left Rome personally committed to Montessori and her method. In her lectures, Parkhurst told her audiences of teachers and parents, "Perhaps no one person is more interested nor has done more to prepare the young child efficiently and practically for life than has the great Italian physician and educator—Maria Montessori. She is many persons in one—her vision is broad, and her aim is not that the child should learn certain cut and dried facts and principles about life, but that he should perfect himself in such a manner that he shall attain the highest possible efficiency of which his personality is capable."[50]

Defending Montessori against her critics, Parkhurst said, "These facts should be considered in the face of the attacks of those educators who have never really studied the method, who do not understand the material, who have not read a single book by the great doctor teacher, and have never visited a school in Rome but who are trying to uphold and protect a faulty system of their own, by condemning and enlarging small imperfections in the great work of others."[51]

After Montessori had completed her assignment in California in November 1915, Parkhurst was making arrangements for her to lecture and conduct a training course at the Teachers College in Steven's Point, Wisconsin. A local committee of forty prominent citizens and businessmen had been established to promote the course to raise funds. The committee needed to raise "approximately $10,000, of which $6,000 or $ 7,000 would be paid to the madame and her corps of assistants" and the balance used for advertising and other expenses. The committee projected that "one hundred students can be secured for the course, each of whom would pay a tuition fee of $100."[52] The indefatigable Anne George even expressed interest in attending the course. George wrote, "The work of Dr. Montessori is to me the most important factor in the world's program today, and my own personal life is completely bound up with its study and development. I studied with Dr. Montessori for eight months in Rome in 1911–12. I wish to take the advanced course whenever it is given. If I can be of any service to you in making the course known, please call upon me."[53] The Steven's Point course did not materialize, because Montessori accepted an offer from regional authorities in Catalonia to provide a training course and establish a school in Barcelona.

With Montessori in Spain, Parkhurst, acting as her official representative, was designated as corresponding secretary of the National Montessori Promotion Fund and as the US Montessori supervisor.[54] Though Parkhurst was educationally prepared for her role, negotiating her way through the confusing situation with the Montessori Educational Association and other Montessori societies in the United States was challenging. Perhaps, even more challenging, as McClure had discovered, was the difficulty in maintaining good relationships with La Dottoressa. Further, Parkhurst, not content to be another person's disciple, had her own ambitions for her future.

In 1915, there were two national Montessori organizations functioning in the United States—Montessori's newly created National Montessori Promotion Fund and the older Montessori Educational Association, which McClure, the Bells, and Anne George had organized in 1912. Unlike the typical educational movement, Montessori education remained focused on its very evident founder, Maria Montessori. With dual but unclear roles in promoting the method, tensions developed between the National Montessori Promotion Fund and the Montessori Educational Association. Without Montessori's approval, the continued existence of the association was tenuous at best. On December 18, 1915, at a meeting of the association, Gilbert Grosvenor, who had earlier warned his mother-in-law about the futility of trying to work with Montessori, moved that the Montessori Educational Association disband. Action on his motion was delayed while Anne George attempted to consult with Montessori.[55] George's efforts failed, and in April 1916, the Montessori Educational Association officially voted to dissolve. Reorganized as the Montessori Association of the District of Columbia, it refocused its activities on supporting Montessori schools in Washington, DC. Mrs. Bell, Grosvenor, and many of their former colleagues in the association continued to work on behalf of the schools, in which Anne George was the principal directress.

On June 10, 1919, Anne Everett George married Robert Wyness Millar, a law professor at Northwestern University in Evanston, Illinois. Known after her marriage as Anne George Millar, she was no longer actively involved in Montessori education. She died in Evanston in August 1973.

As Montessori's officially and legally delegated representative in the United States, Parkhurst, though energetic, had difficulty in coordinating the autonomous local and state Montessori societies, schools, teachers, and publications. Lacking any recognized accreditation, she had little power to supervise Montessori schools and teachers. However, Parkhurst was more successful in establishing and running her own schools than in reining in an unwieldy educational movement that was on a downward trajectory. She established the Children's University School in New York City, in 1916, where she experimented with her own plan for a redesigned school that featured educational laboratories and individualized learning.

From 1917 through 1918, Parkhurst trained directresses at the Montessori Teachers Training College in New York. Montessori had opened the Montessori Teachers Training College in October 1916 and gave some lectures on her method, according to Professor Frank Cyr in his introduction to a 1966 reprint of Parkhurst's *Education on the Dalton Plan*. He also indicated that Montessori was present when the first class graduated in 1918, after which Parkhurst resigned from Montessori education to devote herself to her Children's School.[56] However, Kramer, in her definitive biography of Montessori, simply states that Montessori returned several times to the United States "on unpublicized personal visits, the last one in 1918."[57]

Instead of acting as Montessori's American surrogate, Parkhurst's attention shifted to developing and promoting her own version of Progressive education, the Dalton Laboratory Plan. Prior to her association with Montessori, Parkhurst had taught in one-room ungraded rural schools in Wisconsin with large classes of forty pupils. Seeking to manage students of different ages and abilities, she experimented with arrangements in which some pupils worked individually on their subjects while she guided a small group of students in investigating a particular topic. Pursuing her interest in individualized and small group instruction, Parkhurst, as a teacher educator, developed a plan for a reorganized school in which pupils, between eight and twelve, worked on a unit in a particular subject in educational laboratories. In this new type of school, pupils "would enjoy more freedom" and "their studies" would be organized into sections, or laboratories, in which "each instructor" would be a specialist. Her goal was "to equalize the pupil's individual difficulties and to provide the same opportunity for advancement, to the slow as to the bright child."[58]

In her explanation of the origins of the Dalton Plan, Parkhurst provided a brief account of her involvement in Montessori education. It is interesting that Parkhurst's published one-paragraph account of her association with Montessori, like McClure's short description of his involvement with Montessori in his autobiography, was succinct, terse, and to the point. Parkhurst related that she received a leave from the College at Stevens Point to "go to Italy to investigate the Montessori Method. After that experience I acted as Dr. Montessori's assistant, and while a member of her household I attended four training courses. . . . Between December 1915 and January 1918, having accepted the charge of looking after Dr. Montessori's interests in America, I was obliged to abandon temporarily my experiments with the laboratory idea. But I eagerly resumed them after resigning this charge with the financial support of the Child Education Foundation, which I at that time directed."[59]

Although Parkhurst's educational laboratory concept was oriented to older students of junior high and high school age, it had some parallels to Montessori's emphasis on the freedom of younger children to choose what they wanted to learn. Parkhurst's principle that "the pupil must be free to continue his work upon any subject in which he is absorbed without interruption, because when interested he is mentally keener, more alert, and more capable of mastering any difficulty that may arise in his course of study" resembled the child's freedom to choose his work in the Montessori school. Although Parkhurst's aim to reorganize the school "so that it can function like a community whose essential condition is freedom for the individual to develop himself" had a Montessori-like resonance, she positioned herself as a Progressive educator rather than a Montessorian.[60]

Ernest Jackman, principal of Dalton High School in Dalton, Massachusetts, invited Parkhurst to implement her plan in 1920. In practice, the subjects in the curriculum were divided into units, or "jobs." The student, who signed a contract to complete a particular job within a month, worked cooperatively with other students who had made similar commitments in an educational space, called a laboratory. Each student worked from a "job-book," a guide with instructions, suggestions, questions, and activities related to the monthly contract.[61] The laboratory plan broke the larger classes into smaller groups that, pursuing the same unit or job, engaged in collaborative work. Each laboratory had a teacher, a specialist, to guide the students' progress in completing that job. Though taught according to Parkhurst's Progressive method, the standard secondary curriculum—mathematics, history, science, English, geography, and foreign languages—required in most high schools and tested on college entrance examinations— remained in place.[62] However, the co-relationship of subjects, such as literature to history and science to mathematics, was emphasized as integrated, not isolated, areas of teaching and learning. Based on her work at the Massachusetts school, Parkhurst renamed her method the Dalton Laboratory Plan.

Belle Rennie, a British educator who visited Dalton High School, described the Dalton Laboratory Plan in a highly positive article in the *London Times Educational Supplement* in May 1920. Parkhurst's ideas gained considerable popularity in the United Kingdom where they were implemented in several British schools.[63] In July 1921, Parkhurst arrived in England and spoke about her plan to large and enthusiastic audiences. Her book, *Education on the Dalton Plan*, was published in 1922 in both the United Kingdom and the United States.[64]

The sudden popularity of Parkhurst's Dalton Plan and her movement away from Montessori education did not set well with Maria Montessori. As someone who did not take kindly to revisionists or deviationists from what she regarded as her true method, Montessori now regarded her once trusted protégé as a betrayer.[65] In 1913, Montessori had responded to what she regarded as a similar challenge from Dorothy Canfield Fisher by publishing a letter in the *New York Times* in which she said that Fisher's Montessori Method was not a true version of her method. As Parkhurst's Dalton Plan gained popularity in the United Kingdom, Montessori, in 1922, dispatched a "Circular to the Montessori Societies of Great Britain, labeled "PRIVATE—not to be published." Montessori wrote:

> The sum of my researches may be regarded as an attempt to specify and give precision to a system of pedagogy which shall *correspond exactly* to the *psy-*

> *chology of the child.* It represents, therefore, a departure from the sphere of discussion and theory concerning the emancipation of childhood, in that it *provides the means,* whereby many of the ideas of today of these means, or of the techniques of my method in general, is therefore a retrograde step, depriving my work of that which alone renders it of value. Furthermore, a pedagogy bearing such a relationship to psychic facts, cannot be altered at will.
>
> While, therefore, all are undoubtedly free in their attitude to the many suggested reforms of to-day, the sole justification for the existence of a Society bearing my name is that there should be persons who believe in the efficacy of those methods which I have evolved, and who also desire to propagate these methods in all their integrity.
>
> Therefore, such Societies should endeavour to uphold this aspect of my work, and should do everything possible to prevent confusion in the public mind between this method and others which are fundamentally different, such as the Dalton Plan, "Auto-education in general, "Individual Work," etc., or vague generalizations.
>
> May I call upon all Montessori Societies to do their utmost, not in the sense of depreciating contemporary effort—that would be an offense against freedom itself—but to protect my work from a confusion and a degeneration which would destroy its only value. Signed: MARIA MONTESSORI.[66]

Montessori's Circular echoed her "General Regulations for the Formation of an Authorized Montessori Society" governing authentic Montessori societies that she had handed to Bailey Willis in 1915 in San Francisco. In the Circular, aimed at Parkhurst and her Dalton Plan, Montessori was asserting that educational approaches that claimed to exalt the freedom of the child were an insufficient shadow of her true method, which was based on the psychology of the child.

A copy of Montessori's Circular reached Parkhurst. In a handwritten note on a letter to Dr. Michael O'Shea, a professor at the University of Wisconsin, on November 29, 1922, Parkhurst wrote, "I'm sending you a startling announcement of Montessori's that signs her death warrant as she says *her* contribution is her "*material*." At the bottom of the Circular sent to O'Shea, Parkhurst penned, "The above (including headings) is an exact copy of one just received from London. Isn't it queer that —anyone isn't willing to be helpful with principles and not insist on *materials.* By '*means*' she means materials. HP"[67]

On December 11, 1922, Professor O'Shea responded to Parkhurst, "That circular letter from Dr. Montessori is pathetic, isn't it? I am exceedingly sorry that she has taken the attitude toward the Dalton Plan that she has taken. I suppose, though, it was really inevitable. I have no doubt you will be able to deal with the situation so as to avoid an unseemly personal conflict. Evidently Dr. Montessori feels that she and her system are in danger of being eclipsed."[68]

Deciding that she would no longer delegate authority for Montessori education to others, Montessori, with her son, Mario, as her agent, established the Association Montessori Internationale (AMI) in 1929 as the official organization to control and supervise all Montessori activities, including training programs, throughout the world. The AMI controlled rights to the publication of Montessori's books, recognition of schools, organization of conferences, the manufacture and sale of the materials, and training course fees.[69] In 1936, she made Amsterdam the Association's headquarters where it remains today.

Montessori's lecture tours and the growing number of Montessori schools established between 1910 and 1920 constituted the first wave of Montessori education in the United States. This initial entry of Montessori education in the United States was marked by some short-term successes, but it also revealed serious weaknesses that would jeopardize its long-term success. Montessori's name and method had reached an American audience. She enjoyed the support of some prominent and influential persons, mainly journalists and public figures, who, however, were not well positioned in the educational and academic communities. Although a number of teachers, journalists, and lay people were receptive to Montessori, her impact on the educational establishment—the public schools and the colleges of education—was slight. Montessori's pedagogy failed to make a significant impact on educational psychology as it was conceived of in departments and schools of education in the United States during the first half of the twentieth century.[70] The educational historian W. F. Connell critically assessed her work as a "curious mixture of perceptive and liberal ideas with traditional and mystical nonsense."[71]

By 1920, the first wave of enthusiasm for Montessori education was ebbing severely. The Montessori Method failed to enter the mainstream of American teacher education at the very time when education was being firmly established as a field in American universities. Neither did it enter in any significant way into public schools in the United States. The Montessori school would be located at the periphery of the public educational system but in the 1950s would gain a strong presence in private early childhood education.

Beginning with the 1950s, a second and much more substantial wave of Montessori education occurred in the United States. This second American Montessori movement would lead to the establishment of hundreds of Montessori schools throughout the United States. The Montessori Method was rediscovered by parents seeking a more academically oriented early childhood school than available in many public school kindergartens or Progressive private schools. By the mid-1950s, Progressive education, which had eclipsed the first attempt to introduce the Montessori Method in 1910–1920, was itself declining.

Nancy McCormick Rambusch, founder of the Whitby School in Greenwich, Connecticut, became the central figure in the Montessori revival.[72] Rambusch, who had taken the Montessori training course in England in 1954, believed the method needed to be modernized to incorporate new developments in education and readapted to correspond to American culture. Between 1958 and 1963, when over four hundred Montessori schools were established, Rambusch vigorously led the Montessori revival.[73] The American Montessori Society also conducted training courses, one of the problematic issues during the McClure-Montessori relationship. The AMI, headed by Mario Montessori, was critical of the American version of the method on the grounds that it was deviating from his mother's original ideas and philosophy.

In the second wave of Montessori education in the United States, the demand for Montessori schools exceeded the supply of trained Montessori directresses. As a result, schools and teacher preparation programs proliferated without any accreditation standards. While some schools held closely to Montessori's original method, others made more flexible revisions. As a result of differing perspectives, two organizations came to represent Montessori education in the United States: the Association Montessori Internationale (AMI), which had been founded by Maria and Mario Montessori, and the American Montessori Society (AMS), which had developed from those identified with Nancy McCormick Rambusch.

This schism within Montessori education resembled issues that emerged during its first introduction to the United States when two organizations functioned: the Montessori Educational Association and the Montessori Promotion Fund. Mario Montessori's approach in dealing with the American Montessori Society was a version of Maria Montessori's efforts to guard and protect her method, insisting that only she could properly prepare teachers. Rebuffing those who sought to design a more flexible version of her method, Montessori was convinced that her ideas would be distorted unless implemented exactly as she had developed them.

When Montessori education first came to the United States, the kindergarten had already been institutionalized and was part of public and private education. It was not until its revival in the 1950s that Montessori education became more institutionalized. These Montessori institutions, which came after Maria Montessori's death, were constructed by the later generations of Montessori educators such as Nancy Rambusch in the 1950s, not by McClure, the Bells, and Anne George, the leaders of the first effort in the early twentieth century. Even in its second revival, Montessori education still remained largely outside of the public school systems, teacher education programs in colleges and universities, and state teacher certification requirements. Unlike the kindergarten, which became part of the public school system, Montessori educators, either by choice or necessity, had to create their own institutions, training programs, and approaches to teacher certification. Even when Montessori educators sought to develop organizations such as the International Montessori Association and the American Montessori Society rivalries and conflicts complicated its institutionalization. It would not be until the late twentieth century that Montessori education made a belated and very limited entry into public school systems.

With a few exceptions, Montessori training programs generally did not become part of teacher education programs in college and universities. In some cases, professors of education resisted Montessori education. Montessori's tendency to exert absolute control ran counter to the progressive trends in teacher education that emphasized experimentation, revision, and adaptation. Intent on keeping her method free from others who might alter it through revisions or adaptations, Montessori insisted that only she could train directresses, thus, during her life time, she controlled training programs.

Currently, approximately 6,000 Montessori schools are operating in the United States. Most of these schools are non-public institutions and primarily enroll children between the ages of two and six. The majority of schools offer early childhood and primary programs. A few schools offer programs for intermediate and upper-grade pupils. There has been a recent but still limited movement of the Montessori Method into the public school sector, with some five hundred Montessori magnet schools or divisions operating.[74] The recent trend to charter schools has aided interested groups of parents and teachers to establish Montessori schools in public school districts.

10

McClure and Montessori

The Later Years

After their relationship ended in 1914, McClure, who died in 1949 at the age of 92, lived for another thirty-five years. Montessori, who died in 1952, lived for thirty-eight years after she last saw McClure. The more than three decades since their last meeting took them down different paths. More widely known than Montessori in 1914, McClure, today, is remembered by a few scholars, namely specialists in the history of journalism or American Progressivism. Montessori, in contrast, enjoys a world-wide reputation, not only with educators but with a large audience of parents and students. This chapter that closes the story of the publisher and the pedagogue examines McClure's fading years as a once-famous American journalist and Montessori's rise to the status of an international personage.

During the eleven years that followed his break with Montessori, from 1914 to 1925, McClure's position as a publisher and editor steadily eroded even more. His decline began in 1906 when John Phillips, his closest and most reliable associate; Ida Tarbell, his star writer; and other staff members resigned from *McClure's Magazine*. McClure's financial problems accelerated when he had to reorganize his company to secure the funds to purchase the stock of the departing members of his staff. More than $400,000 in debt, McClure, who did not enjoy sharing authority, was forced by necessity to take Harold Roberts, a New York financier, as his business partner. McClure and Roberts had difficulty in sharing power; Roberts left the partnership in 1907. McClure's indebtedness, now estimated at half a million dollars, escalated, aggravated by a loan from the West Virginia Pulp Wood and Paper Company at sixteen percent interest.

By the fall of 1911, McClure overwhelmed by debt, reluctantly yielded the McClure Company to a board of trustees, headed by Frederick Collins and McClure's son-in-law, Cameron Mackenzie.[1] No longer owner and publisher of the magazine he had founded, McClure, for a time, was retained as the nominal editor. (For McClure's loss of control of his magazine, see chapter 8, "The Montessori-McClure Breakup.")

From 1911 to 1913 when he was promoting Montessori, McClure, as nominal editor, was able to publish the Montessori series of articles in *McClure's Magazine*. He saw his relationship with Montessori as a way of rescuing himself from his desperate financial plight.

Just as the fortunes of its founder sagged under the duress of debt so did *McClure's Magazine*, Inc. For eight years, from 1911 to 1919, Frederick Collins and Charles Hanson Towne, who had succeeded Mackenzie as head of the company, faced an uphill struggle to keep the magazine in publication. Facing an eminent financial collapse, the company went into receivership and a petition for bankruptcy was filed in 1919. In the summer of 1920, Herbert Kaufman, whose brother was president of the American Safety Razor Corporation, purchased the magazine. Only nine months later, in early 1921, Kaufman, like the previous owners, was nearly bankrupt and the magazine went into receivership. *McClure's Magazine*'s assets were to be sold at a public auction.

Obviously distressed by the continuing downward cycle of events that befell his cherished magazine, McClure strenuously objected to the auction. According to the 1911 contract between S. S. McClure and *McClure's Magazine*, Inc., McClure had lost the right to use the name "McClure" in the publishing field; those rights belonged to the owners of *McClure's Magazine*. Also in the 1911 contract, McClure had been guaranteed an annual payment of $10,000. Since Kaufman had not paid McClure his annual stipend, McClure argued that the right to the use of the name "McClure" had reverted back to him. Instead of being auctioned, the company was purchased by Moody B. Gates, the publisher of *The People's Home Journal*, an illustrated magazine that specialized in domestic, agricultural, and fiction reprints. A vindicated McClure was restored to his position as the editor of *McClure's Magazine* in 1921. A new corporation was formed, the McClure Publishing Company, and McClure was named chairman of its board of directors.

Problems over editorial control quickly developed between McClure and Gates. Although McClure was theoretically editor-in-chief and Gates business manager, Gates interfered in making editorial decisions. Throughout his business life, McClure had never been able to share power and authority with another person and that had not changed. Frustrated and following a lifetime habit of exiting when a situation became difficult, McClure left for Europe in December 1922.[2]

While in France, McClure was caught up in a popular craze centered on Emile Coue, an apothecary, who had risen to quick fame. Coue claimed that he was able to cure mental and physical diseases through autosuggestion, in which a person repeated a phrase at certain periods of the day so its message would be lodged in the subconscious. For example, Coue's patients were to repeat the mantra, "Every day in every way I am getting better and better." McClure, who suffered from various illnesses throughout his life and was always looking for cures, was attracted to Coue and his method. Seeking to replicate Montessori's successful lecture tour of 1913 with Coue, McClure attempted to arrange a lecture tour for Coue in 1923. He again turned to Lee Keedick to arrange a national speaking tour for Coue. Unlike their management of Montessori's successful tour ten years earlier, McClure and Keedick's efforts for Coue were a failure.[3]

Returning to the magazine in early 1923, McClure continued his power struggle with Gates over editorial and financial issues. As the magazine's losses increased, Gates, seeking to free himself from what he believed was a futile and insolvent venture, returned control to McClure, its founder in 1924.[4] He managed to publish the *Magazine* from May through August 1924 before running out of funds. When all seemed lost, still another investor, Lewis E. Myers, appeared on the scene to rescue S. S. McClure and his failing magazine. The president of the Children's Foundation, Myer manufactured and sold children's books and Chautauqua equipment on the installment plan.[5] Myers claimed to have a large sales staff that visited six thousand families every day. They would now have an additional product to sell—subscriptions to *McClure's Magazine*. As optimistic as McClure himself, Myers estimated—conservatively— his staff would sell fifty thousand subscriptions a year.[6]

The May 4, 1925, issue of *Time* magazine, in an article titled, "Lost Childhood," commented on McClure's reentry into publishing, "Back to his editorial desk went Samuel Sidney McClure. He has not sat there since 1912, when he turned the magazine that bears his name to Publisher Frederick L. Collins. The 13 years that had passed had been years of trouble for *McClure's*, aching years of middle age, of famine amidst plenty, of dieting and forced feeding at the hands of three rejuvenators in turn. Now the master is back, the earnest wrinkled man with solicitude in his heart and a healing touch in his finger tips." The article continued that the revived *McClure's* featured a new department called "*The Little Magazine*, personally conducted with a Biblical text, by Editor S. S. McClure. Here, for the pleasure and edification of U.S. childhood, were little nature studies by St. Francis of Assisi, one Arthur Mee and the Editor; spring poetry, May songs and three hero stories. Farther on, Mr. Myers advertised his toys. Editor McClure had indeed restored to his magazine its lost childhood."[7]

McClure and Myers were able to publish nine magazine issues before they were forced to close. In early 1926, the magazine was sold to Hearst International Publications, which chose not to employ S. S. McClure. Nor did Hearst honor the contract between Myers and McClure, which stipulated that McClure would receive a salary of one hundred dollars a week for five years. Hearst transformed *Mc-*

Clure's Magazine into *McClure's, The Magazine of Romance*. Then, finally, Hearst sold it to James R. Quirk, the publisher of *Photoplay*. The magazine's last days were as *The New McClure's—A Man's Magazine*. The magazine known as *McClure's* finally died in 1930.

McClure's decline in the publishing world also brought strictures to his private life. To meet expenses, he sold his Connecticut farm, keeping only a small cottage, without plumbing, for his visits. As he had done throughout his life, McClure continued to support family members—his mother, Elizabeth, a patient in the Connecticut State Hospital, and a widowed daughter and her son.

Despite his tightened budget, McClure still managed trips to Europe. While he and his wife, Harriet, were abroad, she was taken seriously ill and was a patient in the American Hospital in Paris. When well enough to return to the United States, she and her adopted son, Enrico, shared a small apartment in Waterbury, Connecticut, with her sister, Mary. After a series of heart attacks, Hattie died on May 29, 1929, with her husband, Sam at her bedside.[8]

As he drifted into obscurity, McClure, who once had a network of friends and associates, became increasingly a man alone. He lived in a small room at the Murray Hill Hotel in New York and was often at the Union League Club, where he held a lifetime membership. Occasionally, he would visit his cottage on the Housatonic River. Although his associates, Phillips and Tarbell, had left his magazine under unpleasant circumstances, there was no animosity between them in later years. In 1936, Phillips, Tarbell, and Roseboro' joined McClure to celebrate his belated birthday at the Union League Club.[9]

In the 1940s, McClure was still remembered as a leading pioneer in progressive journalism. In 1944, McClure and Willa Cather, the author of his *Autobiography*, were jointly honored by the National Institute of Arts and Letters.[10] McClure was awarded the "Order of Merit" for his "work in the furtherance of arts and letters, particularly in the recognition of new talent and in the creation of a new type of journalism."[11] The award brought McClure a gold medal and a check for one thousand dollars. Cather received the Gold Medal for Fiction.

Samuel Sidney McClure, age 92, died in St. Barnabas Hospital in the Bronx, on March 21, 1949. His daughter, Eleanor accompanied his body to Knox College in Galesburg for his funeral. The funeral service attended by faculty, trustees, alumni, students, and friends was held in Beecher Chapel where Dr. John R. Conger, an emeritus professor, gave the eulogy for Knox College's famous graduate. Conger made the point that "possibly" McClure "was born at just the right time, but many others also have been born at the right time but have failed to grasp the opportunities."[12] True to the spirit of his graduation oration seventy-five years earlier, McClure, following his personal philosophy of enthusiasm, seized every opportunity that came his way. McClure was buried in Hope Cemetery in Galesburg in the Hurd family plot area, near the grave of his father-in-law, Professor Albert Hurd, who had steadfastly opposed Sam's marriage to his daughter Harriet.

John Phillips, a Knox Alumnus and associate of McClure in the McClure Syndicate and *McClure's Magazine*, had died at age eighty-seven on February 28, 1949, one month before McClure's death. The *Knox Alumnus* called the deaths of McClure and his friend and associate John Phillips "The Passing of an Era." Knox College's Acting President, Kellogg McClelland, said: "With the passing of these two men, who were the last of the group of Knox College people to be associated in the publication of *McClure's Magazine* and the *American Magazine*, we are conscious of the fact that one of the most remarkable groups, based on accomplishment and character, which has ever been turned out at Knox College, has become entirely a matter of history."[13]

McClure and Phillips, who were members of the Knox graduating class of 1882, formed a friendship and business partnership that lasted for twenty-four years. The *Alumnus* article stated that "Phillips supplied the balance and business judgment, the great attention to detail; McClure was a dynamo of energy and ideas."[14] Near the end of his life, McClure himself acknowledged his enormous obligation to John Phillips, his old friend from college days and his long-time business partner. "From the last year in college all through the years we were together you made it possible for me to do my work. . . . I could never have successfully founded McClure's Magazine but for your help. . . . When you & the staff left me. . . . The irreplaceable man was you. . . . The qualities I lacked were important. In many fields you made up for what I did not have. You were wise and faithful & able. Integrity was your outstanding quality."[15]

One can speculate on the advice Phillips might have given McClure on his relationship with Montessori. Perhaps, he would have cautioned McClure that his place was in journalism, rather than in education. Or, Phillips, an astute judge of character and circumstances, might have been more prudent and less enthusiastic in dealing with the difficult Italian educator. In any event, McClure needed the counsel of the Knox College classmate, who had been his confidant for so many years.

While McClure's last years were a time of decline, Montessori received more and more adulation and acclaim. After Montessori departed from the United States following the Panama-Pacific International Exposition in 1915, her reputation as an educator grew, especially in Europe. In Spain, municipal officials in Barcelona, in 1916, invited her to lecture and establish schools. The Catalan regional government supported the *Escola Montessori*, with infant and primary departments for three to ten year olds and the *Seminari Laboratori di Pedagogia*, an institute for teaching, research, and training in the Montessori Method.[16]

In 1917, Montessori made her first lecture tour in the Netherlands, which led to the establishment of the Netherlands Montessori Society. Later, she made the Netherlands the center for Montessori education and established the headquarters of the Association Montessori Internationale in Amsterdam.

Montessori gave her first lecture and supervised a training course in the United Kingdom in 1919. Between 1920 and 1930, she returned periodically to conduct courses.[17] The British Montessori Society actively supported her work with the result that a large number of Montessori schools and classes functioned in early childhood education, especially in the private school sector.

Montessori's reputation extended to South America. In 1926 she lectured in Argentina, and the following year the Sociedad Argentina Montessoriana was established to promote the Montessori Method and encourage Montessori schools.[18]

In her native Italy, Montessori had an experience that resembled her earlier relationships with Talamo in Rome and McClure in the United States. In 1922, Benito Mussolini established a Fascist regime in Italy. Mussolini's intense Italian nationalism drew the support of some leading Italian intellectuals, such as the Idealist philosopher Giovanni Gentile (1875–1944).[19] Mussolini appointed Gentile Minister of Education in 1923. As President of the Supreme Council of Public Education from 1926 to 1928, Gentile influenced the direction of education in Fascist Italy. Gentile's emphasis of children's self- or auto-education, led him to the Montessori Method.

Gentile arranged a meeting between Mussolini and Montessori in 1924 at which the Duce expressed an interest in establishing Montessori schools. Mussolini was impressed by a method that instilled discipline and order and in which children learned to read and write at age four. He also wanted to use Montessori's name and her associations and societies in other countries to promote his Fascist ideology. Montessori, in turn, was receptive to receiving official support for her educational ideas. In 1926, Montessori was recognized by the *Tessera Fascista*, the Fascist women's organization, and made an honorary party member.[20] The Ministry of Education officially appointed Montessori to conduct a six-month training course for Italian teachers in Milan. Mussolini accepted the honorary presidency of the course and authorized a subsidy for its support. In March 1927, Montessori and Mussolini met again in a private audience. There was more cooperation between Montessori and the Fascist government. The government advised the mayor of Rome to establish a Montessori training school and also supported a monthly publication, *L'Idea Montessori*. By 1929, the Italian government was sponsoring several Montessori enterprises such as the training college, the *Regia Scuola Magistrale di Metodo Montessori* in Rome, Montessori's training course in Milan, and seventy infant and elementary classes in schools throughout Italy.[21]

The years 1929–1930 marked the high point of Montessori's educational work in Italy with the support of Mussolini's government. There was a six-month international training course in Rome in 1930 under the auspices of the *Opera Montessori*. Mussolini accepted the honorary presidency of the fifteenth International Theoretical and Practical Training Course on Child Education, with Gentile as acting president. Mussolini intended to use the international Montessori course to showcase Italy's progress under Fascism.[22] However, Mussolini, like Talamo and McClure before him, had not counted on meeting the steel-like resolve of Maria Montessori to control her own method of education and keep it as she had designed it.

In 1929, Montessori, with her son, Mario, as her agent, had established the Association Montessori Internationale (AMI) as the official international organization that would control and supervise Montessori activities, including training programs, throughout the world. The AMI controlled rights to the publication of Montessori's books and the manufacture and sale of the materials and training course fees.[23]

Mussolini, whose slogan was "Everything in the State, nothing against the State, nothing outside the State," was determined to instill the Fascist ideology throughout Italy, including its schools and youth organizations.[24] The Fascist regime was also tightening its control of Italy's schools with all teachers required to take a loyalty oath.[25]

Cooperation between Mussolini's Fascist government and Montessori was always uneasy. Mussolini wanted to make political capital out of Montessori. Montessori, however, did not accept the Fascist ideology and viewed her role to be that of an international educator rather than a promoter of Italian nationalism. In fact, she believed that the child's nature and stages of development were universal and not determined by national, racial, or ethnic origins. In 1934, the Italian government, seeking to capture publicity, wanted to name Montessori as Italy's children's ambassador. Montessori refused to accept the appointment unless the Italian government recognized her as the sole authority of the AMI. The Fascist government responded to Montessori's intransigence by closing Montessori schools and suppressing Montessori education.[26] Maria Montessori left her native Italy as an exile.

In an interesting coincidence, McClure, too, became involved with Mussolini. By 1926, McClure was seventy years old, and his efforts to regain and revitalize *McClure's Magazine* were behind him. McClure, however, still irrepressible, was open to new possibilities. When his friend, Dr. Edward Rumely, suggested that Il Duce would be a good subject for articles, McClure was enthusiastic. Just as he had done in their early years, McClure shared his idea with his wife, Harriet. In June 1926, he told her that he was "working on a big idea . . . to get a series of signed articles by Mussolini. I am pulling all the wires to get the right influences, & if I succeed I will go on to Rome."[27]

Was history about to repeat itself for McClure with a new opportunity with a famous Roman? Reminiscent of his trip to persuade Montessori to come to the United States thirteen years earlier, McClure, in July 1926, sailed to Rome with letters of introduction to Mussolini. McClure, fascinated by Fascism, naively proclaimed the Italians as the world's "one free people" . . . living in "a new and dawning civilization." He extolled the Fascist dictator as "the masterful man who had brought the trade unions to heel and who promised the same for industry."[28]

Successful in arranging an interview with Mussolini at the Chigi Palace, McClure offered his services to Il Duce. As had been true earlier with Montessori, Mussolini, aware that McClure had been a well-connected American publisher and editor, believed McClure could popularize his Fascist ideology in the United States. After all, Mussolini, who began his career as a journalist like McClure, felt a common thread with the elderly publisher. Writing of his meeting with Mussolini to Harriet, McClure reported, "We had a beautiful talk. . . . [Mussolini] is full of force & charm & kindliness. It made my heart beat hard for a long time after I left him."[29]

McClure spent eighteen months in Italy, from July 1926 through December 1927, researching Fascist Italy. He concluded that "Mussolini ranks with the nation-builders like Washington. He has organized democracy for the Italian people. . . . In truth, Mussolini is making democracy work.'"[30] Although naive about Mussolini and Fascism, McClure was not alone in giving his approval to the Italian strong man. Mussolini had only been in power for four years in 1926. He was being praised for bringing order to Italy's chaotic politics, for his rapprochement with the Vatican, and for making the Italian trains run on time

Despite his advanced years, McClure, once a door-to-door salesman as a student, was still persuasive. He secured Mussolini's agreement to "put his name to a series of articles about his rise to power."[31] However, Mussolini insisted that Signora Margharita Sarfatti, his biographer and former mistress, would have to approve the manuscript. Sarfatti, with her own agenda, demanded a stipend for giving her approval. Estimates of the payment to her range from ten to forty thousand dollars.[32]

A further complication occurred. Kenneth Roberts had been sent by *The Saturday Evening Post* to ghostwrite Mussolini's autobiography. After Roberts's request for forty personal interviews with Mussolini was rejected, he declined the assignment. The job was turned over to Richard Washburn Child, a journalist who had been the US ambassador to Italy from 1921 to 1924. Child says in the foreword to Mussolini's *My Autobiography* that "For his autobiography I am responsible."[33] Child, who claimed that he persuaded Mussolini to write his autobiography, did not mention S. S. McClure.

Kenneth Roberts disputed Child's version of the origins of the Mussolini autobiography. While Child claimed that the idea for Mussolini's autobiography had originated with him, Kenneth Roberts asserted that the idea came from McClure. In Roberts's account, McClure found that Mussolini would sign his name as author if the autobiography was written by a journalist approved by the *Post*. When he arrived in Rome, Roberts learned that Mussolini's biographer and former mistress Margharita Sarfatti was to serve as Mussolini's go-between. Sarfatti told him that the autobiography would be compiled from her own book on Il Duce and from various other documents she would supply. Her demands for a stipend of tens of thousands of dollars further complicated an already complex scenario. Although McClure offered Roberts an additional subsidy to conform to these conditions, he refused and went back to New York.[34] Lyon exonerates McClure from trying to bribe Roberts, saying that he offered to revise his own contract with *The Post* so as to make an additional five thousand dollars available for Roberts's expenses. Robert chose to construe the offer as a bribe. Overpayment was a McClure characteristic but, if the story is true, he displayed no awareness of his dire financial situation. Lyon says that McClure was "able to sell the series to *The Saturday Evening Post* for a handsome fee."[35]

McClure and Mussolini had something in common. They each authored an "autobiography" written by someone else. Similar to the method used in Willa Cather's autobiography of S. S. McClure, Child says that Mussolini dictated his life story to him. The Mussolini autobiography was published as a series in *The Saturday Evening Post* and then published as a book by Charles Scribner's Sons in 1928.

With her prospects for working in Italy finished by her break with Mussolini, Montessori relocated her activities to the Netherlands. In 1936, Montessori, accompanied by her son, Mario, made Amsterdam the headquarters of the Association Montessori Internationale. She continued her world-wide activities, addressing Montessori congresses and conferences, lecturing, and conducting training classes.

In October 1939, Montessori, at age sixty-nine, was in India to conduct a training school, sponsored by the Theosophical Society at Adyar in Madras. When Italy, a member of the Axis, invaded France and entered World War II in 1940 on the side of the Germans, Italian nationals in Great Britain and its colonies were interned. Montessori, an Italian national, was not actually interned by the British authorities in India but was confined to the compound of the Theosophical Society. The British easily decided that Montessori posed no security threat and released her to carry on her educational activities in India.[36] When World War II ended, Montessori returned to Europe, arriving on July 30, 1946, in Amsterdam, at the AMI headquarters. In 1947, the aging Montessori delegated many of the administrative responsibilities of the international society to Mario Montessori, her trusted son, confidant, and aide. Maria Montessori died on May 6, 1952, in Noorwijk aan Zee, a small village near the Hague, and was buried in the local Catholic cemetery.

The issue of institutionalizing Montessori education surfaced in the plans of both Montessori and McClure. During her 1913 tour, Montessori referred to her plan for an international institute in Rome while McClure envisioned himself as the president of a Montessori Institute in the United States. McClure wanted to be a change agent in education. He had unfulfilled ambitions to create an Abraham Lincoln Institute for practical studies at Knox College and a University of the Mind where great inventors, scientists, writers, and artists would be the professors. When McClure's proposal was presented to Montessori in 1914, she adamantly rejected it. If McClure's plan for a Montessori Institute had been implemented, it just might have been a positive step in institutionalizing Montessori education, following the path of the kindergarten, as an integral part of the American school system.

Notes

Chapter 1

1. Willa Cather, *The Autobiography of S. S. McClure* (Lincoln, Nebraska: University of Nebraska Press, 1997), 37. Though written by Cather, the book was originally published as *My Autobiography* by S. S. McClure (New York: Frederick A. Stokes, 1914). The University of Nebraska book was reprinted from the original. Subsequent references are cited as McClure, *Autobiography*.

2. *History of Porter County, Indiana*, Vol. 1 (Chicago: Lewis Publishing Co., 1912), 357.

3. McClure, *Autobiography*, 37.

4. Ibid., 41–42.

5. Ibid., 40.

6. Ibid., 44–45.

7. Ibid., 48.

8. Ibid., 51–52.

9. Ibid., 57–59.

10. Ibid., 60–61.

11. Ibid., 62.

12. Ibid., 65.

13. Unidentified newspaper clipping, "Coeducation at Galesburg," translated by Mary C. Hurd, 2. Special Collections and Archives, Knox College Library, Galesburg, Illinois.

14. Extract from *McClure's Magazine*, May 1895, by Madame Blanc, "A Prairie College: An Eminent Frenchwoman's Study of Co-Education in America," 2–4. Special Collections and Archives, Knox College Library, Galesburg, Illinois.

15. McClure, *Autobiography*, 68, 69.

16. Ibid., 128.

17. Ibid., 128.

18. Ibid., 130–31.

19. Extract from *McClure's Magazine*, May 1895, by Madame Blanc, "A Prairie College: An Eminent Frenchwoman's Study of Co-Education in America," 5. Special Collections and Archives, Knox College Library, Galesburg, Illinois.

20. McClure, *Autobiography*, 78.

21. Peter Lyon, *Success Story: The Life and Times of S. S. McClure* (New York: Charles Scribner's Sons, 1963), 19.

22. McClure, *Autobiography*, 87.

23. Ibid., p. 96.

24. S. S. McClure, editor-in-chief, "Editorial," *The Knox Student*, Vol. 4, No. 3. Galesburg, IL (December 1881), 35. Special Collections and Archives, Knox College Library, Galesburg, Illinois.

25. McClure, *Autobiography*, 137.

26. Ibid., 135.

27. Ibid., 133–35.

28. S. S. McClure, editor-in-chief, "Editorial," *The Knox Student*, Vol. 4, No. 4. Galesburg, IL (January 1881), 75–76. Special Collections and Archives, Knox College Library, Galesburg, Illinois.

29. "Constitution of the Western College Press Association," S. S. McClure, editor-in-chief, *The Knox Student*, Vol. 4, No. 8. Galesburg, IL (May 1882), 118–19. Special Collections and Archives, Knox College Library, Galesburg, Illinois.

30. "History of College Journalism," S. S. McClure, editor-in-chief, *The Knox Student*, Vol. 4, No. 8. Galesburg, IL (May 1882), 120. Special Collections and Archives, Knox College Library, Galesburg, Illinois.

31. S. S. McClure, ed., *A History of College Journalism* (Chicago: Orville Brewer & Co., 1882).

32. S. S. McClure, editor-in-chief, "Editorial," *The Knox Student*, Vol. 4, No. 3. Galesburg, IL (December 1881), 33–34. Special Collections and Archives, Knox College Library, Galesburg, Illinois.

33. Commencement Program, Knox College and Seminary, June 22, 1882. Special Collections and Archives, Knox College Library, Galesburg, Illinois.

34. "Commencement Exercises," S. S. McClure, editor-in-chief, *The Knox Student*, Vol. 4, No. 9. Galesburg, IL (June, 1882), 139. Special Collections and Archives, Knox College Library, Galesburg, Illinois.

35. McClure, *Autobiography*, 139.

36. McClure, "The Greatness of Knox College," undated and unattributed clipping. Special Collections and Archives, Knox College Library, Galesburg, Illinois.

37. McClure, *Autobiography*, 140–41.

38. Ibid., 138, 142–43.

39. Ibid., 143–44.

40. Forgotten stories.net/tag/pope-manufacturing-company (accessed 5/13/2014).

41. *The Wheelman: An Illustrated Magazine: Cycling, Literature and News*, Vol. 1 (October 1882–March 1883) (Boston: The Wheelman Col., 1883).

42. McClure, *Autobiography*, 150.

43. Ibid., 159.

44. Ibid., p. 158.

45. "Alumni File No. 417, Knox College, Galesburg, IL, Nov. 95, Special Collections and Archives, Knox College Library, Galesburg, Illinois.

46. McClure, *Autobiography*, 168.

47. Ibid., 169.

48. Douglas Gilbert, "Crusading Editor: Famous Writings in Britain and America Introduced First by S. S. McClure," *New York World-Telegram* (1944). Clipping. Special Collections and Archives, Knox College Library, Galesburg, Illinois.

49. McClure, *Autobiography*, 180–82.

50. Ibid., 203–4.

51. Ibid., 208–9.

52. Ibid., 245–47.

53. Lyon, *Success Story*, 126.

54. McClure, *Autobiography*, 215.

55. Ibid., 221–22.

56. Ibid., 222–32.

57. Ibid., 224–25.

58. Ibid., 234–35.

59. Ibid., 228–29.

60. Ibid., 230.

61. Ibid., 243.

62. Ibid., 244.

63. J. Leonard Bates, *The United States 1898–1928: Progressivism and Society in Transition* (New York: McGraw-Hill Books Co. 1976), 52.

64. Books about Tarbell are Steven Weinberg, *Taking on the Trust: The Epic Battle of Ida Tarbell and John D. Rockefeller*, 2008; and Kathleen Brady, *Ida Tarbell: Portrait of a Muckraker*, 2004.

65. Ida Tarbell, *Madame Roland: A Biographical Study* (New York: Scribner's, 1896); and Tarbell, *A Short Life of Napoleon* (New York: McClure, 1895).

66. McClure, *Autobiography*, 220.

67. Ibid., 237–40.

68. Ibid., 237–40.

69. Ibid., 237–40.

70. Bates, *The United States 1898–1928*, 110.

71. For his career, see Lincoln Steffens, *Autobiography of Lincoln Steffens* (New York: Harcourt and Brace, 1958); and Justin Kaplan, *Lincoln Steffens: A Biography* (New York: Simon and Schuster, 1974).

72. Lincoln Steffens "The Shame of Minneapolis: The Rescue and Redemption of a City that was Sold Out." From the cover page of *McClure's Magazine*, Vol. XX, No. 3 (January 1903).

73. McClure, *Autobiography*, 237–40.

74. Ibid., 244–45.

75. Ibid., 244–45.

76. "Talk of Mr. S. S. McClure before the members of the 57th Street Branch of the Y. M. C. A.," Monday, April 19, 1911, 1–4, McClure Mss., Manuscript Collections, Lilly Library, Indiana University, Bloomington, Indiana.

77. Ellery Sedgwick, "The Metropolis against Me," *The Atlantic Monthly*, 97. Third in-

stallment excerpted from Sedgwick, *A Happy Profession* (1946). Special Collections and Archives, Knox College Library, Galesburg, Illinois.

78. Ibid., 98–99.

79. Ibid., 99.

80. Ibid.

81. McClure, *Autobiography*, 156–57.

82. Ibid., 253–55.

83. Lyon, *Success Story*, 255.

84. Ibid., 261.

85. Letter from Ida Tarbell to John Phillips in Lyon, *Success Story: The Life and Times of S. S. McClure*, 258–61.

86. Lyon, *Success Story*, 224, 233.

87. Ibid., 277.

88. Ida M. Tarbell, *All in the Day's Work: An Autobiography* (Urbana and Chicago, University of Illinois Press, 2003), 255.

89. Tarbell, *All in the Day's Work: An Autobiography*, 256.

90. Ibid., 256.

91. Harold S. Wilson. *McClure's Magazine and the Muckrakers* (Princeton, NJ: Princeton University Press. 1970), 174–78.

92. Wilson, *McClure's Magazine and the Muckrakers*, 174–78.

93. S. S. McClure to John S. Phillips, April 5, 1906; McClure Mss., Manuscript Collections, Lilly Library, Indiana University, Bloomington, Indiana.

94. Frederick L. Collins, "*People*," *Good Housekeeping*, Vol. 85, No. 6, 37.

95. Wilson, *McClure's Magazine and the Muckrakers*, 188–89.

96. Ibid., 188–89.

97. S. S. McClure to Harriet McClure, March 25, 1911, McClure Mss., Manuscript Collections, Lilly Library, Indiana University, Bloomington, Indiana.

98. Hermann R. Muelder, *Missionaries and Muckrakers: The First Hundred Years of Knox College* (Urbana and Chicago: University of Illinois Press, 1984) p. 165.

99. Robert Mather to S. S. McClure, May 29, 1911, McClure Mss., Manuscript Collections, Lilly Library, Indiana University, Bloomington, Indiana.

100. S. S. McClure to Harriet McClure from London, July 17, 1911, McClure Mss., Manuscript Collections, Lilly Library, Indiana University, Bloomington, Indiana.

101. Harriet McClure to S. S. McClure on Hotel Powers, Paris Letterhead, July 21, 1911, McClure Mss., Manuscript Collections, Lilly Library, Indiana University, Bloomington, Indiana.

102. Wilson, *McClure's Magazine and the Muckrakers*, 188–89.

103. Cameron Mackenzie to S. S. McClure in London, on *McClure's Magazine* Letterhead. McClure Mss., Manuscript Collections, Lilly Library, Indiana University, Bloomington, Indiana.

104. Harriet McClure to S. S. McClure, August 23, 1911, McClure Mss., Manuscript Collections, Lilly Library, Indiana University, Bloomington, Indiana.

105. Sales Contract between S. S. McClure and the McClure Publications, Inc., May

14, 1912. McClure Mss., Manuscript Collections, Lilly Library, Indiana University, Bloomington, Indiana.

106. Ibid.

107. S. S. McClure to Willa Cather, October 14, 1911, McClure Mss., Manuscript Collections, Lilly Library, Indiana University, Bloomington, Indiana.

108. Harriet Hurd McClure to Helen McClure, November 24, 1911, McClure Mss., Manuscript Collections, Lilly Library, Indiana University, Bloomington, Indiana.

Chapter 2

1. Josephine Tozier, "An Educational Wonder-Worker: The Methods of Maria Montessori," *McClure's Magazine*, Vol. XXXVII, No. 1 (May 1911), 3–19.

2. Phyllis Povell, *Montessori Comes to America: The Leadership of Maria Montessori and Nancy McCormick Rambusch* (New York: University Press of America, 2010).

3. Rita Kramer, *Maria Montessori: A Biography* (Reading, MA: Perseus Books, 1988, originally published Chicago: University of Chicago, 1976), 22–24.

4. Kramer, *Maria Montessori*, 33.

5. Dorothy Canfield Fisher, *A Montessori Mother* (New York: Henry Holt and Co., 1912), 213.

6. Margaret Naumburg,"Maria Montessori: Friend of Children," *Outlook*, (December 13, 1913), 790.

7. Fisher, *Montessori Mother*, 212.

8. Lena L. Gitter, *The Montessori Way* (Seattle, WA: Special Child Publications, 1978), 7.

9. Kramer, *Maria Montessori*, 48.

10. More information about Anne George, Josephine Tozier, and Ellen Yale Stevens is provided in later chapters. This chapter focuses on Montessori's life prior to her lecture tour in the United States in 1913.

11. Kramer, *Maria Montessori*, 34–35.

12. Povell, *Montessori Comes to America*, 30–31.

13. Anne E. George, "Dr. Maria Montessori: The Achievement and Personality of an Italian Woman Whose Discovery Is Revolutionizing Educational Methods," *Good Housekeeping*, Vol. 55, No. 1 (July 1912), 28.

14. Kramer, *Maria Montessori*, 72.

15. Povell, *Montessori Comes to America*, 33.

16. Robert Gardner, "The Maria Montessori No One Knows: A Heartbreaking Betrayal," http://www.northhillmontessori.com/the-maria-montessori-no-one-knows -a heartbreaking-betrayal (9/27/2013).

17. Povell, *Montessori Comes to America*, 34.

18. Kramer, *Maria Montessorii*, 55.

19. Ibid., 79–81.

20. Ibid., 92–93.

21. Ibid., 185.

22. Tozier, "An Educational Wonder-Worker," *McClure's Magazine*, (May 1911), 4.

23. George, "Dr. Maria Montessori: The Achievement and Personality of an Italian Woman Whose Discovery Is Revolutionizing Educational Methods," 28.

24. Fisher, *A Montessori Mother*, 212, 213, 216.

25. Maria Montessori, *Pedagogical Anthropology* (New York: Frederick A. Stokes, 1913).

26. Tozier, "An Educational Wonder-Worker," 4.

27. Ibid., 4.

28. Maria Montessori, *The Montessori Method* (New York: Frederick A. Stokes, 1912), 51.

29. Fisher, *A Montessori Mother*, 229.

30. Montessori's quotes are from an interview that Montessori gave in 1947, in an unidentified newspaper clipping in archives of the AMI, as quoted by Kramer, *Maria Montessori*, 145–46, 387.

31. Fisher, *A Montessori Mother*, 225–26.

32. Josephine Tozier, "The Montessori Schools in Rome: The Revolutionary Work of Maria Montessori as Carried Out in Her Own Schools," *McClure's Magazine* Vol. 38, No. 2 (December 1911), 129.

33. Fisher, *A Montessori Mother*, 229–30.

34. Tozier, "The Montessori Schools in Rome," 132.

35. Ibid.

36. Ibid., 135.

37. Fisher, *A Montessori Mother*, 10, 30.

38. Helen Parkhurst notes, Montessori 5th lecture, March 20, 1914, 15–16. Helen Parkhurst Collection, University Archives, University of Wisconsin, Stevens Point, Wisconsin

39. Ibid.

Chapter 3

1. Helen Parkhurst notes, Montessori 6th lecture, March 23, 1914, 22. Helen Parkhurst Collection, University Archives, University of Wisconsin, Stevens Point, Wisconsin.

2. Parkhurst notes, Montessori 5th lecture, March 20, 1914, 19.

3. Parkhurst notes, Montessori 7th lecture, March 25, 1914, 30.

4. Tozier, "An Educational Wonder-Worker," 3.

5. Two accounts of Itard's experiment with the wild boy of Aveyron were published: *De l'education d'un homme sauvage ou des premiers developpements physiques et moraux du jeune sauvage de l'Aveuron* (1801) and *Rapport sur les nouveaux developpements et l'etat actuel du sauvage de l'Aveyron* (1807). For an English version, see Jean Marc Gaspard Itard, *The Wild Boy of Aveyron* (New York: McGraw-Hill/Appleton & Lange, 1962).

6. Itard's major work was the two volume *Traite des maladies de l'oreille et de l'audition* (1821).

7. Timothy D. Seldin, "Montessori," in James Guthrie, ed. *Encyclopedia of Education*, 2nd ed. (New York: Macmillan Reference USA/Thomson Gale, 2003), 1676.

8. Maria Montessori, *The Montessori Method*, trans. Anne E. George (New York: Frederick A. Stokes Co., 1912), 33–34.

9. Seguin's major work was *Traitement Moral, Hygiene et Education des Idiots*, which was published in France in 1846. After his immigration to the United States, it was re-published in English in 1886 as *Idiocy and its Treatment by the Physiological Method* (New York: W. Wood & Co. 1886)

10. Seguin immigrated to the United States and established schools in Ohio and New York. His *Idiocy and its Treatment by the Physiological Method* (New York: W. Wood & Co. 1866) made his ideas available to American readers.

11. Anne E. George, "Dr. Maria Montessori: The Achievement and Personality of an Italian Woman Whose Discovery Is Revolutionizing Educational Methods," *Good Housekeeping*, Vol. 55, No. 1 (July 1912), 28.

12. Katherina Myers, "Seguin's Principles of Education as Related to the Montessori Method," *Journal of Education*, 77 (May 1913), 538–41.

13. Mattie Crumpton Hardy, "The Derivation of the Montessori Didactic Apparatus," accessed at http:archive.org/stream/jstor-994050/994050_djvu.txt. (9/24/2013), 2.

14. Hardy, "The Derivation of the Montessori Didactic Apparatus," 2.

15. Maria Montessori, *The Montessori Method*, trans. Anne E. George (New York: Frederick A. Stokes Co., 1912), 37.

16. Tozier, "An Educational Wonder-Worker," 3.

17. Parkhurst notes, Montessori 5th lecture, March 20, 1914, 19.

18. Ibid., 18.

19. Rita Kramer, *Maria Montessori: A Biography* (Reading, MA.: Perseus Books, 1988), 73–76.

20. Kramer, *Maria Montessori*, 68–69.

21. Ibid., 68, 96–99.

22. Parkhurst notes, Montessori lecture, March 9, 1914, 9–10, 15.

23. Maria Montessori, *The Montessori Method* (New York: Schocken Books, 1964), 1–3.

24. Ibid., 29.

25. Parkhurst notes, Montessori 8th lecture, March 30, 1914, 42–43.

26. Parkhurst notes, Montessori 8th lecture, March 25, 1914, 36–37.

27. Parkhurst notes, Montessori 8th lecture, March 30, 1914, 37–39.

28. Maria Montessori, *The Absorbent Mind* (New York: Henry Holt and Co., 1995), 19–20.

29. Maria Montessori, *The Absorbent Mind*, 51.

30. Ibid., 167.

31. Kramer, *Maria Montessori*, 180–81.

32. Maria Montessori, *The Absorbent Mind*, 189.

33. Montessori, *The Montessori Method*, trans. Anne E. George (New York: Frederick A. Stokes Co., 1912), 63.

34. Ibid., 60–61.

35. George, "Dr. Maria Montessori: The Achievement and Personality of an Italian Woman Whose Discovery Is Revolutionizing Educational Methods," *Good Housekeeping*, Vol. 55, No. 1 (July 1912), 28.

36. Tozier, "An Educational Wonder-Worker," 5.

37. Ibid., 5–6.

38. Ibid., 6.

39. Parkhurst notes, Montessori's Lecture on the School, April 20, 1914, 44–45.

40. Ibid., 45.

41. Dorothy Canfield Fisher, *A Montessori Mother* (New York: Henry Holt and Co, 1913), 23.

42. Parkhurst, "Notes," 3.

43. Kramer, *Maria Montessori*, 209–10.

44. Parkhurst notes, Montessori's Lecture on the School, April 20, 1914, 46–48.

45. Parkhurst notes, Montessori's Lecture on Movement, April 22, 1914, 52–55.

46. Josephine Tozier, "The Montessori Schools in Rome: The Revolutionary Work of Maria Montessori as Carried Out in Her Own Schools," *McClure's Magazine* Vol. 38, No. 2 (December 1911), 134.

47. Josephine Tozier, "The Montessori Schools in Rome: The Revolutionary Work of Maria Montessori as Carried Out in Her Own Schools." *McClure's Magazine*, Vol. 38, No. 2 (December 1911), 132

48. Ibid., 135.

Chapter 4

1. Dorothy Canfield Fisher, *A Montessori Mother* (New York: Henry Holt and Co., 1912), viii-ix.

2. Ibid., 224.

3. Ibid., 48.

4. Ibid., 176.

5. Ibid., vi.

6. Ibid., 123.

7. Ibid., 131.

8. Ibid., 162.

9. Ibid., 77.

10. Ibid., 174–75, 180, 182.

11. Dorothy Canfield Fisher, *The Montessori Manual for Teachers and Parents* (New York: W. E. Richardson Co. 1913), 20.

12. Ibid., 23.

13. Ibid., 30.

14. Fisher, *A Montessori Mother*, 49.

15. Fisher, *The Montessori Manual for Teachers and Parents*, 30.

16. Fisher, *A Montessori Mother*, 91.

17. Fisher, *The Montessori Manual for Teachers and Parents*, 36–37.

18. Fisher, *A Montessori Mother*, 105.

19. Ibid., 111.

20. Rita Kramer, *Maria Montessori: A Biography* (Reading, MA.: Perseus Books, 1988), 174.

21. Maria Montessori, Letter to the Editors, *Times Educational Supplement* (London), September 1, 1914, as quoted in Kramer, *Maria Montessori*, 174.

22. Maria Montessori, *The Advanced Montessori Method*, trans. F. Simmonds and I. Hutchinson (London: Heinemann, 1919).

23. Paul Willcott, "The Initial American Reception of the Montessori Method," *The School Review*, Vol. 76, No. 2 (June, 1968), 146.

24. Maria Montessori, *The Montessori Method: Scientific Pedagogy As Applied to Child Education in "The Children's Houses" With Additions and Revisions by The Author*, translated from the Italian by Anne E. George (New York: Frederick A. Stokes, 1912).

25. Montessori, *The Montessori Method*, (New York: Frederick A. Stokes, 1912), viii.

26. The Chautauquan (September 1912), clipping in the Chautauqua Institution Archives.

27. Earl Barnes, "Dr. Montessori Explains," *The Chautauquan* (December 1913), 1913; Maria Montessori, *Educational Anthropology*, Trans. Frederic T. Cooper (New York: Frederick T. Stokes Co. 1913).

28. "The Montessori Method and the Home," *The Chautauquan* (December 1913) clipping in the Chautauqua Institute Archives.

29. *New York Times* (Letter to the editor from Dr. Montessori), August 10, 1913, sec. 2, 10 as quoted in Paul Willcott, "The Initial American Reception of the Montessori Method," *The School Review*, Vol. 76, No.2 (June, 1968), 161.

30. Henry W. Holmes, "Introduction," in Montessori, *The Montessori Method* (New York: Frederick A. Stokes, 1912), xvii.

31. Ibid., xvii.

32. Ibid., xviii.

33. Ibid., xx.

34. Ibid., xxi–xxiii.

35. Ibid., xxxv–xxxvi.

36. Ibid., xxxvi–xxxvii.

37. Margaret Naumburg, "Maria Montessori: Friend of Children," *Outlook* CV (December 13, 1913), 796–99, as quoted in Paul Willcott, "The Initial American Reception of the Montessori Method," *The School Review*, Vol. 76, No. 2 (June, 1968), 156–57.

38. Ruth M. French, "The Working of the Montessori Method," *Journal of Education* LXXVII (October 1913), 423.

39. Parkhurst notes, Montessori 5th lecture, March 20, 1914 15–16.

40. John M. McAllister and Laura B. Tandy, eds., *Genealogies of the Lewis and Kindred Families* (Columbia, MO: E.W. Stephens Publishing Co., 1906), 82.

41. Anne E. George, "Dr. Maria Montessori: The Achievement and Personality of an Italian Woman Whose Discovery is Revolutionizing Educational Methods," *Good Housekeeping*, Vol. 55, No. 1 (July 1912), 25.

42. Ibid., 25.

43. Ibid., 25.

44. Anne E. George, "The First Montessori School in America," *McClure's Magazine* 39, No.2 (June 1912), 178.

45. Ibid., 178.

46. George, "Dr. Maria Montessori," *Good Housekeeping*, 26.

47. Florence Ward, *The Montessori Method and the American School* (New York: Macmillan, 1913), 31.

48. Anne E. George, "The Montessori Movement in America," *Report of the U.S. Commissioner of Education*, Vol. 1, Chapter XV (Washington, DC: US Government Printing Office, 1914), 362.

49. George, "Dr. Maria Montessori: The Achievement and Personality of an Italian Woman Whose Discovery is Revolutionizing Educational Methods," *Good Housekeeping*, 28.

50. Anne E. George, "The Montessori Movement in America," *Report of the U.S. Commissioner of Education*, 358.

51. George, "The First Montessori School in America," *McClure's Magazine*, 178.

52. George, "The Montessori Movement in America," *Report of the U.S. Commissioner of Education*, 359.

53. Ellen Yale Stevens, "The Montessori Movement in America" *McClure's Magazine* 40 (February 1913), 222.

54. George, "The Montessori Movement in America," *Report of the U.S. Commissioner of Education*, 359.

55. Ibid., 357.

Chapter 5

1. *Concerning McClure's* (New York: S. S. McClure Co., 1901), 5. McClure Mss., Manuscript Collections, Lilly Library, Indiana University, Bloomington, Indiana.

2. Maria Montessori, "Preface, "*The Montessori Method: Scientific Pedagogy as Applied to Child Education in "The Children's Houses" with Additions and Revisions by the Author* (New York: Frederick A. Stokes Co., 1912), viii.

3. Ellen Yale Stevens, "The Montessori Method and the American Kindergarten," *McClure's Magazine*, Vol. 40, No. 1 (November 1912), 77.

4. Josephine Tozier, "An Educational Wonder-Worker: The Methods of Maria Montessori," *McClure's Magazine*, Vol. 37, No. 1 (May, 1911), 3–19.

5. Josephine Tozier, *Susan in Sicily; Her Adventures and Those of her Friends during Their Travels and Sojourns in the Garden of the Mediterranean* (Boston: L.C. Page, 1910).

6. Willa Cather, *The Autobiography of S. S. McClure* (Lincoln and London: University of Nebraska Press, 1997), 251–52.

7. Josephine Tozier, *Among English Inns: The Story of a Pilgrimage to Characteristic Spots of Rural England* (Boston: L.C. Page, 1904); *The Traveler's Handbook: A Manual for Transatlantic Tourists* (New York: Funk and Wagnalls Co., 1905); *A Spring Fortnight in France* (Boston: L.C. Page, 1907).

8. Cather, *Autobiography of S. S. McClure*), 252–53.

9. Montessori's didactic apparatus and materials are identified in chapter 3, The Montessori Method.

10. Tozier's biographical sketch and discussion of the origins of the Case dei Bambini are discussed in chapter 2, "Maria Montessori, 'An Educational Wonder-Worker,'" and chapter 3, "The Montessori Method."

11. Tozier, "An Educational Wonder-Worker: The Methods of Maria Montessori," *McClure's Magazine*, 13.

12. Ibid., 6.

13. Ibid., 10.

14. Ibid., 11.

15. Ibid., 11.

16. Ibid., 18.

17. Ibid., 18.

18. Ibid., 19.

19. Editor's untitled note on Montessori developments, *McClure's Magazine*, Vol. 38 No. 2 (December 1911), 123.

20. Josephine Tozier, "The Montessori Schools in Rome: The Revolutionary Educational Work of Maria Montessori as Carried Out in Her Own Schools," *McClure's Magazine*, Vol. 38 No. 2, (December 1911), 123–37.

21. Ibid., 123.

22. Ibid., 124.

23. Ibid., 124.

24. Ibid., 124.

25. Ibid., 124.

26. Ibid., 124.

27. Ibid., 128.

28. Ibid., 130.

29. Ibid., 128.

30. Ibid., 136.

31. Editor's note on Montessori developments, *McClure's Magazine,* Vol. 38, No. 2 (December 1911), 137.

32. Josephine Tozier, "Montessori Apparatus," *McClure's Magazine*, Vol. 39, No. 1 (January, 1912), 289–302.

33. Dorothy Canfield Fisher, *The Montessori Manual: For Teachers and Parents* (New York: W. E. Richardson Co., 1913).

34. Tozier, "Montessori Apparatus," *McClure's Magazine*, 289.

35. Ibid., 294.

36. Ibid., 295.

37. Ibid., 296–97.

38. Ibid., 299.

39. Ibid., 300–301.

40. Ibid., 300.

41. Ibid., 298.

42. Ibid., 301.

43. Anne E. George,"The Montessori Movement in America," *Report of the U.S. Com-*

missioner of Education, Vol. 1, Chapter XV (Washington, DC: US Government Printing Office, 1914), 356–57.

44. Maria Montessori, "Disciplining Children," *McClure's Magazine*, Vol. 39, No. 1 (May 1912), 95–102. The article carried the note that it would be reproduced in the English translation of Montessori's *Pedagogia Scientifica*, which was scheduled for publication by the Frederick A. Stokes Company.

45. Montessori, "Disciplining Children," *McClure's Magazine*, 95.

46. Ibid., 96.

47. Ibid., 98.

48. Ibid., 101.

49. Ibid., 96.

50. Ibid., 98.

51. Ibid., 100.

52. Anne E. George, "The First Montessori School in America," *McClure's Magazine*, Vol. 39, No. 2 (June 1912), 177–87.

53. Kramer, *Maria Montessori*, 163.

54. George, "The First Montessori School in America," 178.

55. Ibid., 178.

56. Ibid., 180.

57. Ibid., 183.

58. Ibid., 184–85.

59. Ibid., 185–86.

60. Ibid., 187.

61. Ibid.

62. Ibid.

63. Montessori, *The Montessori Method,* 162.

64. Ibid., 171.

65. Ellen Yale Stevens, "The Montessori Method and the American Kindergarten," *McClure's Magazine* 40, No. 1 (November 1912), 77–82.

66. Ibid., 77.

67. Ibid., 78.

68. Ibid., 78.

69. Ibid., 78.

70. Ibid., 78.

71. Ibid., 80.

72. Ibid., 78.

73. Ibid., 81.

74. Henry R. Holmes, "Introduction," in Maria Montessori, *The Montessori Method*, trans. by Anne E. George (New York: Frederick A. Stokes Co., 1912), xx.

75. Stevens, "The Montessori Method and the American Kindergarten," *McClure's Magazine*, 81.

76. Ellen Yale Stevens, "The Montessori Movement in America," *McClure's Magazine*, Vol. 40, No. 4 (February 1913), 222.

77. Ibid., 227.

78. Ibid., 222.

79. Stevens, "The Montessori Movement in America, Plan for an International Institute by Dr. Maria Montessori," *McClure's Magazine*, Vol. 40, No. 5 (March 1913), 221.

80. Ibid., 226.

81. Stevens, "A Mother's Experiment, The Montessori Movement in America," *McClure's Magazine*, Vol. 40, No. 6 (April 1913), 222–24.

82. Ibid., 224.

83. Ibid.

84. Anne E. George, "Rhythm Work in the Children's House at Washington," in Ellen Yale Stevens, "The Montessori Movement," *McClure's Magazine*, Vol. 40, (May 1913), 182–86.

85. Ibid., 186.

86. Janet S. Townsend, "A Letter from Rome," in Ellen Yale Stevens, "The Montessori Movement," *McClure's Magazine*, Vol. 40 (June 1913), 184–94.

87. Ibid., 184.

88. Ibid., 186.

89. Ibid., 189.

90. Ibid., 194.

91. Stevens, "The Montessori Movement," 201.

Chapter 6

1. Anne E. George, "The Montessori Movement in America," *Report of the U.S. Commissioner of Education,"* Vol. 1, Chapter XV (US Government Printing Office, 1914), 359.

2. Kramer, *Maria Montessori*, 172.

3. Telegram, Maria Montessori to S. S. McClure, June 5, 1912, McClure Mss., Manuscript Collections, Lilly Library, Indiana University, Bloomington, Indiana.

4. Kramer, *Maria Montessori*, 172.

5. "The World We Live in: The Montessori American Committee," *McClure's Magazine*, Volume 39, No. 1 (May 1912), 238.

6. George, "Montessori Movement," 359.

7. Minutes apparently written by Anne George: "Memorandum regarding formal meeting of members of the Montessori American Committee, at 335 Lexington Avenue, New York City, Tuesday, April 23, at 6:15." McClure Mss., Manuscript Collections, Lilly Library, Indiana University, Bloomington Indiana.

8. Anne E. George to S. S. McClure, May 4, 1912, McClure Mss., Manuscript Collections, Lilly Library, Indiana University, Bloomington, Indiana.

9. Edith Sharon to S. S. McClure, May 1912, McClure Mss., Manuscript Collections: Lilly Library, Indiana University, Bloomington, Indiana.

10. Ellen Yale Stevens, "The Montessori Movement: A McClure Department," *McClure's Magazine*, July 1913, 174.

11. Sol Cohen, "Montessori Comes to America, 1911–1917," *Notre Dame Journal of Education*, Vol. 2, No. 4 (Winter 1972), 366.

12. Ibid.

13. Robert V. Bruce, *Bell: Alexander Graham Bell and the Conquest of Solitude* (Boston: Little, Brown and Co., 1973), 462–63.

14. George, "Montessori Movement," 359.

15. *Beinn Breagh Recorder*, XIII, July 25, 1913, 208, as quoted in Cohen, "Montessori Comes to America, 1911–1917," *Notre Dame Journal of Education*, 366.

16. Bruce, *Bell*, 462–63; and Cohen, "Montessori Comes to America," 366.

17. From the association's articles of incorporation, quoted by George, "Montessori Movement," 360.

18. George, " Montessori Movement," 360.

19. Cohen, "Montessori Comes to America," 367.

20. From Zoe Russell Bateman to S. S. McClure, January 10, 1914. Letterhead of The Montessori Educational Association, 1840 Kalorama Road, Washington, DC.

Chapter 7

1. Kramer, *Maria Montessori*, 187.

2. "Dr. Montessori Talks of her Mode of 'Autoeducation,'" *New York Times* (December 7, 1913).

3. Ibid.

4. Ibid.

5. Ibid.

6. Ibid.

7. Ibid.

8. Ibid.

9. Ibid.

10. Ibid.

11. For Montessori and the women's movement, see Phyllis Povell, *Montessori Comes to America: The Leadership of Maria Montessori and Nancy McCormick Rambusch* (Lanham, MD.: New York: University Press of America, 2010), 35–41.

12. Kramer, *Maria Montessori*, 55, 79–81.

13. Maria Montessori, *The Montessori Method*, trans. Anne E. George (New York: Frederick A. Stokes Co., 1912), 60–61.

14. "Dr. Montessori Talks of Her Mode of 'Auto-education,'" *New York Times* (December 7, 1913).

15. Ibid.

16. Kramer, *Maria Montessori*, 191.

17. Ibid., 192,

18. Ibid.

19. "Her School Reforms," *Washington Post* (December 5, 1913), 15.

20. Ibid.

21. Ibid.

22. Ibid.

23. Ibid.

24. Mabel Bell to Margaret Woodrow Wilson, November 1913; Alexander Graham Bell Family Papers; Library of Congress, Washington, DC.

25. Kramer, *Maria Montessori*, 343–44.

26. The descriptions of the photographs are based on the captions in Josephine Tozier, "An Educational Wonder-Worker: The Methods of Maria Montessori," *McClure's Magazine*, Vol. 38, No. 1 (May 1911), 3–19; "The Montessori Schools in Rome: The Revolutionary Educational Work of Maria Montessori as Carried Out in Her Own Schools," *McClure's Magazine*, Vol. 38, No. 2 (December 1911), 123–37; "The Montessori Apparatus: A Description of the Material and Apparatus Used in Teaching by the Montessori Method," *McClure's Magazine*, Vol. 39, No. 1 (January 1912), 289–302.

27. "Entertain Dr. Montessori," Special to the *New York Times* (December 7, 1913).

28. "Montessori System Impresses Claxton," *The Washington Herald* (December 8, 1913).

29. "Montessori System Impresses Claxton," *The Washington Herald* (December 8, 1913).

30. George, "Montessori Movement," and Elizabeth Harrison, *The Montessori Method and the Kindergarten* (Washington, DC. US Bureau of Education, 1914).

31. *New York Times* (December 9, 1913).

32. Ibid.

33. Helen Keller with Anne Sullivan and John Macy, *The Story of My Life* (New York: Doubleday and Page, 1903; see also Dorothy Herrmann, *Helen Keller: A Life* (New York: Alfred Knopf, 1998).

34. "When Montessori Met Helen Keller," *The Literary Digest*, Vol. 48 (January 17, 1914), 134. The *Digest* attributed the account of the meeting to a special reporter of the *Boston Herald*.

35. "When Montessori Met Helen Keller," pp. 134, 137.

36. Ibid. 135.

37. Ibid., 135.

38. Ibid., 135.

39. Ibid.,137.

40. "Dr. Montessori Returns," *New York Times* (December 11, 1913).

41. As quoted in the *Brooklyn Daily Eagle* (December 12, 1913) in Kramer, *Maria Montessori*, 197, 390.

42. Anne E. George, "Interpretation of Dr. Montessori's Lecture, Delivered at the Academy of Music, Brooklyn, December 11, 1913," McClure Mss., Manuscript Collections, Lilly Library, Indiana University, Bloomington, Indiana.

43. George, "Interpretation of Dr. Montessori's Lecture," 2.

44. Ibid.

45. George, "Interpretation of Dr. Montessori's Lecture," 3–4.

46. Ibid., 5.

47. Ibid., 6.

48. Ibid., 8.

49. Kramer, *Maria Montessori*, 198.

50. Ibid.

51. "Give Child Liberty, Says Dr. Montessori." *New York Times* (December 16, 1913).

52. Ibid.

53. Ibid.

54. Ibid.

55. Ibid.

56. *New York Tribune* (December 16, 1913),

57. Ibid.

58. The *Honesdale (PA) Citizen* (December 30, 1913).

59. "New Ideas on the Teaching of Children," *Chicago Daily Tribune* (December 19, 1913).

60. Ibid.

61. Ibid.

62. Ibid.

63. Ibid.

64. Ibid.

65. Ibid.

66. Ibid.

67. "Jurist's View of Montessori," *Chicago Daily Tribune* (December 19, 1913).

68. S. S. McClure to Mabel Bell, December 20, 1913, in Alexander Graham Bell Family Papers, Box 84, Library of Congress, Washington, DC.

69. Advertisement for the Battle Creek Sanitarium, *The Literary Digest*, Vol. 48 (January 17, 1914), 135.

70. Montessori as quoted in the *New York Times* (December 14, 1913), in Kramer, *Maria Montessori*, 202, 390.

Chapter 8

1. Maria Montessori to S. S. McClure; June 29, 1913; in French translated by Anie Sergis; McClure Mss., Manuscript Collections, Lilly Library, Indiana University, Bloomington Indiana.

2. Maria Montessori, *The Montessori Method: Scientific Pedagogy as Applied to Child Education in the Children's Houses*, translated from the Italian by Anne E. George (New York: F. A. Stokes, 1912, p. viii.

3. Henry Holmes, "Introduction," in Montessori, *The Montessori Method*, p. xvii.

4. Maria Montessori, "The History and Growth of Montessori's Method," Lecture 1, 7 May 1915, in Robert G. Buckenmeyer, ed. *The California Lectures of Maria Montessori, 1915: Collected Speeches and Writings*. (Oxford, UK: Clio Press, 1997), 6.

5. Robert James Bennett, *Carl Byoir: Public Relations Pioneer*, MA thesis (journalism), University of Wisconsin, Madison, 1.

6. Bennett, *Carl Byoir: Public Relations Pioneer*, 14–15.

7. Bennett, *Carl Byoir: Public Relations Pioneer*, 15.

8. Josephine Tozier, "An Educational Wonder-Worker: The Methods of Maria Montessori," *McClure's Magazine*, Vol. 37, No. 1 (May, 1911), 19.

9. Tozier, "An Educational Wonder-Worker: The Methods of Maria Montessori," 19.

10. Tozier, "An Educational Wonder-Worker: The Methods of Maria Montessori," 19.

11. Bennett, *Carl Byoir: Public Relations Pioneer*, 17.

12. Roberts Walker to Edith Lewis, July 18, 1912, McClure Mss., Manuscript Collections, Lilly Library, Indiana University, Bloomington, Indiana.

13. Bennett, *Carl Byoir: Public Relations Pioneer*, p. 17–18.

14. Ibid., 18.

15. Ibid., 18.

16. *McClure's Magazine*, Vol. 39, No. 1 (May 1912), 238.

17. Carl Byoir to S. S. McClure; July 16, 1912, McClure Mss., Manuscript Collections, Lilly Library, Indiana University, Bloomington, Indiana.

18. Josephine Tozier, "The Montessori Apparatus, A Description of the Material and Apparatus Used in Teaching by the Montessori Method," *McClure's Magazine*, Vol. 39, (January 1912), 302.

19. Maria Montessori. *The Montessori Method* (New York, Frederick A. Stokes Company, 1912), v.

20. T. L. Smith, "Dr. Maria Montessori and Her Houses of Childhood." *Pedagogical Seminary*, Volume 18 (December 1911), 542.

21. Theodate L. Smith, *The Montessori System in Theory and Practice: An Introduction to the Pedagogic Methods of Dr. Maria Montessori* (New York: Harper & Brothers. 1912), 70, 73.

22. Bennett, *Carl Byoir: Public Relations Pioneer*, 20.

23. Florence Elizabeth Ward, *The Montessori Method and the American School* (New York: Macmillan Co., 1913), ix.

24. Mrs. C. H. Mann to S. S. McClure, December 12, 1913, McClure Mss., Manuscript Collections, Lilly Library, Indiana University, Bloomington, Indiana,

25. Undated document probably published in *McClure's Magazine* in 1913, McClure Mss. Manuscript Collections, Lilly Library, Indiana University, Bloomington, Indiana.

26. Maria Montessori to S. S. McClure, April 14, 1914, translated from Italian by Dorina Spiering. McClure Mss., manuscript collections, Lilly Library, Indiana University, Bloomington, Indiana.

27. Maria Montessori to S. S. McClure, April 14, 1914, translated from Italian by Dorina Spiering. McClure Mss., manuscript collections, Lilly Library, Indiana University, Bloomington, Indiana.

28. Silas L. Egly to S. S. McClure, December 17, 1913, McClure Mss., Manuscript Collections, Lilly Library, Indiana University, Bloomington, Indiana.

29. S. S. McClure to Harriet McClure, December 22 or 23, 1913, McClure Mss., Manuscript Collections, Lilly Library, Indiana University, Bloomington, Indiana.

30. Maria Montessori to S. S. McClure, January, 1914, in French translated by Sabine Haenen, McClure Mss., Manuscript Collections, Lilly Library, Indiana University, Bloomington, Indiana.

31. Maria Montessori to S. S. McClure, January 1914, in French translated by Sabine Haenen, McClure Mss., Manuscript Collections, Lilly Library, Indiana University, Bloomington, Indiana.

32. Telegram, Maria Montessori to S. S. McClure, January 7, 1914, McClure Mss. Manuscript Collections, Lilly Library, Indiana University, Bloomington, Indiana.

33. Maria Montessori to S. S. McClure, January 1914, in French translated by Sabine Haenen, McClure Mss., Manuscript Collections, Lilly Library, Indiana University, Bloomington, Indiana.

34. Harriet Hurd McClure to Robert B. McClure, unsigned, undated, probably April 1914. McClure Mss., Manuscript Collections, Lilly Library, Indiana University, Bloomington, Indiana.

35. Maria Maraini to S. S. McClure, January 10, 1914, McClure Mss. Manuscript Collections, Lilly Library, Indiana University, Bloomington Indiana,

36. Ibid.

37. Ibid.

38. Telegram, Maria Montessori to S. S. McClure, January 7, 1914, McClure Mss. Manuscript Collections, Lilly Library, Indiana University, Bloomington Indiana.

39. Maria Montessori to S. S. McClure, April 14, 1914, translated from Italian by Dorina Spiering. McClure Mss., Manuscript collections, Lilly Library, Indiana University, Bloomington, Indiana.

40. Robert B. McClure to S. S. McClure, April 8, 1914, McClure Mss., Manuscript Collections, Lilly Library, Indiana University, Bloomington, Indiana,

41. S. S. McClure to Harriet McClure, March 18, 1914, McClure Mss., Manuscript Collections, Lilly Library, Indiana University, Bloomington, Indiana.

42. S. S. McClure to Harriet McClure, March 18, 1914, McClure Mss., Manuscript Collections, Lilly Library, Indiana University, Bloomington, Indiana.

43. Silas L. Egly to S. S. McClure, March 31, 1914, McClure Mss., Manuscript Collections, Lilly Library, Indiana University, Bloomington, Indiana.

44. S. S. McClure to Mrs. Harvey W. Wiley, February 14, 1914, McClure Mss., Manuscript Collections, Lilly Library, Indiana University, Bloomington, Indiana.

45. Maria Montessori to S. S. McClure, March 25, 1914, McClure Mss., Manuscript Collections, Lilly Library, Indiana University, Bloomington, Indiana.

46. Maria Maraini to S. S. McClure, January 10, 1914, McClure Mss., Manuscript Collections, Lilly Library, Indiana University, Bloomington, Indiana.

47. Robert B. McClure to S. S. McClure, April 8, 1914, McClure Mss., Manuscript collections, Lilly Library, Indiana University, Bloomington, Indiana.

48. Alfredo Bruno to S. S. McClure, April 14, 1914. In Italian. Translated by Dorina Spiering and Patricia A. Gutek. McClure Mss., Manuscript Collections, Lilly Library, Indiana University, Bloomington, Indiana.

49. Alfredo Bruno to S. S. McClure, April 14, 1914. Translated by Dorina Spiering and Patricia A. Gutek. McClure Mss., Manuscript Collections, Lilly Library, Indiana University, Bloomington, Indiana.

50. Harriet Hurd McClure to Robert B. McClure, undated, unsigned; probably dated

April 1914 ; McClure Mss., Manuscript Collections, Lilly Library, Indiana University, Bloomington, Indiana.

51. Ibid.

52. Ibid.

53. S. S. McClure to Anne George, June 11, 1914, McClure Mss. Manuscript Collections, Lilly Library, Indiana University, Bloomington, Indiana.

54. Harriet McClure to S. S. McClure, June 30, 1914, McClure Mss., Manuscript Collections, Lilly Library, Indiana University, Bloomington, Indiana.

55. Sol Cohen. "Montessori Comes to America, 1911–1917," *Notre Dame Journal of Education*, Vol. 2, No. 4 (Winter 1972), 370.

56. S. S. McClure to Harriet McClure, November 15, 1913, McClure Mss, Manuscript Collections, Lilly Library, Indiana University, Bloomington, Indiana.

57. S. S. McClure to Harriet McClure, November 10, 1913. McClure Mss., Manuscript Collections, Lilly Library, Indiana University, Bloomington Indiana.

58. Ibid.

59. S. S. McClure to Harriet McClure, November 11, 1913, McClure Mss, Manuscript Collections, Lilly Library, Indiana University, Bloomington, Indiana.

60. S. S. McClure to Harriet McClure, November 15, 1913, McClure Mss, Manuscript Collections, Lilly Library, Indiana University, Bloomington, Indiana.

61. Ibid.

62. Contract between S. S. McClure and Maria Montessori, November 14, 1913, McClure Mss., Manuscript Collections, Lilly Library Indiana University, Bloomington Indiana.

63. S. S. McClure to Harriet McClure, November 15, 1913, McClure Mss., Manuscript Collections, Lilly Library, Indiana University, Bloomington, Indiana.

64. S. S. McClure to Harriet McClure, November 18, 1913, McClure Mss., Manuscript Collections, Lilly Library, Indiana University, Bloomington, Indiana.

65. S. S. McClure to Harriet McClure, November 15, 1913, McClure Mss., Manuscript Collections, Lilly Library, Indiana University, Bloomington, Indiana.

66. S. S. McClure to Harriet McClure, November 12, 1913, McClure Mss., Manuscript Collections, Lilly Library, Indiana University, Bloomington, Indiana.

67. S. S. McClure to Harriet McClure, December 22 or 23, 1913, McClure Mss., Manuscript Collections, Lilly Library, Indiana University, Bloomington, Indiana.

68. Maria Montessori to C. Bang, January 3, 1914, translation from Italian. McClure Mss., Manuscript Collections, Lilly Library, Indiana University, Bloomington, Indiana.

69. Maria Montessori to S. S. McClure, January 1914, in French translated by Sabine Haenen, McClure Mss., Manuscript Collections, Lilly Library, Indiana University, Bloomington, Indiana.

70. C. Bang to S. S. McClure, January 7, 1914, McClure Mss., Manuscript Collections, Lilly Library, Indiana University, Bloomington, Indiana.

71. Telegram, Maria Montessori to S. S. McClure, January 5, 1914, McClure Mss. Manuscript Collections, Lilly Library, Indiana University, Bloomington Indiana.

72. Telegram, Maria Montessori to S. S. McClure, January 7, 1914, McClure Mss. Manuscript Collections, Lilly Library, Indiana University, Bloomington Indiana.

73. Robert B. McClure to S. S. McClure, April 8, 1914, McClure Mss., Manuscript Collections, Lilly Library, Indiana University, Bloomington Indiana.

74. Maria Montessori to S. S. McClure, April 14, 1914, in Italian, Translated by Dorina Spiering. McClure Mss. Lilly Library, Bloomington, Indiana.

75. Alfredo Bruno to S. S. McClure, April 14, 1914, in Italian, translated by Dorina Spiering and Patricia A. Gutek. McClure mss, Manuscript Collections, Lilly Library, Indiana University, Bloomington, Indiana.

76. Maria Montessori to S. S. McClure, April 15, 1914, McClure Mss. Manuscript Collections, Lilly Library, Indiana University, Bloomington Indiana.

77. Harold S. Wilson, *McClure's Magazine and the Muckrakers* (Princeton, NJ: Princeton University Press 1970), 321.

78. S. S. McClure to Dr. McClelland, April 3, 1912, McClure Mss., Manuscript Collections, Lilly Library, Indiana University, Bloomington Indiana.

79. S. S. McClure to Eleanor McClure, dated 1911, prior to September, McClure Mss., Manuscript Collections, Lilly Library, Indiana University, Bloomington, Indiana.

80. S. S. McClure to Harriet McClure, November 10, 1913, McClure Mss., Manuscript Collections, Lilly Library, Indiana University, Bloomington Indiana.

81. Ibid.

82. S. S. McClure to Harriet McClure, November 11, 1913, McClure Mss., Manuscript Collections, Lilly Library, Indiana University, Bloomington, Indiana,

83. S. S. McClure to Harriet McClure, November 12, 1913, McClure Mss., Manuscript Collections, Lilly Library, Indiana University, Bloomington, Indiana.

84. Memoranda of Agreements entered into between the Dottoressa Maria Montessori and S. S. McClure, November 14, 1913, McClure Mss., Manuscript Collections, Lilly Library, Indiana University, Bloomington, Indiana.

85. S. S. McClure to Harriet McClure, November 12, 1913, McClure Mss., Manuscript Collections, Lilly Library, Indiana University, Bloomington, Indiana,

86. Telegram, Maria Montessori to S. S. McClure, March 5, 1914, McClure Mss., Manuscript Collections, Lilly Library, Indiana University, Bloomington, Indiana.

87. Unsigned letter, Maria Maraini to S. S. McClure, March 8, 1914, McClure Mss., Manuscript Collections, Lilly Library, Indiana University, Bloomington Indiana.

88. Maria Montessori to S. S. McClure, March 25, 1914, translated from Italian by Dorina Spiering. McClure Mss., Manuscript collections, Lilly Library, Indiana University, Bloomington, Indiana.

89. Lee Keedick to S. S. McClure, March 10, 1914, McClure Mss., Manuscript Collections, Lilly Library, Indiana University, Bloomington, Indiana,

90. Alfredo Bruno to S. S. McClure, April 14, 1914, in Italian, Translated by Dorina Spiering and Patricia A. Gutek. McClure Mss., Manuscript Collections, Lilly Library, Indiana University, Bloomington, Indiana.

91. Robert B. McClure to S. S. McClure, April 8, 1914. McClure Mss., Manuscript Collections, Lilly Library, Indiana University, Bloomington Indiana.

92. Ibid.

93. Financial statement from Lee Keedick's office; Josephine B. Huauer to S. S. McClure, January 28, 1914, McClure Mss., Manuscript Collections, Lilly Library, Indiana University, Bloomington, Indiana.

94. S. S. McClure to Harriet McClure, January 16, 1914, McClure Mss., Manuscript Collections, Lilly Library, Indiana University, Bloomington, Indiana.

95. S. S. McClure to Harriet McClure, March 12, 1914, McClure Mss. Manuscript Collections, Lilly Library, Indiana University, Bloomington, Indiana.

96. Maria Montessori to S. S. McClure, March 25, 1914, in Italian, translated by Dorina Spiering and Patricia A. Gutek, McClure mss., Manuscript Collections, Lilly Library, Indiana University, Bloomington, Indiana.

97. Harriet Hurd McClure to Robert B. McClure, undated but probably April 1914, unsigned; McClure Mss., Manuscript Collections, Lilly Library, Indiana University, Bloomington, Indiana.

98. S. S. McClure to Harriet McClure, March 12, 1914, McClure Mss., Manuscript Collections, Lilly Library, Indiana University, Bloomington, Indiana.

99. S. S. McClure to Harriet McClure, March 7, 1914, McClure Mss., Manuscript Collections, Lilly Library, Indiana University, Bloomington, Indiana.

100. S. S. McClure to Harriet McClure, March 18, 1914, McClure Mss., Manuscript Collections, Lilly Library, Indiana University, Bloomington, Indiana.

101. S. S. McClure to Harriet McClure, March 7, 1914, McClure Mss., Manuscript Collections, Lilly Library, Indiana University, Bloomington, Indiana.

102. S. S. McClure to Harriet McClure, March 10, 1914, McClure Mss., Manuscript Collections, Lilly Library, Indiana University, Bloomington, Indiana.

103. S. S. McClure to Robert L. McClure, March 22, 1914, McClure Mss., Manuscript Collections, Lilly Library, Indiana University, Bloomington, Indiana.

104. S. S. McClure to Harriet McClure, March 7, 1914, McClure Mss., Manuscript Collections, Lilly Library, Indiana University, Bloomington, Indiana.

105. S. S. McClure to Harriet McClure, March 12, 1914, McClure Mss., Manuscript Collections, Lilly Library, Indiana University, Bloomington, Indiana.

106. S. S. McClure to Robert L. McClure, March 22, 1914, McClure Mss., Manuscript Collections, Lilly Library, Indiana University, Bloomington, Indiana.

107. S. S. McClure to Harriet McClure, March 18, 1914, McClure Mss., Manuscript Collections, Lilly Library, Indiana University, Bloomington, Indiana.

108. S. S. McClure to Robert L. McClure, March 22, 1914, McClure Mss., Manuscript Collections, Lilly Library, Indiana University, Bloomington, Indiana.

109. Ibid.

110. S. S. McClure to Harriet McClure, March 18, 1914, McClure Mss., Manuscript Collections, Lilly Library, Indiana University, Bloomington, Indiana.

111. S. S. McClure to Harriet McClure, March 12, 1914, McClure Mss., Manuscript Collections, Lilly Library, Indiana University, Bloomington, Indiana.

112. S. S. McClure to Harriet McClure, March 7, 1914, McClure Mss., Manuscript Collections, Lilly Library, Indiana University, Bloomington, Indiana.

113. Maria Montessori to S. S. McClure, February 19, 1914, written in French, translated by Sabine Haenen, McClure Mss., Manuscript Collections, Lilly Library, Indiana University, Bloomington, Indiana.

114. Maria Montessori to S. S. McClure, February 19, 1914, in French, translated by Sabine Haenen, McClure Mss., Manuscript Collections, Lilly Library, Indiana University, Bloomington, Indiana.

115. Ibid.

116. Telegram, Zoe Bateman to S. S. McClure, January 13, 1914, McClure Mss., Manuscript Collections, Lilly Library, Indiana University, Bloomington, Indiana.

117. S. S. McClure to Harriet McClure, March 7, 1914, McClure Mss., Manuscript Collections, Lilly Library, Indiana University, Bloomington, Indiana.

118. Charles A. Brodek to S. S. McClure, undated, approximately March 16, 1914, McClure Mss., Manuscript Collections, Lilly Library, Indiana University, Bloomington, Indiana.

119. Charles A. Brodek to S. S. McClure, March 20, 1914, McClure Mss., Manuscript Collections, Lilly Library, Indiana University, Bloomington, Indiana.

120. S. S. McClure to Harriet McClure, March 18, 1914, McClure Mss., Manuscript Collections, Lilly Library, Indiana University, Bloomington, Indiana.

121. S. S. McClure to Robert L. McClure, March 22, 1914, McClure Mss., Manuscript Collections, Lilly Library, Indiana University, Bloomington, Indiana. The deletions are McClure's. "Montessori society" in this context refers to his Montessori Company.

122. Telegram, Maria Montessori to S. S. McClure, March 26, 1914, McClure Mss., Manuscript Collections, Lilly Library, Indiana University, Bloomington, Indiana.

123. Maria Montessori to S. S. McClure, March 25, 1914, in Italian, translated by Dorina Spiering and Patricia A. Gutek, McClure Mss., Manuscript Collections, Lilly Library, Indiana University, Bloomington, Indiana.

124. Ibid.

125. Maria Montessori to S. S. McClure, April 14, 1914, in Italian, translated by Dorina Spiering, McClure Mss., Manuscript Collections, Lilly Library, Indiana University, Bloomington, Indiana.

126. Harriet McClure to S. S. McClure, October 21, 1913, McClure Mss., Manuscript Collections, Lilly Library, Indiana University, Bloomington, Indiana.

127. Robert B. McClure to S. S. McClure, April 8, 1914, McClure Mss., Manuscript Collections, Lilly Library, Indiana University, Bloomington, Indiana.

128. Ibid.

129. Ibid.

130. Ibid.

131. Ibid.

132. Ibid.

133. S. S. McClure to Harriet McClure, March 10, 1914, McClure Mss. Manuscript Collections, Lilly Library, Indiana University, Bloomington, Indiana.

134. Robert B. McClure to S. S. McClure, April 8, 1914, McClure Mss., Manuscript Collections, Lilly Library, Indiana University, Bloomington, Indiana.

135. Alfredo Bruno to S. S. McClure, April 14, 1914; in Italian, translated by Dorina Spiering and Patricia A. Gutek, McClure Mss., Manuscript Collections, Lilly Library, Indiana University, Bloomington, Indiana.

136. Ibid.

137. Telegram from S. S. McClure to Harriet McClure, April 8, 1914, McClure Mss., Manuscript Collections, Lilly Library, Indiana University, Bloomington, Indiana.

138. Harriet McClure to S. S. McClure, April 14, 1914; McClure Mss. Manuscript Collections, Lilly Library, Indiana University, Bloomington, Indiana.

139. Ibid.

140. Alfredo Bruno to S. S. McClure, April 4, 1914, in Italian, translated by Dorina Spiering and Patricia A. Gutek; McClure Mss. Manuscript Collections, Lilly Library, Indiana University, Bloomington, Indiana.

141. S. S. McClure to Harriet McClure, April 11, 1914, McClure Mss., Manuscript Collections, Lilly Library, Indiana University, Bloomington, Indiana.

142. Alfredo Bruno to S. S. McClure, April 14, 1914, in Italian, translated by Dorina Spiering and Patricia A. Gutek, McClure Mss., Manuscript Collections, Lilly Library, Indiana University, Bloomington, Indiana,

143. Harriet McClure to S. S. McClure, April 14, 1914, McClure Mss., Manuscript Collections, Lilly Library, Indiana University, Bloomington, Indiana.

144. Norman Hopgood, May 25, 1914, McClure Mss., Manuscript Collections, Lilly Library, Indiana University, Bloomington, Indiana.

145. Peter Lyon, *Success Story: The Life and Times of S. S. McClure* (New York: Everett/ Edwards, Inc., 1963), 352.

146. Mabel Bell to S. S. McClure, June 5, 1914, McClure Mss., Manuscript Collections, Lilly Library, Indiana University, Bloomington, Indiana.

147. Harriet McClure to S. S. McClure, June 19, 1914, McClure Mss., Manuscript Collections, Lilly Library, Indiana University, Bloomington, Indiana.

Chapter 9

1. Walter N. Halsey, "A Valuation of the Montessori Experiments," *Journal of Education* 77 (January 1913), 63.

2. William H. Kilpatrick, *The Montessori Method Examined* (Boston: Houghton Mifflin Co., 1914), 8–9.

3. Ibid.

4. S. S. McClure, *My Autobiography* by S. S. McClure (New York: Frederick A. Stokes, 1914).

5. Robert Thacker, "Introduction," Willa Cather, *The Autobiography of S. S. McClure* (Lincoln: University of Nebraska Press, 1997), v.

6. Llewellyn Jones, "The Life Story of a Genius," *The Chicago Evening Post* (September 18, 1914). Special Collections and Archives, Knox College Library, Galesburg, Illinois.

7. Willa Cather, *The Autobiography of S. S. McClure* (Lincoln: University of Nebraska Press, 1997), 251–53.

8. Cather, *Autobiography of S. S. McClure*, 253.

9. Promotional material from Lee Keedick's office, Samuel S. McClure, (March 17, 1914). Special Collections and Archives, Knox College Library, Galesburg, Illinois.

10. Robert G. Buckenmeyer, ed., *The California Lectures of Maria Montessori, 1915: Collected Speeches and Writings* (Oxford, UK: Clio Press, 1997), xiii. Also, see Kramer, *Maria Montessori*, 212.

11. Sol Cohen, "Montessori Comes to America," *Notre Dame Journal of Education*, Vol. 2, No. 4 (Winter 1972), 368.

12. Ibid., 368–69.

13. *Stevens Point Pointer* (college newspaper), April 30, 1915, Helen Parkhurst Collection, University Archives, University of Wisconsin—Stevens Point.

14. Cohen, "Montessori Comes to America," 369.

15. Acting as her stenographer, Adelia Pyle typed Montessori's lectures while she was delivering them. Montessori's lectures were edited by Robert G. Buckenmeyer and published as *The California Lectures of Maria Montessori, 1915: Collected Speeches and Writings* (Oxford, UK: Clio Press, 1997). Buckenmeyer provides a much more complete record of Montessori's 1915 lectures than exists of her 1913 lectures, which have to be reconstructed from newspaper articles.

16. Kramer, *Maria Montessori,* 212–17.

17. Noah W. Sobe, "Challenging the Gaze: The Subject of Attention and a 1915 Montessori Demonstration Classroom," *Educational Theory*, Vol. 54, No.3 (2004), 282, 284–85.

18. Maria Montessori, *Dr. Montessori's Own Handbook* (New York: Frederick A. Stokes, 1914).

19. Dorothy Canfield Fisher, *The Montessori Manual for Teachers and Parents* (New York: W. E. Richardson Co., 1913); Theodate L. Smith, *The Montessori System in Theory and Practice: An Introduction to the Pedagogic Methods of Dr. Maria Montessori* (New York: Harper & Brothers, 1912); Florence Ward, *The Montessori Method and the American School* (New York: Macmillan, 1913).

20. John Dunlop, secretary, Announcement of Annual Meeting of the Montessori Educational Association, April 14, 1914, Alexander Graham Bell Family Papers, Library of Congress, Washington, DC.

21. Mabel B. Brooks, Minutes of the Executive Committee of the Montessori Educational Association, October 15, 1914, Alexander Graham Bell Family Papers, Library of Congress, Washington, DC.

22. Ibid.

23. Copy of an unsigned letter addressed to Miss Anne George, November 2, 1914, in the Alexander Graham Bell Family Papers, Library of Congress, Washington, DC. Based on the sequence of events, it is to George from Chancellor Hamilton of the American University. Since it is unsigned, it could also be a copy of a letter from Grosvenor to George. In any event it makes clear that the American University was not proposing to sponsor paid lectures by Montessori.

24. Minutes—Special Meeting. Montessori Educational Association, Saturday, November 29, 1914, Alexander Graham Bell Family Papers, Library of Congress, Washington, DC.

25. Gilbert H. Grosvenor to Mabel Bell, December 4, 1914, Alexander Graham Bell Family Papers, Library of Congress, Washington, DC. Because of its importance, the letter has been reproduced in much of its entirety. Two short personal comments about his wife have been deleted. The underlining is Grosvenor's. Grosvenor's handwritten corrections of one sentence appear as print.

26. Minutes, Board of Trustees, Montessori Educational Association, December 10, 1914, Alexander Graham Bell Family Papers, Library of Congress, Washington, DC.

27. Kramer, *Maria Montessori,*) 222–23.

28. Margaret (Baker) Willis was the daughter of Dr. Frank Baker, a professor at Georgetown University, who was also superintendent of the national zoo in Washington, DC.

29. Mabel Bell to Bailey Willis, August 21, 1915, Alexander Graham Bell Papers, Box 65, Library of Congress, Washington, DC.

30. Willis's correspondence with Mabel Bell in the Alexander Graham Bell Papers, Box 65, Library of Congress, Washington, DC.

31. Bailey Willis, Copy of Report on Meeting with Maria Montessori, 1 (undated, late August 1915), Alexander Graham Bell Papers, Box 65, Library of Congress, Washington, DC.

32. Ibid.

33. Ibid.

34. Ibid.

35. Ibid.

36. Ibid., 2.

37. Ibid., 4.

38. Ibid., 5.

39. Ibid.

40. "General Regulations for the Formation of an Authorized Montessori Society," sent by Bailey Willis to Mabel Bell, undated typescript, late August 1915 1, Alexander Graham Bell Family Papers, Box 65, Library of Congress, Washington, DC. On the document's first page Willis had written "Provisional" and "Drawn up for Dr. Montessori, by some of her students, I presume."

41. Ibid.

42. Ibid., 2.

43. Ibid., 3

44. Ibid.

45. Mabel Bell to Bailey Willis (September 25, 1915), Alexander Graham Bell Family Papers, Box 65, Library of Congress, Washington, DC.

46. Ibid.

47. Ibid.

48. Helen Parkhurst "Biographical Material," Helen Parkhurst Collection, University Archives, University of Wisconsin—Stevens Point.

49. Kramer, *Maria Montessori*, 214–15.

50. Helen Parkhurst lecture to the Northwestern Teachers Association at Eau Claire, Wisconsin, October 1914, as reported in "Montessori System: Member of Normal Faculty Spent Time in Rome Studying This System," *Stevens Point Daily Journal* (May 15,

1915), Helen Parkhurst Collection, University Archives, University of Wisconsin—Stevens Point.

51. Ibid.

52. *Stevens Point Gazette* (October 6, 1915), Helen Parkhurst Collection, University Archives, University of Wisconsin—Stevens Point.

53. *Stevens Point Daily Journal* (November 2, 1915), Helen Parkhurst Collection, University Archives, University of Wisconsin—Stevens Point.

54. Cohen, "Montessori Comes to America," 370.

55. Ibid.

56. Frank W. Cyr, "Introduction" to Helen Parkhurst, *Education on the Dalton Plan* (New York: E.P. Dutton, 1922), reprinted by Cedric Chivers, Ltd. Portway, Bath, UK, 1966.

57. Kramer, *Maria Montessori*, 221.

58. Helen Parkhurst, *Education on the Dalton Plan* (New York: E.P. Dutton, 1922), 12–13.

59. Ibid.,13.

60. Ibid., 17, 19.

61. Beverly A. Blois, "The Development and Implementation of Helen Parkhurst's Dalton Plan," (May 10, 1983), 2, Helen Parkhurst Collection, University Archives, University of Wisconsin—Stevens Point.

62. Parkhurst, *Education on the Dalton Plan*, 34–36.

63. Ibid., xv, 16.

64. Parkhurst, *Education on the Dalton Plan*.

65. Kramer, *Maria Montessori*, 225–26.

66. Maria Montessori, "CIRCULAR TO THE MONTESSORI SOCIEITIES OF GREAT BRITAIN" (1922); Handwritten on the circular and signed with the initials H. P. (Helen Parkhurst), included in a letter from Parkhurst to Dr. Michael Vincent O'Shea, dated Nov. 29, 1922, on letterhead: Children University School, 18 West 72nd Street, New York; Education Director, Helen Parkhurst. Helen Parkhurst Collection, University Archives, University of Wisconsin—Stevens Point.

67. Helen Parkhurst to Professor M. V. O. Shea (November 29, 1922), Helen Parkhurst Collection, University Archives, University of Wisconsin–Stevens Point.

68. Professor M. V. O. Shea to Helen Parkhurst (December 11, 1922), Helen Parkhurst Collection, University Archives, University of Wisconsin–Stevens Point.

69. Kramer, *Maria Montessori*, 317.

70. J. McV. Hunt, "Introduction," in Maria Montessori, *The Montessori Method* (New York: Schocken Books, 1964), xiv.

71. W. F. Connell, *A History of Education in the Twentieth Century* (New York: Teachers College Press, 1980), 133–34.

72. For Rambusch and the Montessori revival, see Phyllis Povell, *Montessori Comes to America: The Leadership of Maria Montessori and Nancy McCormick Rambusch* (Lanham, CO, University Press of America, 2010).

73. Povell, *Montessori Comes to America*, 78; Kathy Ahlfeld, "The Montessori Revival: How Far Will It Go?" *Nation's Schools* 85 (January 1970), 75–80.

74. Timothy D. Seldin, "Montessori," in James W. Guthrie, ed., *Encyclopedia of Education*, 2nd ed. Vol. 5 (New York: Macmillan Reference USA/Thomson Gale, 2003), 1697.

Chapter 10

1. Harold S. Wilson, *McClure's Magazine and the Muckrakers* (Princeton, NJ: Princeton University Press, 1970), 188–89.

2. Peter Lyon, *Success Story: The Life and Times of S. S. McClure* (New York: Charles Scribner's Sons, 1963), 392–94.

3. Ibid., 394.

4. Ibid., 394–95.

5. Ibid., 395.

6. Ibid.

7. "Lost Childhood," *Time* (May 4, 1925), Alumni file No. 512, Special Collections and Archives, Knox College Library, Galesburg, Illinois.

8. Lyon, *Success Story*, 399–403,

9. Ibid., 409–11.

10. "Ceremonial Program," American Academy of Arts and Letters. Special Collections and Archives, Knox College Library, Galesburg, Illinois.

11. "The Passing of an Era," *The Knox Alumnus* Vol. XXXII, No. 4 (April 1949), 75. Special Collections and Archives, Knox College Library, Galesburg, Illinois.

12. "Memorial Services for S. S. McClure," *Daily Register-Mail*, Galesburg, IL (March 28, 1949), 2. Special Collections and Archives, Knox College Library, Galesburg, Illinois.

13. "The Passing of an Era," *The Knox Alumnus* Vol. XXXII, No. 4 (April 1949), 74–75. Special Collections and Archives, Knox College Library, Galesburg, Illinois.

14. "The Passing of an Era," *The Knox Alumnus* Vol. XXXII, No. 4 (April, 1949), 74. Special Collections and Archives, Knox College Library, Galesburg, Illinois.

15. S. S. McClure to John S. Phillips, June 25, 1942, McClure Mss., Manuscript Collections, Lilly Library, Indiana University, Bloomington Indiana.

16. *Maria Montessori: A Centenary Anthology, 1870–1970* (Amsterdam, Netherlands: Association Internationale, 1970), 27, American Montessori Records. Archives & Special Collections at the Thomas J. Dodd Research Center, University of Connecticut Libraries; and Kramer, *Maria Montessori*, 249.

17. *Montessori: A Centenary Anthology*, 31.

18. Ibid., 37.

19. Giovanni Gentile (1875–1944) was a noted Italian philosopher and educator who was a proponent of Idealism in philosophy and education. He was professor of the history of philosophy at the University of Rome and supported Mussolini's Fascist regime, serving as its first minister of education. His books include: *The Theory of Mind as Pure Art* (1916), *The Reform of Education*, trans. G. Bigongiari (London: Benn, 1923), and *Genesis and Structure of Society* (1943). For an interpretation of Gentile's Idealism, see *The Social Philosophy of Giovanni Gentile* (Urbana, IL: University of Illinois Press, 1960).

20. Kramer, *Maria Montessori*, 300.

21. Ibid., 302–4.

22. Ibid., 311–12.

23. Ibid., 317.

24. Benito Mussolini, *Fascism: Doctrine and Institution* (Rome: Ardita, 1935), p. 40.

25. W. F. Connell, *A History of Education in the Twentieth Century World* (New York: Teachers College Press, 1980), 250–54.

26. Kramer, *Maria Montessori*, 326–27.

27. Lyon, *Success Story*, 400.

28. Ibid., 400.

29. Ibid., 401.

30. "McClure Plans Study of Cities," *The Michigan Daily* (March 21, 1926), Special Collections and Archives, Knox College Library, Galesburg, Illinois.

31. Lyon, *Success Story*, 401.

32. While Lyon states that Sarfatti's approval was dependent on a payment of $10,000, William L. Vance in *America's Rome: Catholic and Contemporary Rome*, New Haven: Yale University Press, 1989, 328, puts Sarfatti's fee at $40,000.

33. Benito Mussolini and Richard Washburn Child, *My Autobiography*, New York: Scribner's Sons, 1928.

34. Vance: *America's Rome*, 328.

35. Lyon, *Success Story*, 401.

36. Kramer, *Maria Montessori*, 343–44.

Bibliography

Manuscripts and Letters

Alexander Graham Bell Family Papers, Library of Congress, Washington, DC.

McClure Mss. Manuscript Collections, Lilly Library, Indiana University, Bloomington, Indiana.

Helen Parkhust Collection, University Archives, University of Wisconsin, Stevens Point, Wisconsin.

Special Collections and Archives, Knox College Library, Galesburg, Illinois.

American Montessori Records, Archives & Special Collections at the Thomas J. Dodd Research Center, University of Connecticut Libraries.

Books

Bruce, Robert V. *Bell: Alexander Graham Bell and the Conquest of Solitude*. Boston: Little, Brown and Co., 1973.

Buckenmeyer, Robert G., ed. *The California Lectures of Maria Montessori, 1915: Collected Speeches and Writings*. Oxford, UK: Clio Press, 1997.

Cather, Willa. *The Autobiography of S. S. McClure*. Lincoln: University of Nebraska Press, 1997. Originally published as *My Autobiography* by S. S. McClure. New York: Frederick A. Stokes, 1914. Reprinted from the original. Page references are to the 1997 edition.

Fisher, Dorothy Canfield. *The Montessori Manual for Teachers and Parents*. New York: W. E. Richardson Co. 1913.

———. *A Montessori Mother*. New York: Henry Holt and Co., 1912.

Gitter, Lena L. *The Montessori Way*. Seattle, WA: Special Child Publications, 1978.

Harrison, Elizabeth. *The Montessori Method and the Kindergarten*. United States Bureau of Education, Bulletin, 1914, No. 28. Washington: Government Printing Office, 1917.

Itard, Jean Marc Gaspard. *The Wild Boy of Aveyron*. New York: McGraw-Hill/Appleton & Lange, 1962.

Kilpatrick, William H. *The Montessori Method Examined*. Boston: Houghton Mifflin Co., 1914.

Kramer, Rita. *Maria Montessori: A Biography*. Reading, MA: Perseus Books, 1988, originally published Chicago: University of Chicago Press, 1976.

Lyon, Peter. *Success Story: The Life and Times of S. S. McClure*. New York: Charles Scribner's Sons, 1963.

McClure, S. S. *My Autobiography by S. S. McClure*. New York: Frederick A. Stokes, 1914.

——, ed. *A History of College Journalism*. Chicago: Orville Brewer & Co., 1882.

Montessori, Maria. *The Absorbent Mind*. Translated by Claude A. Clermont. Madras, India: Theosophical Press, 1949.

———. *The Absorbent Mind*. New York: Henry Holt and Co., 1995.

———. *The Montessori Method: Scientific Pedagogy, as Applied to Child Education in "The Children's Houses."* Translated by Anne E. George, New York: Frederick A. Stokes Company, 1912.

———. *Pedagogical Anthropology*. Translated by Frederic T. Cooper. New York: Frederick A. Stokes, 1913.

———. *Spontaneous Activity in Education*. Translated by Florence Simmonds. New York: Frederick A. Stokes, 1917.

———. *Dr. Montessori's Own Handbook*. New York: Frederick A. Stokes, 1914.

Mussolini, Benito and Richard W. Child. *My Autobiography*. New York: Scribner's Sons, 1928.

Parkhurst, Helen. *Education on the Dalton Plan*. New York: E. P. Dutton, 1922.

Povell, Phyllis. *Montessori Comes to America: The Leadership of Maria Montessori and Nancy McCormick Rambusch*. Lanham, CO: University Press of America, 2010.

Rambusch, Nancy McCormick. *Learning How to Learn*. Baltimore: Helicon Press, 1962.

Seguin, Edouard. *Idiocy: and Its Treatment by the Physiological Method*. New York: W. Wood & Co., 1866.

Smith, Theodate L. *The Montessori System in Theory and Practice: An Introduction to the Pedagogic Methods of Dr. Maria Montessori*. New York: Harper & Brothers, 1912.

Standing, E. M. *Maria Montessori: Her Life and Work*. New York: New American Library, 1962.

Stevens, Ellen Yale. *A Guide to the Montessori Method*. New York: Frederick A. Stokes Co., 1913.

Vance, William L. *America's Rome: Catholic and Contemporary Rome*. New Haven: Yale University Press, 1989.

Ward, Florence E. *The Montessori Method and the American School*. New York: Macmillan, 1913.

Wilson, Harold S., *McClure's Magazine and the Muckrakers*. Princeton, NJ: Princeton University Press, 1970.

Sections and Selected Chapters in Books

Cyr, Frank W. "Introduction." In Helen Parkhurst, *Education on the Dalton Plan*. New York: E. P. Dutton, 1922.

George, Anne E. "The Montessori Movement in America," *Report of the U.S. Commis-*

sioner of Education, Vol.1, Chapter XV. Washington, DC: US Government Printing Office, 1914.

Gutek, Gerald L. "Maria Montessori: Contributions to Educational Psychology." In *Educational Psychology: A Century of Contributions,* edited by Barry J. Zimmerman and Dale H. Schunk. New York: Lawrence Erlbaum Associations, Publishers, 2003.

Hunt, J. McV. "Introduction: Revisiting Montessori." In Maria Montessori, *The Montessori Method*. New York: Schocken Books, 1964.

Seldin, Timothy D. "Montessori." In *Encyclopedia of Education*, 2nd ed., edited by Barry J. Zimmerman and Dale H. Schunk. New York: Macmillan Reference USA/Thomson Gale, 2003.

Suzzallo, Henry. Editor's Introduction." In *The Montessori System Examined*, by William H. Kilpatrick. Boston: Houghton Mifflin Co., 1914.

Thacker, Robert. "Introduction." In *The Autobiography of S. S. McClure*, by Willa Cather. Lincoln: University of Nebraska Press, 1997.

Articles in Magazines and Journals

Ahlfeld, Kathy. "The Montessori Revival: How Far Will It Go? *Nation's Schools* 85 (January 1970), 75–80.

Barnes, Earl. "Comparison of Froebelian and Montessorian Methods and Principles," *Kindergarten Review*, XXIII (April, 1913), 487–90.

Cohen, Sol. "Educating the Children of the Urban Poor: Maria Montessori and Her Method," *Education and Urban Society*, Vol. 1 (November, 1968), 61–79.

———. "Montessori Comes to America," *Notre Dame Journal of Education*, Vol. 2, No. 4 (Winter, 1972), 358–72.

———. "Maria Montessori: Priestess or Pedagogue?" *The Record*, Teachers College, Columbia University, Vol. 71, No. 2 (December, 1969), 313–26.

George, Anne E. "The First Montessori School in America," *McClure's Magazine* 39 (June 1912), 177–87.

———. "Dr. Maria Montessori: The Achievement and Personality of an Italian Woman Whose Discovery Is Revolutionizing Educational Methods," *Good Housekeeping*, Vol. 55, No. 1(July, 1912).

———. "Rhythm Work in the Children's House at Washington," *McClure's Magazine* 41 (May 1913), 182–86.

Gruenberg, Sidonie M., "What Is the Montessori Method?" *Scientific American* CVI (June 22, 1912), 564–65.

Hailmann, W. N. "The Montessori Method and the Kindergarten," *Kindergarten-Primary Magazine* XXV (September, 1912), 6–7.

Halsey, Walter N. "A Valuation of the Montessori Experiments," *Journal of Education* 77 (January 1913), 63–64.

Holmes, Henry W. "Promising Points in the Montessori System," *Kindergarten Review* XXIII (April, 1913), 481–86.

"Information about the Montessori Method," *McClure's Magazine* 37 (October 1911), 702–4.

Kilpatrick, William H. "Montessori and Froebel," *Kindergarten Review* XXIII (April, 1913), 491–96.

———. "What Can We Learn from the Montessori System?" *Kindergarten Review* XXIII (December, 1912), 270.

Margulies, A. Reno "Dr. Montessori and Her Method," *American Annals of the Deaf* LVIII (October, 1913), 497.

"The Montessori American Committee," *McClure's Magazine* 39 (June 1912), 238.

Montessori, Maria, "Disciplining Children," *McClure's Magazine* 39 (May 1912), 95–102.

Montessori, Maria. "Plan for an International Institute," *McClure's Magazine* 40 (March 1913), 221.

Myers, Kathrina, "Seguin's Principles of Education as Related to the Montessori Method," *Journal of Education*, 77 (May 1913), 538–41.

Naumburg, Margaret. "Maria Montessori: Friend of Children," *Outlook* CV (December 13, 1913), 796–99.

O'Shea, M. V. "The Montessori Method of Teaching," *Dial* LII (May 16, 1912), 393.

Shaw, Elizabeth. "The Effect of the Scientific Spirit in Education upon the Kindergarten in Relation to the Distinctive Characteristics of the Montessori Method," *School Journal* LXXX (October, 1913), 373–74;

Sobe, Noah W. "Challenging the Gaze: The Subject of Attention and a 1915 Montessori Demonstration Classroom," *Educational Theory* Vol. 54, No. 3 (2004), 282–85.

Stevens, Ellen Yale. "The Montessori Method and the American Kindergarten," *McClure's Magazine* 40 (November 1912), 77–82.

———. "The Montessori Movement: A New McClure Department," *McClure's Magazine* 40 (March 1913), 221.

———. "The Montessori Movement in America: A New McClure Department," *McClure's Magazine* 40 (February 1913), 222–27.

———. "The Montessori Movement: A McClure Department, Answers to Correspondents," *McClure's Magazine* 40 (July 1913), 222–27.

Tozier, Josephine. "An Educational Wonder-worker: Maria Montessori's Methods," *McClure's Magazine* 37 (May 1911), 3–19.

———. "Montessori Schools in Rome," *McClure's Magazine* 38 (December, 1911), 123–37.

———. "Montessori Apparatus," McClure's *Magazine* 38 (January, 1912), 289- 302.

"When Montessori Met Helen Keller," *The Literary Digest* 48 (January 17, 1914), 134–37.

Whitescarver, Keith, and Jacqueline Cossentino. "Montessori and the Mainstream: A Century of Reform on the Margins," *Teachers College Record*110, no. 12, (2008), 2571–2600.

Willcott, Paul, "The Initial Reception of the Montessori Method," *The School Review*76, no. 2 (June 1968), 147–65.

Witmer, Lightner. "A Caution on Montessori," *Journal of Education*, LXXVI (July 4, 1912), 39.

Newspaper Articles

"Dr. Montessori Returns," *New York Times* (December 11, 1913).

"Dr. Montessori Talks of Her Mode of 'Autoeducation,'" *New York Times* (December 7, 1913).

"Entertain Dr. Montessori," Special to the *New York Times* (December 7, 1913).
"Her School Reforms," *Washington Post* (December 5, 1913).
The Honesdale (PA) Citizen (December 30, 1913).
"Jurist's View of Montessori," *Chicago Daily Tribune* (December 19, 1913).
"Montessori System Impresses Claxton," *The Washington Herald* (December 8, 1913).
"New Ideas on the Teaching of Children," *Chicago Daily Tribune* (December 19. 1913).

Thesis

Bennett, Robert James. *Carl Byoir: Public Relations Pioneer*, MA thesis (journalism), University of Wisconsin, Madison.

Web Sites

Hardy, Mattie Crumpton Hardy, "The Derivation of the Montessori Didactic Apparatus," www.archive.org/stream/jstor-994050/994050_djvu.txt. (Accessed September 24, 2013.)
Robert Gardner, "The Maria Montessori No One Knows: A Heartbreaking Betrayal." www.northhillmontessori.com/the-maria-montessori-no-one-knows-a heartbreaking-betrayal. (Accessed September 27, 2013.)
Association Montessori Internationale. www.montessori-ami.org.htm. (Accessed September 24, 2013.)
American Montessori Society. www.amshq.org.html. (Accessed September 24, 2013.)

Index